The Elements of Pascal

A Problem Solving Approach
for Business

by

Chris Sherman

and

Steven L. Holder

Interactive Technologies Corporation

Publisher: Gary Carlson
Editor: Matt Danielson
Managing Editor: Lorie Rothstein
Technical Editors: Steven Levy
                   Lew Hollerbach
Product Manager: Bill Rosen

Printed in the United States of America

UCSD Pascal is a registered trademark of the Regents of the University of
California.

IBM, IBM PC, and IBM Personal Computer Pascal are trademarks of International Business Machines, Inc.

Apple, and Apple Pascal are trademarks of Apple Computer, Inc.

MT + 86 is a trademark of Digital Research, Inc.

Library of Congress Cataloging in Publication Data

Sherman, Chris.
    The elements of Pascal.

    Includes index.
    1. PASCAL (Computer program language)   2. Business—
Data processing.   I. Holder, Steven L.   II. Title.
HF5548.5.P14S54 1984   001.64'24   84-3673
ISBN 0-471-80651-X

Dedication: To my parents, James and Merlene Sherman, with love and thanks.

—C.S.

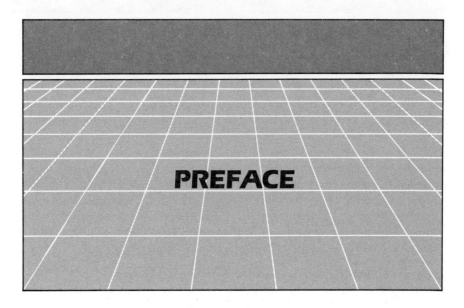

PREFACE

The Elements of Pascal is an introductory programming text emphasizing the principles of problem solving, and the fundamentals of writing solutions in the form of a Pascal program. For the student with no previous computer experience, this text establishes a firm foundation of problem solving skills that can be generalized to any programming language.

The Elements of Pascal is a concise introduction to problem solving with Pascal. Using common business examples, we present a variety of techniques for developing solutions that can be translated into computer programs. Although the emphasis is on microcomputers, the concepts covered apply to all kinds of computers, from large mainframes to lap-sized portables.

Features

The Elements of Pascal has several unique features not found in other programming texts:

Motivating Problem.   Each chapter begins with a motivating problem designed to stimulate the student's interest. We systematically introduce the concepts and programming fundamentals needed to solve the problem, making the student a partner in the development of a solution. At the end of the chapter, all new concepts are combined in a Pascal program which solves the motivating problem.

Highlighted Key Ideas.   Each new concept begins with a concise statement of the key idea, highlighted for emphasis. The key idea is followed by detailed explanation, with abundant examples illustrating its uses and application. After three or four new key ideas have been introduced, questions and exercises are provided for the student to test their understanding.

Software Supplement.   Free to adopter's of this text, the software supplement contains the programming solutions to the motivating problems. Also on the diskette are the authors' solutions to the exercises found at the end of the programming chapters. The instructor is encouraged to copy these programs for student use. The software supplement is formatted for both the IBM PC and the Apple II/IIe microcomputers.

Overview

Because it is short and inexpensive, *The Elements of Pascal* is a perfect companion text to any data processing or information science text book, or it may be used independently of any other text. The writing is clear and conversational, with each chapter introducing essential concepts in a logical sequence.

Chapters 1 and 2 lay the groundwork for the rest of the book. Chapter 1 discusses the top-down approach to problem solving, focusing on the development of algorithms that can be easily translated into Pascal. Chapter 2 introduces the fundamentals of Pascal, by examining the structure of a "generic" program.

Chapters 3 through 6 put the student in the role of a consultant who works with businesses to computerize various tasks. Each chapter begins with a motivating problem—the task the student "consultant" is to computerize for the client—and by the end of the chapter the student has seen how to systematically analyze the problem and translate the resulting algorithm into a Pascal program. Each motivating problem was chosen to highlight and complement the presentation of specific Pascal concepts for each chapter.

In short, *The Elements of Pascal* is an ideal introduction to problem solving and the Pascal programming language for any student.

To the Student

Each chapter in *The Elements of Pascal* is divided into sections. Each section in turn is divided into several parts. Each part introduces a new "key idea" in a shaded box.

Example: A Key Idea

THE *WRITE* AND *WRITELN* STATEMENTS

WRITE and WRITELN can be used to print the values of variables or constants, or strings of "literal" text.

At first, the key idea introduces a new concept by briefly summarizing the following paragraphs. Later, you should use shaded key ideas as a "quick reference" when reviewing. Each key idea heading is listed in the Table of Contents, making it easy for you to find the material you wish to study.

All Pascal programs and program segments appear in this special computer printout typestyle. All examples used in this book can be run on a computer. You are encouraged to use and modify these programs as you learn.

Acknowledgements

The authors would like to thank Matt Danielson, Gary Carlson, and Lorie Rothstein at Wiley for their unflagging enthusiasm and support, and Elliott Derman, Scott Krakoff, and crew at Graphic Typesetting Service for their patience and expert advice. We also appreciate the efforts of Rick Grunsky, Patrick Mahoney, Marilyn Correa, George Gintowt, Stan Benedict, Randall B. Baker, Shaman Hoop, and Tess Eracte for their reviews and suggestions.

We would especially like to thank Dr. Charlotte Chell of Carthage College for her insight, dedication, and enthusiasm in reading the manuscripts, and for teaching us the meaning of "structured authoring."

Dr. Richard A. Walker generously provided the opportunity to carry out this project. We are grateful to Dr. Walker, and Tom Fetter, Jack Speigelberg, Mary Breach, Rod Daynes, and Beverly Butler at Interactive Technologies Corporation for providing a stimulating and cooperative work environment.

Finally, special thanks to Lauralee Butler for frequent warm meals, persistent support during bleak moments, and listening, and listening, and listening . . .

Chris Sherman
Steven L. Holder
February 29, 1984

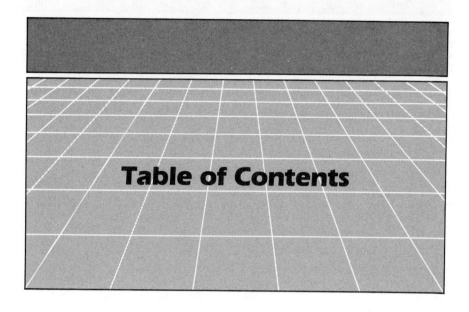

Table of Contents

CHAPTER 1

Problem Solving
and Pascal

CHAPTER OBJECTIVE

To introduce the *top-down* approach to problem solving, and to describe the general structure of a Pascal program.

CHAPTER OVERVIEW

The purpose of this book is to introduce the two parts involved in developing useful computer programs: the problem solving process, and actual use of a programming language to implement a solution on a computer. This chapter introduces both aspects of programming.

In the first part of this chapter, we discuss the *top-down* approach to the problem solving process. The careful formulation of solution steps to a problem—independent of any programming language—is the heart of this problem solving technique. Many questions should be asked during the problem solving process, such as: What is the program to do? What kind of information will be processed? How should the output be presented? These questions can and should be answered long before a single line of a computer program is written.

The second part of the chapter introduces the Pascal programming language by describing the basic structure of an actual program. Chapter 2 continues this discussion of the elements of Pascal in greater detail.

This chapter has two sections:

- **The Approach to Problem Solving**
- **The Structure of a Pascal Program**

Section 1. The Approach to Problem Solving

INTRODUCTION

There are many ways to solve problems with a computer. Some people simply sit down and throw together a slapdash solution in the form of a program in just a few minutes. While this method works for some, a far better approach is to use a systematic process called *top-down* problem solving. This involves breaking down the problem into small, manageable parts, then explicitly listing all the steps needed to solve the problem. The list of solution steps is called an *algorithm*. Well-designed algorithms are easily translated into Pascal programs.

The process for formulating an algorithm described in this section is a general outline of one approach to problem solving. Algorithms describing the solution to a particular problem can vary widely from person to person; there is no "right" or "wrong" way to create an algorithm. With practice, you should be able to develop your own problem solving style, and your algorithms will be as unique as your fingerprints.

This section has six parts:

- The Computer as a Problem Solving Tool
- Top-Down Problem Solving
- How to Develop an Algorithm
- Stepwise Refinement of Algorithms
- Algorithms and Pseudocode
- From Algorithms to Programs

THE COMPUTER AS A PROBLEM SOLVING TOOL

Computers are a *system* of components, and their true power lies in the *interaction* between the components.

Modern computers are useful for two main reasons: they are capable of processing tremendous amounts of information, and they can process information at very high speeds with a great deal of reliability.

There are three fundamental mechanical, or *hardware*, components common to all computer systems: The input/output system, the computer's memory, and the central processing unit.

Most people experience computers solely through the input/output system. This system allows us to communicate with the computer, and provides a means for the computer to return the results of its work to us.

Memory is the storage space for computer programs and data.

The central processing unit, or CPU, controls all arithmetic and logic functions performed by the computer. The CPU accepts input, figures out what to do with it, and provides for output; it also manages the memory system.

Computers use prewritten instructions, called *programs,* to carry out processes. Completed programs are commonly called *software* applications.

Computer programs are lists of specific, precise instructions that direct the computer to perform certain actions on information, or *data.* These instructions are written in a programming language—languages similar to English in that they have rules for syntax and usage, but severely limited in other respects. These limitations are extremely useful to a skilled programmer, allowing much more precision of expression than an ambiguous language like English.

Programming languages such as Pascal, BASIC, FORTRAN, and COBOL were developed so that people could instruct the computer in a language similar to English, without having to worry about the mechanical details of the computer's operation. Because of this, the programmer can devote much more energy to problem solving, instead of worrying about details having nothing to do with the solution of the problem at hand.

TOP-DOWN PROBLEM SOLVING

***Top-down* problem solving is an effective method for developing solutions that can be easily translated into Pascal.**

In daily life we usually approach problems informally, without analyzing them in detail, or forming a deliberate plan of attack for their solution. Problem solving for computers, on the other hand, requires much more fore-thought. Computers won't do what we desire unless they are programmed with unambiguous instructions—thus the need for a careful, systematic approach to problem solving.

What is top-down problem solving? Simply stated, it is starting at the beginning, or "top" of a problem, working from general to specific, breaking down the problem into smaller and smaller parts. As one works "down" through the problem, the smaller parts are easier to deal with, making the entire problem seem more managable. Top-down problem solving is a technique that can be applied to the solution of almost any problem, with or without a computer.

The first step in formulating a top-down solution: make sure you have an overall understanding of the problem. This requires extracting three pieces of information from the problem. First: What exactly are you starting with? Second: What will the solution look like?—in other words, what is the required (or desired) result? Third: What action is necessary to achieve this desired result? If you can state the problem to answer these three questions, you have begun the process of formulating a top-down solution. The result of the top-down process is an algorithm—a precise list of steps that solve the problem—which can then be translated into Pascal.

Solving problems using the top-down approach has several advantages. As we mentioned, a top-down approach makes the problem solving process easier, because it is easier to deal with many small problems than a single large one. Also, algorithms can be tried out with test data before the actual computer program is written; this saves time and energy. If the algorithm works for all test situations, chances are good that the program formulated from the algorithm will also work properly. And finally, carefully designed algorithms can usually be easily translated into Pascal.

HOW TO DEVELOP AN ALGORITHM

Algorithms are formulated in several stages, beginning with a general list of the solution steps.

Don't be intimidated by the word "algorithm." Algorithm simply means "an explicit list of instructions." A detailed list of all steps involved in driving to the market and buying groceries is an algorithm to solve the problem "Get Food." Algorithms are simply detailed descriptions of the steps required to solve a problem.

Because there are many ways to solve a particular problem, there are many possible algorithms that describe solution steps for the problem. As you gain skill in problem solving, you will see many alternative ways of developing an algorithm for a problem. Your algorithmic techniques will also become more refined as you learn Pascal.

How does one go about developing an algorithm using a top-down approach? As an example, let's say our problem is to cook dinner. Most of us could solve the problem without much thought—by simply putting a frozen dinner in the oven. However, if our goal is to create an algorithm that can be translated into a functional computer program, we need to describe the process of cooking dinner in greater detail.

The first step in creating an algorithm is to list each major process involved in cooking dinner. The top-down approach emphasizes working from general to specific, so the initial algorithm should list only major steps, with few specific details. The general, non-specific algorithm for cooking dinner can be written this way:

Algorithm for Cooking Dinner

1. Gather the ingredients
2. Mix the ingredients together
3. Cook the meal
4. Serve the meal

This is a good, all-purpose algorithm for cooking dinner. We can customize this general algorithm for most kinds of cooked meals by filling in more details. In its current state, however, the algorithm is not specific enough to be translated into Pascal. It leaves some questions unanswered: "Which ingredients should be used?" "How do I cook the meal?" and "By the way, what is food, anyway?" The next step in the top-down process is to add detail—in other words, make the instructions more specific. This process of *refinement* will answer many of our questions.

STEPWISE REFINEMENT OF ALGORITHMS

Stepwise refinement **is the process of specifying more and more detail for each algorithm step.**

The phrase "stepwise refinement" is a formal way of saying that we "break down the problem into smaller and smaller parts." Stepwise refinement is a part of the top-down problem solving process, focusing on the analysis and development of each individual algorithm step. During stepwise refinement, details are added to each algorithm step, one step at a time.

We need to ask some questions before we can begin the stepwise refinement of the "cooking dinner" algorithm. First, what is on the menu, and how will we cook it? How about cream of mushroom soup? By deciding what we will cook, we automatically answer several unasked questions. We now know what ingredients we need, and how we will cook them. In other words, we've figured out additional details for algorithm steps 1 and 3, *"Gather the ingredients"* and *"Cook the meal."*

Let's jump into an initial refinement of our algorithm. Our goal is to fill in as many details as possible for each step. Notice that the original algorithm remains intact, but now there are more substeps in this refined version.

Refined Algorithm for Cooking Mushroom Soup

1. *Gather the ingredients*
   1.1 *Get milk and mushrooms from the refrigerator*
   1.2 *Get flour and spices from the cupboard*
   1.3 *Get a pan out of the dishwasher*

2. *Mix the ingredients together*
   2.1 *Pour the milk into the pan*
   2.2 *Add the mushrooms, flour, and spices*

3. *Cook the meal*
   3.1 *Turn on the stove*
   3.2 *Put the pan on the stove*
   3.3 *If the soup is done*
        then remove the pan
        or else repeat:
             3.3.1 *Stir the soup*
             3.3.2 *If the soup needs thickening,*
                    add flour
        Until the soup is done

4. *Serve the Meal*

As you see, each major algorithm step has been refined to include a list of sub-steps specifying in detail what is required. We have numbered each step of the algorithm for reference. As we continue refining this algorithm, we can refer to each sub-step by its number.

Another goal of stepwise refinement is to make our language increasingly precise, so that the translation into Pascal will be easy. Next, we talk about enhancing the precision of our problem solving language by using *pseudocode.*

ALGORITHMS AND PSEUDOCODE

As algorithms are refined, they are expressed in Pascal-like English, or *pseudocode.*

Pseudocode is a transitional "language" somewhere between English and Pascal. Pseudocode varies from programmer to programmer, depending on personal techniques for refining algorithms. Pseudocode will not run on a computer. Its purpose is to help the programmer express ideas in a manner similar to Pascal without worrying about technical details. Pseudocode is not a predefined language; it is a programmer-invented language not quite as terse as Pascal, but without many of the ambiguities of English.

There is no specific point in the refinement process when you switch from English to pseudocode. As you learn about Pascal, your algorithms will probably use more and more pseudocode. Refining algorithm steps into pseudocode statements makes them easier to translate into Pascal.

Since we haven't introduced any Pascal to you yet, our pseudocode version of the cooking dinner algorithm will be simplified, and may seem rather silly—especially since Pascal has no built-in means of manipulating kitchen objects!

The pseudocode version of our algorithm has particular value, however, in showing you how pseudocode works as a cross between English and Pascal. Notice how each major step of the algorithm has become a *procedure.* Also, notice how we have changed such phrases as "Pour the milk into the pan" to "Pan gets the milk." As you will see in later chapters, "Pan gets the milk" is a way of expressing an action closer to Pascal than the original phrase. Here's our pseudocode version of the "mushroom soup" algorithm.

Pseudocode Version of Mushroom Soup Algorithm

1. *Procedure GetIngredients*
    1.1   *Open refrigerator; get mushrooms and milk*
    1.2   *Open cupboard; get flour and spices*
    1.3   *Open dishwasher; get pan*

2. *Procedure MixIngredients*
   2.1   *Pan gets the milk*
   2.2   *Pan gets the mushrooms, flour, and spices*

3. *Procedure CookMeal*
   3.0   *Soup is done = false*
   3.1   *Initialize stove*
   3.2   *Stove gets the pan*
   3.3   *If Soup is done then remove pan*
        else
            repeat
                3.3.1   *Stir the soup*
                3.3.2   *If the soup needs thickening then*
                        add flour
        Until Soup is done = true

4. *Procedure ServeMeal*

This pseudocode refinement of the "mushroom soup" algorithm is still too general to be translated directly into a Pascal program. Most of the substeps could be refined much further. However, it gives you a good idea of the general process of stepwise refinement.

FROM ALGORITHMS TO PROGRAMS

The final step in the problem solving process is to write the actual Pascal program, then to test the program on a computer.

Stepwise refinement, or the process of working from the general to the specific is fundamental to successful problem solving in any programming language. It is impossible to translate our algorithm in its current state into a fully functioning Pascal program—many more levels of refinement are necessary first. This example illustrates how complicated even the seemingly simplest actions can be when we try to break them down into instructions a computer can follow. A considerable part of learning how to program is devoted to observing details that might ordinarily go unnoticed.

TEST YOUR UNDERSTANDING

1. What is top-down problem solving?
2. What is an algorithm?
3. What is stepwise refinement?
4. What is the purpose of pseudocode?

Section 2. The Structure of a Pascal Program

INTRODUCTION

Now that we have introduced the top-down process to help break down large problems into manageable parts, we will apply the top-down approach in describing Pascal for you.

Our first step is to outline the general *structure* of a typical Pascal program, because all Pascal programs have a similar structure. Then we will describe each part of the program, discussing the finer points of how the language is used.

The remainder of this chapter is devoted to illustrating the overall structure of a Pascal program; Chapter 2 will be devoted to detailed explanations of concepts and terminology.

Look at Figure 1.1. This sample Pascal program doesn't accomplish anything useful or productive, but it will run if you want to try it on your own computer. Its lack of pragmatic function makes it useful as an example because it allows us to focus on concepts rather than on details.

Read this section as a general introduction to Pascal. Everything introduced here will be elaborated in Chapter 2 and the rest of the book. As you read, concentrate on understanding the general points we discuss; don't worry yet about what the sample program does, or how it works. For now, we are only concerned with describing the overall structure of a Pascal program.

This section has five parts:

- The Four Parts of a Pascal Program
- The Program Heading
- The Definition Part
- The Declaration Part
- The Statement Part

THE FOUR PARTS OF A PASCAL PROGRAM

A Pascal program has four parts, each performing a specific and unique function.

There are four parts to a Pascal program: the *program heading*, the *definition part*, the *declaration part*, and the *statement part.* Each part is dis-

```pascal
program Sample (input, output);

const
  TaxRate =          0.06;
  MinnesotaLakes = 10000;
type
  colors = (blue, green, red);
  matrix = array [1..10] of real;
var
  Apples, Oranges, Total : integer;
  Dollars : real;
  RegisteredVoter : boolean;
  LetterGrade : char;
  HotelRooms : matrix;
begin
  Total := 0;
  RegisteredVoter := false;
  read (Dollars);
  if (Dollars * TaxRate) >= 100.0 then
    LetterGrade := 'A'
  else
    LetterGrade := 'F';
  read (Oranges);
  for Apples := 0 to MinnesotaLakes do
      Total := Total + 1;
  writeln ('Have a Nice Day!');
end.
```

Figure 1.1   A Sample Pascal Program

tinct and separate from the others. They must appear in a program in the order we listed. The definition part and the declaration part are optional, although it is not common to see programs without them. Here the four parts are illustrated:

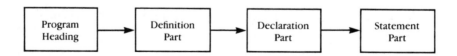

Figure 1.2   The Structure of a Pascal Program

Here is the sample program from Figure 1.1. again, with each part clearly indicated:

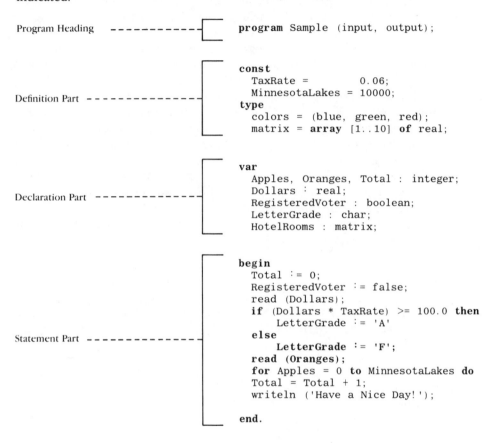

Program Heading

```
program Sample (input, output);
```

Definition Part

```
const
    TaxRate =           0.06;
    MinnesotaLakes = 10000;
type
    colors = (blue, green, red);
    matrix = array [1..10] of real;
```

Declaration Part

```
var
    Apples, Oranges, Total : integer;
    Dollars : real;
    RegisteredVoter : boolean;
    LetterGrade : char;
    HotelRooms : matrix;
```

Statement Part

```
begin
    Total := 0;
    RegisteredVoter := false;
    read (Dollars);
    if (Dollars * TaxRate) >= 100.0 then
        LetterGrade := 'A'
    else
        LetterGrade := 'F';
    read (Oranges);
    for Apples = 0 to MinnesotaLakes do
    Total = Total + 1;
    writeln ('Have a Nice Day!');
end.
```

Figure 1.3   Sample program, with parts identified.

THE PROGRAM HEADING

Every Pascal program must have a program heading.

The function of the program heading is simply to tell the computer the program's name, and what to do about input and output. Let's consider the program heading for the program Sample in detail:

```
program Sample (input, output);
```

In a program heading, the word program is followed by the program name (in this case, "Sample" is the name of the program). Following the program name are the words input and output enclosed in parentheses. A program heading is completed with a semi-colon.

What do the parts of the program heading mean? The word program is special word in Pascal, known as a *reserved word.* We discuss reserved words and their use in Pascal programs in Chapter 2.

The words input and output are the names of special built-in processes, or *procedures*, used by Pascal to provide input and output operations for your program. All program headings in this book will use these built-in procedures. It's possible to use something other than these procedures, but that subject is beyond the scope of this book.

Finally, the semi-colon is one of the most important parts of Pascal, because its proper use is vital to the successful execution of programs. The semi-colon is called the *statement separator.* Its function is to separate each unique *statement* in a program. Chapter 2 discusses statements and the statement separator in detail.

THE DEFINITION PART

The definition part is where constants, data structures, and user-specified data types are defined.

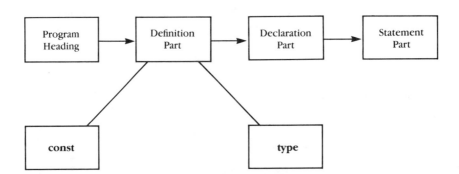

Here is the definition part from the program Sample:

```
const
    TaxRate =          0.06;
    MinnesotaLakes = 10000;
```

```
type
   colors = (blue, green, red);
   matrix = array [1..10] of real;
```

Pascal has many features that allow information, or *data,* to be represented in a way easy for humans to understand. For example, Pascal allows you to give a literal name to a number used repeatedly in a program. This *constant* name can be used in place of the actual number anywhere in a program, making the meaning and purpose of the represented value immediately apparent. Chapter 2 discusses the use of constants in a Pascal program in greater detail.

The definition of a new *data type,* colors, is also a way to make programs easier to read. Chapter 2 explores the data type concept, and Chapter 5 discusses how to create and use your own data type.

The definition part of the program is also where data *structures* are defined. Data structures are features of Pascal that allow you to organize quantities of information efficiently and effectively. The use of data structures is an advanced programming topic, but we introduce them and focus on one structure, the *array,* in Chapter 6.

THE DECLARATION PART

The declaration part of a program is where all variables and procedures used by a Pascal program are declared.

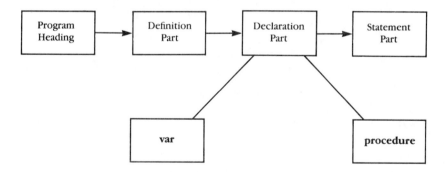

Here is the declaration part from the program Sample:

```
var
   Apples, Oranges, Total : integer;
   Dollars : real;
```

```
RegisteredVoter : boolean;
LetterGrade : char;
HotelRooms : matrix;
```

A *variable* is a symbolic name that represents a changeable value. All words to the left of colons under the word var in the example above are variable names. Variables provide a handy way to store and reference data. Pascal requires that all variables used by a program be declared, or listed, in the declaration part of the program. Variables are discussed in detail in Chapter 2.

Procedures are also declared in the declaration part of a program. There is no procedure declaration in the above example; Chapter 4 is devoted to discussing procedures and their uses.

THE STATEMENT PART

The statement part of a Pascal program is where the actual work, or *action,* of a program is specified.

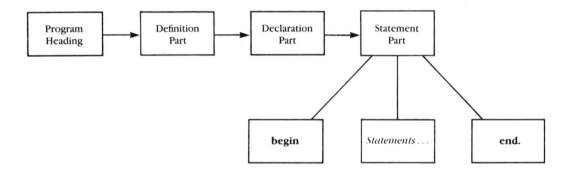

Here is the statement part of the program Sample:

```
begin
   Total := 0;
   RegisteredVoter := false;
   read (Dollars);
   if (Dollars * TaxRate) >= 100.0 then
      LetterGrade := 'A'
   else
      LetterGrade := 'F';
   read (Oranges);
```

```
    for Apples := 0 to MinnesotaLakes do
        Total := Total + 1;
    writeln ('Have a Nice Day!');
end.
```

The *actions* of a Pascal program are expressed as statements. Each statement in a program is separated from all others by a semi-colon.

We will spend much time discussing the statement part of programs. Notice that the statement part starts with the reserved word begin, and finishes with the reserved word end followed by a period. The period is a program terminator, and is only used once in a program, after the final end.

The reserved words begin and end are *action brackets*. They delineate the start and finish of a group of logically related statements—statements that must be performed as a unit for the program to function properly. Therefore, a begin must always be paired with an end.

Chapter 2 discusses statements and their components: *reserved words, expressions,* and so on.

We have covered a good deal of information in this chapter. Don't worry if it doesn't all fit together yet. The rest of this book is devoted to describing in detail everything we have just introduced.

TEST YOUR UNDERSTANDING

   5. What are the four parts of a Pascal program?
   6. What is the function of the program heading?
   7. What is the purpose of the definition part of a program?
   8. What is the purpose of the declaration part of a program?
   9. What is the function of the statement part of a program?

EXERCISES

Exercise 1:

Using a top-down approach, write an algorithm that describes the steps involved in learning a new subject in school. Be as specific as possible—include details about registering for class, buying books, allocating study time, preparing for examinations, and so on.

Exercise 2:

Extract some of the words and phrases you used more than once from the algorithm you wrote in Exercise 1. Write these words in a list, and see if you can add other words that are useful in writing instructions to solve problems. The goal is to create your own personal *pseudocode* for solving problems and creating algorithms.

ANSWERS TO THE TEST YOUR UNDERSTANDING EXERCISES

1. Top-down problem solving is an approach that involves starting at the beginning of a problem, breaking down the problem into smaller and smaller parts. Such breaking down into smaller parts makes problems easier to work with.

2. An algorithm is an explicit list of instructions that specifies a solution to a problem.

3. Stepwise refinement is the process of adding more and more detail to each algorithm step.

4. Pseudocode helps the programmer express ideas in a manner similar to Pascal without worrying about technical details.

5. The four parts of a Pascal program are the *program heading,* the *definition part,* the *declaration part,* and the *statement part.*

6. The program heading lists the program's name, and tells the computer what to do about input and output.

7. The definition part is where constants, data structures, and user-specified data types are defined.

8. The declaration part is where variables and procedures used by a Pascal program are declared.

9. The statement part is where the actual work or action of a program is specified.

CHAPTER 2

The Elements of
Pascal

CHAPTER OBJECTIVE

To discuss the fundamentals of the Pascal programming language.

CHAPTER OVERVIEW

Last chapter, we described the basic structure of Pascal programs. This chapter elaborates on many of those concepts, and introduces other fundamental elements of the language.

We begin with a discussion of the conceptual operation of a Pascal program. Programs are made up of *data* and *action*. We discuss techniques for representing data, and the rules for describing action.

Programs should be easily understood by anyone who reads them; Section 4 focuses on methods for making programs readable. Finally, we talk about how Pascal programs are translated into a form that can be understood by a computer.

This chapter has five sections:

- **The Elements of Pascal**
- **More About Data and Action**
- **The Rules for Making Calculations**
- **Making Programs Understandable**
- **Pascal Operating Environments**

Section 1. The Elements of Pascal

INTRODUCTION

Pascal, like any other "language," has extremely specific rules concerning "syntax," "punctuation," and "semantics."

For purposes of illustration, let's compare Pascal to English. On the most fundamental level, Pascal syntax consists of certain words representing very explicit instructions to the computer. The components of this syntax are called *reserved words* and *special symbols*.

Some of the words in Pascal represent *data* (corresponding to nouns in English), and some represent *action* (the domain of verbs in English). This section discusses the concepts of data and action, and introduces the two most basic ways of representing data in a program: with variables and constants.

This section has five parts:

- The Concept of Data
- The Concept of Action
- Reserved Words and Special Symbols
- Variables and Constants
- Naming Variables and Constants

THE CONCEPT OF DATA

Computer programs perform *action* on *data*.

Data is a specific kind of information—namely, information that can be operated on by the computer.

Examples of Data:

— The number of people in Zambesi
— The text of this book
— Mailing lists
— Information gathered by a weather satellite

There are many ways to represent data. However, Pascal has some specific rules for representing data. You must understand these rules before you can write successful programs.

First of all, what do we mean by "representation of data"? Let's look at some of the different ways we can represent the number "3."

Examples:

3 : The number "3," printed without a decimal point or fractional part, is called an *integer* value. An integer representation is useful for data values that have no fractional parts. A count of people in a room would be represented as an integer.

3.00 : The number "3.00" is called a *real* number, Notice that it is written with its fractional part shown. Real numbers are useful for representing data that have fractional parts, such as dollar amounts.

Three : The word "Three" is a textual representation made up of *characters.* We would use data in this form to represent the concept "3" in the dictionary.

As you see, we can represent the number "3" in several ways, depending on our purpose. The form of representation, whether *integer, character,* or *real,* is called the *data type.*

The *actions* occuring in a Pascal program are designed to operate on data of a specific type. The most efficient program will be one supplying data of the type best suited for each action—just as humans add "523 + 16" more efficiently than "fivehundredtwentythree plus sixteen," and find "three" in the dictionary more easily than "3."

An individual unit of data is called a *data item,* and each data item in a program has one and only one *data type,* specified by the programmer. We will consider data types in greater detail later in this chapter.

THE CONCEPT OF ACTION

Action consists of the processes that occur to manipulate data. Data is *acted* on.

Action is fundamental to a computer program. The concept of "action" should be familiar from sci-fi movies where the computer speaks the familiar phrase, "COMPUTING." All basic computer operations are examples of action.

Examples of Action:

— Adding two numbers
— Comparing two results
— Printing a program listing
— Reading an input value

Thus, Pascal programs consist of data and action. A data item of a specific type is acted on in a manner designed to deliver appropriate results.

RESERVED WORDS AND SPECIAL SYMBOLS

Pascal has a set of *reserved words* and *special symbols* used to describe data and control action in a program.

Reserved words and *special symbols* are the syntactical units of Pascal. Reserved words are used to describe or define data, or to control action. Other words used in programs, typically English words used by the programmer, are not as strictly regulated as reserved words.

Reserved words and special symbols may only be used for specific purposes in a program. Figure 2.1 shows Pascal's reserved words. Throughout this text reserved words always appear in this special `computer printout` typestyle.

It is not necessary to memorize all of these words. Anytime you're in doubt as to whether a word is reserved, just refer to this list.

In addition to reserved words, Pascal also makes use of special symbols that work in conjunction with reserved words. Like reserved words, special symbols must only be used for specific purposes. You may be familiar with many of these symbols from mathematics. Figure 2.2 shows Pascal's special symbols.

We will always point out reserved words and special symbols when we describe the various ways they are used in a program.

and	end	mod	repeat
array	file	nil	set
begin	for	not	then
case	forward	of	to
const	function	or	type
div	goto	packed	until
do	if	procedure	var
downto	in	program	while
else	label	record	with

Figure 2.1 Pascal's Reserved Words

'+'	'–'	'*'	'/'	':='
'['	']'	'('	')'	'='
'<'	'>'	'<='	'>='	'<>'
';'	':'	','	'.'	'..' '↑'

Figure 2.2 Pascal's Special Symbols

VARIABLES AND CONSTANTS

A *variable* is a symbolic name that represents a changeable value; a *constant* is a symbolic name that represents a single unchangeable value.

Variables in Pascal are similar in form and function to variables used in algebra problems. Variables are useful for representing data because they let us create a single meaningful name, or *identifier,* that will represent one or many values, though only one at a time.

The *value* of a variable can change as often as necessary in a program. However, the variable name, or identifier, always stays the same regardless of how many times its value changes. This is because a variable identifier is always associated with one specific memory location. The variable identifier in effect becomes the name of an actual memory "cell" in the computer that will store some value. The following illustration shows the relationship between a variable identifier and a memory location in the computer:

Variable Identifier   **Memory Location**

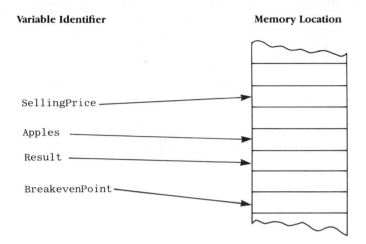

SellingPrice

Apples

Result

BreakevenPoint

Fortunately, we don't need to worry about assigning particular memory location to a variable—Pascal takes care of that for us. However, we must give each variable a unique identifier in the declaration part of a program. We will discuss the rules for declaring variables in the next section.

A *constant* is a symbolic name representing an unchanging value. The significance of a value is immediately clear to the reader of a program from the descriptive symbolic name representing the value. For example, the expression "TaxRate * CostOfItem" indicates quite clearly why the calculation is being performed, whereas the expression "0.06 * CostOfItem" does not give us the same information (although it may perform the same computation).

Constants are easy to define. The reserved word const begins the definition. Then, the literal name for a constant value is associated with its actual value with the equal sign. Here is the constant definition part from the program Sample:

```
const
   TaxRate =          0.06;
   MinnesotaLakes = 10000;
```

This definition creates two constants, TaxRate and MinnesotaLakes. Each has been assigned a specific value. Now the literal name TaxRate can be used *in place of* the number 0.06, and the literal name MinnesotaLakes can be used in place of the number 10000. These names should be far more meaningful to the reader of a program than the numbers they represent.

The primary difference between variables and constants, as their names imply, is that a variable can change values during a program, whereas a constant maintains a single value. Variables and constants in Pascal simplify the manipulation of data, because they associate a meaningful name with a specific value.

NAMING VARIABLES AND CONSTANTS

Variables and constants must have a unique name, called an *identifier.*

Every working person in America has a unique identifier—his or her social security number. Similarly, every variable or constant in Pascal must have a unique identifier. A judicious choice of identifiers for variables and constants can significantly enhance the readability of a program—that is, if the function or purpose of a variable or constant is clear from its identifier.

Variables and constants are not the only parts of Pascal that have identifiers. The name of a program is called the *program identifier.* Later, we will see that we must create an identifier whenever we need to give something a unique name.

There are several rules for forming identifiers, regardless of whether they will name variables, constants, programs, or anything else:

1. Pascal requires that identifiers begin with a letter (A–Z or a–z).
2. Punctuation marks are not allowed. Identifiers must consist exclusively of upper or lowercase letters and numbers.
3. An identifier cannot contain blank spaces.
4. Reserved words may not be used as identifiers.

Example:

Legal Identifiers	Illegal Identifiers	
PrimeRate	Prime.Rate	{"." not a letter or number}
Start	Begin	{reserved word}
FourthPlace	4thPlace	{begins with a number}
NumberOne	#One	{"#" not a letter or number}
BreakevenPoint	Stock Market Analysis	{no blank spaces}

The length of an identifier (the number of characters or numerals) is not restricted, but many versions of Pascal only recognize the first eight characters as significant. Therefore, the first eight characters of each identifier within a program must be unique, regardless of whether the identifier is used to name a variable, a constant, or a program. The identifiers `CalculateMortgage` and `CalculateDepreciation` conform to all of the rules for forming identifiers, but they may not be recognized as two individual entities in a program—their first eight characters, "Calculat," are identical.*

TEST YOUR UNDERSTANDING

1. What is data?
2. What is action?
3. What is a variable?
4. What is a constant?
5. Which of the following are legal identifiers?
   R2D2 MegaMillion %Rate fOuR5678 Test.Time

Section 2. More About Data and Action

INTRODUCTION

In Chapter 1, we talked about representing information as a variable or constant of a specific data type. This section discusses data types and how they make the representation of data efficient. And, as promised, we show how to declare variables.

We also talk about how action is specified in Pascal, with expressions and statements.

This section has four parts:

- The Simple Data Ttypes
- The Type `real`
- Declaring Variables
- Expressions and Statements

*In particular, Apple Pascal only recognizes the first eight characters of an identifier as significant, whereas IBM Personal Computer Pascal will recognize the first 31 characters as significant.

THE SIMPLE DATA TYPES

A variable or constant of a simple data type can represent only one value at a time.

Every variable or constant in a program represents a value of a specific data type. We illustrated the differences between data types by showing how the value "3" could be represented as an *integer* (with no fractional part), as a *real* value (with a fractional part), and as a *character* value (or a word). Pascal requires that we specify the data type for each variable used by a program.

Pascal has four "simple" data types: `integer`, `char`, `boolean`, and `real`. A variable or constant of a simple data type can represent only one value at a time. Other types of variables, different from simple types, can represent more than one value at a time. These *structured* variables are discussed in Chapter 6.

Three of the simple data types, `integer`, `char`, and `boolean`, are *scalar*. The values represented by a variable of a scalar data type can be ordered according to a sequence. Think of a number line: each value has a unique position on the line, and that value is either greater than or less than all other values.

Example: A Number Line

1 . . . 2 . . . 3 . . . 4 . . . 5 . . . 6 . . . 7 . . . 8 . . . 9 . . . 10 . . . 11 . . . 12 . . . 13 . . .

↑

The scalar value "8" is *greater than* "3", and *less than* "11".

Scalar data values have fixed positions in a *scale*. Checking the scalar position of a variable's value allows us to make comparisons that might influence action. For example, you can decide if employees should receive overtime pay by comparing the value of a standard work week (40 hours) with the number of hours they actually worked. If they worked more than 40 hours, they should receive overtime pay.

The first scalar data type we will discuss is type `integer`. Integers are whole numbers, such as 3, 12368, and −49. The range of `integer` values allowed by most versions of Pascal is typically from −32767 to +32767. Notice that no commas are used in values of type `integer`.

The other two simple scalar data types in Pascal are the type `char` and the type `boolean`. Each `char` variable represents one character, such as the letter "h" or the number "5" (if "5" is used as a character, rather than as a numeric value).

Variables of the boolean data type can represent only one of two values: they are either *true* or *false*.

Both char and boolean data types are useful for a variety of purposes, but the problems in this text do not require their use. See an advanced programming text for their description.

THE TYPE *real*

A *real* number must have a decimal point and at least one digit to the left and right of the decimal point, or alternatively, must be expressed in scientific notation.

Variables of type real are used often in Pascal because many problems require numbers with fractional parts. real values can be expressed in traditional scientific notation (1.0 E12) or as standard decimal numbers, with an integer part, a decimal point, and a fractional part (4.2735). The range of real values in most Pascal systems is $\pm\ 1.7\ E\pm38$.

Here are some real numbers. Note that all real numbers less than 1.0 must have a zero on the left side of the decimal point.

Legal *real* Values	Illegal *real* values
3.0	.03 {a zero must precede the decimal point}
4.60000 E −0.7	0.046 E 74 {not in the allowed range of real numbers}
−1237.0378	
1489036471.3	

DECLARING VARIABLES

All variables must be declared in the declaration part before they can be used.

The primary reason for declaring every variable is to specify its data type. You need to indicate whether it is type integer, real, char, or boolean. A variable declaration is also important because it associates a symbolic name, or identifier, with a unique memory location in the computer.

Here is the declaration part of the program `Sample`:

```
var
  Apples, Oranges, Total : integer;
  Dollars : real;
  RegisteredVoter : boolean;
  LetterGrade : char;
```

A variable declaration begins with the reserved word var. Next, all identifiers of a single data type are listed. This list is followed by a colon and a data type specification—the type of values that the variables will represent. A semi-colon must separate the variable declarations for each different data type.

As you see in this example, it is permissible to declare all the variables of the same data type with a single declaration. In the following example, we show two equivalent ways of declaring the variables `Apples`, `Oranges`, and `Total`.

Two Equivalent Variable Declarations

Example 1:

```
var
  Apples  : integer;
  Oranges : integer;
  Total   : integer;
```

Example 2:

```
var
  Apples, Oranges, Total : integer;
```

It is important to realize that all variables declared in a single declaration must be of the same data type. Variables of different data types must have separate declarations, with semi-colons separating each declaration. Notice below how two variables, one of type integer and one of type real, can be declared.

Two Equivalent Variable Declarations

Example 1:

```
var
  PayRate : real;
  HoursWorked : integer;
```

Example 2:

```
var
  PayRate : real; HoursWorked : integer;
```

This is a good example of Pascal's indifference to the way we format a program. Even though in Example 2 two variable declarations are on the same line, they are separated by a semi-colon. Thus, Pascal interprets each declaration separately.

There are many valid ways to format a program. The computer doesn't care if we are conservative or liberal in our use of blank space. The important thing is that the program be easily read and understood by humans. Of course, a program must use valid Pascal syntax, but the free-format characteristic of Pascal can be a tremendous advantage in making programs understandable.

By the way, although it is not necessary to specify a data type for constants, all constants nevertheless have an implicit data type. Pascal infers the data type from the constant definition: if a value has no decimal point, the constant is of type `integer`. If the constant value is defined with a decimal point, or in scientific notation, it is type `real`.

EXPRESSIONS AND STATEMENTS

Expressions and statements are combinations of words and symbols which allow us to specify *action* to be performed on *data*.

An *expression* is the representation of a single value. An expression can be a number, such as "27, " or a calculation which when evaluated will yield a single value, such as "328 + 47. " Variables and constants can replace numeric values in expressions; "Apples + Oranges" is a valid expression, as is "Apples + 92075. " Expressions can be compared or evaluated.

Expressions are always part of a *statement.* A Pascal *statement* is a complete description of action. Statements are set apart from each other by the statement separator, the semi-colon. Statements are made up of expressions and one or more reserved words and special symbols.

Let's look at some examples to illustrate the difference between expressions and statements:

Expressions	Statements
`Total`	`Total := 0;`
`(Dollars)`	`read (Dollars);`

```
(Dollars * TaxRate) = 100.0      if (Dollars * TaxRate) >= 100.0
                                 then
                                   LetterGrade := 'A'
                                   else LetterGrade := 'F';

Total + 1                        Total := Total + 1;

780 + 927                        Total := 780 + 927;
```

As you can see in the above examples, expressions are the component parts of statements. An expression can be a number, a variable, or a comparison between two values, but ultimately an expression represents a single value. Statements, on the other hand, are complete descriptions of *action* that the program is to perform.

Once again, we must stress the importance of the statement separator, the semi-colon. All statements must be separated from one another with a semi-colon at the end of the statement. Blank spaces will not do. The semi-colon is an important special symbol, because Pascal is a free-format language. Pascal ignores spaces, tabs, and blanks for the most part. The semi-colon is specifically used to separate statements, no matter how many lines a statement may require.

TEST YOUR UNDERSTANDING

6. What is a "simple data type"?
7. What's the difference between `integer` values and `real` values?
8. What are the two parts of a variable declaration?
9. What is an *expression?*
10. What is a Pascal *statement?*

Section 3. The Rules for Making Calculations

INTRODUCTION

Calculations and comparisons are the fundamental operations performed by computers on data. The basic rules for making calculations in Pascal are similar in many ways to the rules for standard mathematical calculations. One can add, subtract, multiply, and divide, or perform any combination of these operations. There are two significant differences in making calculations with Pascal, as opposed to making them "by hand" or with a calculator. The first difference concerns the symbols used for the arithmetic operators, and the second has to do with the way results are stored, or *assigned,* to variables.

This section has five parts:

- Pascal's Arithmetic Operators
- The Hierarchy of Operations
- The Assignment Operator
- Initializing Variables
- Assigning Results to Variables

PASCAL'S ARITHMETIC OPERATORS

The six arithmetic operators available in Pascal are addition, subtraction, multiplication, real division, integer division, and modulo.

Pascal uses the standard arithmetic operators (+) and (−) to perform addition and subtraction.

However, because the keyboard used to input symbols on most computers does not use standard multiplication (× or •) symbols, Pascal uses the asterisk (*) for multiplication. The addition, subtraction, and multiplication operators can be used with either `integer` or `real` values.

`real` division is performed by the slash (/) symbol. The result of division with this symbol will always be a `real` value, that is, a value having a fractional part. As in mathematics, division by zero is undefined and therefore not allowed in Pascal.

The Arithmetic Operators

Algebra	Pascal
+	+
−	−
× or •	*
real division	/
integer division	`div, mod`

Examples:

The following are all legitimate calculations in Pascal. `Amount` and `Quantity` are variables that may have any `real` value.

```
Addition:    5 + 3
             5 + Quantity
             Amount + Quantity
Subtraction: 5 - 3
             Quantity - 5
             Amount - Quantity
```

Multiplication: `5 * 3`
                  `5 * Quantity`
                  `Amount * Quantity`

real Division: `5 / 3`
                  `Quantity / 5`
                  `Amount / Quantity`

The division of `integer` values is a special situation. One of Pascal's design goals was to restrict calculations as much as possible to values of the same data type. Division of `integer` values, then, should not yield a fractional value, because the dividend would be of type `real`. To solve this problem, integer division makes use of two other operators, `div` (integer division) and `mod` (the modulus operator).

The operator `div` divides one integer by another, returns the whole number part of the result, and throws away the remainder if there is one. The result is *not* rounded; the remainder is simply discarded.

The operator `mod` will return the remainder portion of an `integer` division operation. `mod` divides two integers, throws away the whole number part, and assigns only the remainder part to the expression.

Examples:

integer division: `25 `**`div`**` 5`   `{result = 5}`
                     `100 `**`div`**` 10`   `{result = 10}`
                      `37 `**`div`**` 6`   `{result = 6}`

Modulus: `10 `**`mod`**` 2`   `{result = 0}`
                     `10 `**`mod`**` 3`   `{result = 1}`
                     `10 `**`mod`**` 4`   `{result = 2}`

Pascal allows us to make calculations (or evaluate expressions) between constant values, variable values, or any mixture of the two.

THE HIERARCHY OF OPERATIONS

In the process of evaluating an expression, Pascal performs multiplication and division before it performs addition and subtraction.

As in mathematics, you can use parentheses to alter the standard order of operations. Any expression enclosed between parentheses will be evaluated first—then the standard order of evaluation is used to complete the calculation.

Examples:

Perform addition before multiplication:

```
(5 + 3) * Quantity

(5 + Quantity) * (Amount + Quantity)
```

Perform subtraction before division:

```
(5 - 3) / Quantity

(5 - Quantity) / (Amount - Quantity)
```

Mixed order of operation:

```
((5 - 3) * Quantity) / (Amount + 5)

Quantity * ((Amount + 5) / (Amount + 3))
```

THE ASSIGNMENT OPERATOR (:=)

The *assignment operator,* (:=), is used to assign the value of an expression to a variable.

The assignment operator evaluates the expression on its right side, then assigns the result to the variable on the left side. The assignment operator is read "gets the value of," not "equals."

Examples:

```
NewValue := 10;
```
{The variable "NewValue" gets the value "10"}

```
Fruit := Apples + Oranges;
```
{"Apples" and "Oranges" are added; the variable "Fruit" gets the value of the result}

```
Counter := Counter + 10;
```
{"10" is added to the *value* of "Counter"; then "Counter" gets the new result}

For those algebra purists who find the notion of the expression "Counter := Counter + 10" hard to accept, just remember that "Counter" does not *equal* "Counter plus ten." This example shows an assignment statement, so the expression "Counter + 10" is evaluated first, *then* "Counter" *gets the value of* the expression.

The distinction between the equal sign (=) and the assignment operator (: =) is crucial. In Pascal, the equal sign (=) is used to test for equality between two expressions. If we wanted to know whether the value of Apples was equivalent to the value of Oranges, we would use the equal sign. The equal sign is also used to define the value of a constant, which cannot change thereafter.

INITIALIZING VARIABLES

Every variable must be given an initial, or starting value before it can be used in a calculation or comparison. This is called *initialization*.

A variable is considered to be undefined until it has been initialized. Initialization of each variable ensures that the program uses a correct starting value. If variables were not initialized, random values could be associated with the variable, possibly causing undesirable results. The necessity of initializing variables is another way Pascal encourages programmers to use forethought in the programming process.

There are several ways to initialize variables within a program. One way is to assign an explicit value to the variable with an assignment statement.

Example:

```
Apples := 10;
Oranges := 20;
Apples := Oranges;
```

Each variable is the above example is being assigned a single value. In the first two cases, Apples and Oranges are assigned numeric values. In the third case, Apples is assigned the value of Oranges, thus, both variables store the same value—the number "20".

The result of evaluating an expression can similarly be assigned to a variable. When the expression has been evaluated, the result is assigned to the variable on the left side of the assignment operator, effectively initializing that variable.

Example:

```
Total := 175 + Oranges;
Apples := 10 + (Oranges / Total );
Result := (LowValue + HighValue) / 35.0;
```

At first glance, these three examples may seem to contradict the rule that variables must be initialized before use in a calculation. However, we are initializing *only* the variables Total, Apples, and Result. The variables Oranges, LowValue, and HighValue must have been previously initialized.

ASSIGNING RESULTS TO VARIABLES

The assignment operator can *assign* the result of a calculation to a variable.

When an expression is evaluated, the result can be assigned to a variable, but *not* to a constant. This is supported by the definitions of constants and variables: constants are assigned a value once, in the definition part of a program, and cannot be changed thereafter. Variables can be assigned the value of any expression at any time. In Example 1 below, the variables LowValue, HighValue, and Result have been declared as integer variables.

Example 1: integer **calculations**

```
Result := 10 + 2;
Result := (LowValue + HighValue) div 35;
Result := (1000 - LowValue) * (185 mod HighValue);
```

Example 2: real **calculations**

```
Result := 10 + 2.398;
Result := LowValue + HighValue;
Result := (HighValue + LowValue) / 0.089
```

In example 2, the variables LowValue and HighValue can be either type integer or type real, but the variable Result *must* be type real, because Pascal will not assign a real value to a variable of type integer.

It is permissible to make calculations between integer and real values; Pascal automatically converts values of type integer to type real before the calculation is made. However, the result of any calculation that uses even a single real value, or uses the real division operator (/), can only be *assigned* to a real variable.

TEST YOUR UNDERSTANDING

   11. Evaluate the following expressions:

   A.   100 **div** 10
   B.   98 **div** 5
   C.   13 **mod** 4
   D.   150 **mod** 10

   12. Evaluate the following expressions:

   A.   19 * 7 + 3
   B.   (100 + 45) / 10
   C.   (425 **mod** 15) + (2850 **div** 75)
   D.   ((1467 – 321) * 5) – (653/4)

   13. What is the difference between the equal sign (=) and the assignment operator (:=)?

   14. Why must variables be initialized?

Section 4. Making Programs Understandable

INTRODUCTION

One of the goals of program design is to make programs easy to understand. A program should be easy for you as a programmer to read—and for anyone else who might happen to read it as well.

   Program readability is vital for purposes of *documentation.* If a program is designed to be used by more than one person, it should be well documented. Documentation helps make the purpose of a program clear to anyone who reads it, thus making the program easier to change at a later date.

   This section has three parts:

   • The Importance of Readability
   • Inventing Meaningful Identifiers
   • Adding Comments to a Program

THE IMPORTANCE OF READABILITY

Programs should be easy to read and understand.

The last part of this chapter is going to touch on an issue already mentioned often—and which will continue to be mentioned often. Programs intended to be used frequently—say, in a business environment—often require modification after the program has been written. A new function may be required, or the program might need to be adapted to a new computer.

A common error made by many programmers involves thinking that documentation is unnecessary; the programmer should be able to remember what the program does. When a change is required months or years after a program has been written, however, even the programmer with a very good memory can find it difficult to remember how a program works. This problem compounds if the original programmer is not available to make the changes.

There are several methods for making programs readable. Two common techniques include inventing meaningful identifiers, and adding comments that explain a program's action.

INVENTING MEANINGFUL IDENTIFIERS

Meaningful, or "self-explanatory," identifiers enhance the readability of programs.

Identifiers should indicate the nature of the information they represent. Variable identifiers like "a, " "m1, " or "ED" may be easy for the programmer to type when writing the program, but give absolutely no indication of what they represent. Whenever possible, try to create identifiers that are complete words or phrases describing the purpose of the value they represent.

Meaningful Identifiers	Non-Meaningful Identifiers
AccountsReceivable	AR
January	M1
EndOfData	ED

ADDING COMMENTS TO A PROGRAM

Another way to enhance program readability is to include *comments* explaining data or action.

Comments can explain action in a program that might not have an obvious purpose. They can also explain the significance of a variable, or the type of result expected from a calculation, and so on.

Anything enclosed between braces (the symbols "{" and "}") is considered to be a comment by Pascal and is ignored, even if the comment contains a valid Pascal statement. If your computer keyboard does not have braces, comments can be enclosed between the symbols "(*" and "*)".

Examples: Using Comments

```
{ This is a Comment. }

(* This is also a Comment *)

Apples := Apples + Oranges; { This comment follows a
                                             statement }


Total := Apples; { This comment also follows a statement,
                          but is spread out over two lines. }
```

Comments can appear on the same line as a statement, but should be placed either before or after the complete statement. An error that might be difficult to spot arises when a closing brace is forgotten. This error turns the rest of the program into a comment!

Because comments are ignored by Pascal and won't affect the execution of your program in any way, they should be used liberally.

TEST YOUR UNDERSTANDING

15. Why should identifiers be meaningful?
16. Name two ways of putting comments into a program.

Section 5. Pascal Operating Environments

INTRODUCTION

After you have written a Pascal program, you must prepare it to run on your computer. First, the program must be entered into the computer's memory, usually with a text editing program. Then you need to begin a process called "compilation," which makes sure that your program conforms to the syntactical rules of Pascal, and, if it does, readies the program for execution.

The process of executing programs varies among computers. As you begin to work with Pascal, you should familiarize yourself with the compiler and run-time system available to you.

This section has three parts:

- Compilers Detect Syntactical Errors
- Standard Pascal Systems
- UCSD Pascal

COMPILERS DETECT SYNTACTICAL ERRORS

A compiler translates Pascal instructions into *machine language* instructions that can be directly executed by the computer.

A *compiler* is a specialized program designed specifically to make the translation from Pascal into machine language. Compilers perform several functions; the first is to check your program to make sure it conforms to Pascal's syntactical rules.

Checking the program's syntax as a first step toward compilation is very important. A syntax check will reveal action that doesn't make sense, or action that may be ambiguous or is simply impossible. The compiler detects these conditions and indicates that you have an error to correct before compiling and running the program successfully.

The syntax check performed by the compiler is the first step in the process of "debugging," or getting the mistakes out of your programs. Almost all programs, even those written by Pascal experts, have syntax errors the compiler detects the first time.

If the syntax of a program is correct, the program will probably run. However, just because a program is syntactically correct does not guarantee it will do what you intended. The compiler cannot check your use of the language, or *semantics*.

We all know it is possible to construct a sentence in English that is syntactically correct but is semantic nonsense—such as "The pickle shuddered menacingly across the moon." It is equally possible to construct syntactically correct but semantically meaningless statements in Pascal. Correct semantics can only be assured by rigorous planning and testing of programs.

If the compiler has found no syntactical errors in the program, it goes on to translate the program into instructions that can be executed by your particular computer. How Pascal programs are executed is typically a function of the particular operating system used by your computer. Many compilers produce a "run-time" module allowing a Pascal program to be executed independently of any other program. UCSD Pascal, on the other hand, interprets your compiled programs each time they are run. Next, we discuss the features and advantages of each type of process.

STANDARD PASCAL SYSTEMS

Some Pascal compilers produce an independent "run-time" module allowing programs to be executed independently of any other program.

A "run-time" module is a complete Pascal program. All machine instructions to carry out your program, as well as a comprehensive set of instructions that handle input and output operations, are included in a run-time module.

Pascal compilers that produce this kind of module are commonly called "standard" Pascal systems. Standard Pascal conforms to the specifications of the International Standards Organization. While the definition of what constitutes "standard" and "non-standard" systems could take up an entire book, it is sufficient to say that most Pascal systems available for microcomputers adhere closely to standard Pascal. UCSD Pascal, while conforming to the standard, has included several "extensions," or additions, to the language considered "non-standard."

There are several versions of "standard" Pascal available for microcomputers; two popular versions are *IBM Personal Computer Pascal,* and *MT+,* manufactured by Digital Research.

UCSD PASCAL

UCSD Pascal is a component of the *p-system,* a powerful group of software tools including a Pascal compiler and a run-time interpreter.

As we mentioned above, UCSD Pascal is considered "non- standard" because it supports several features not considered standard. Among these are enhanced capabilities for text processing and graphics.

The UCSD Pascal compiler is just one part of the p-system. Also included are an editor for processing text, a filer for managing disks, and so on. The p-system has an advantage over many other Pascal systems; programs written in UCSD Pascal will run on *any* computer system using the p-system, with no modifications needed.

This *portability* feature is possible because programs are translated by the compiler into "p-code," rather than machine language. The p-code instructions are then interpreted by a program simulating an "optimal" computer. In other words, the p-code interpreter is a *software* program simulating *hardware.* Therefore, the p-code interpreter program must be written in machine language for every different type of computer.

A full discussion of the details of UCSD Pascal and the p-system is beyond this text. The p-system is available for most kinds of microcomputers. For example, Apple Pascal is a version of UCSD Pascal and the p-system designed to run on Apple computers.

TEST YOUR UNDERSTANDING

17: Why is the syntax check performed by a compiler important?

EXERCISES

Exercise 1:

If you have access to a computer, find out the manufacturer of the Pascal system. Read the documentation that comes with the compiler, and determine if yours is a standard Pascal or UCSD Pascal system.

Exercise 2:

If you have access to a computer, type in the program Sample listed in Chapter 1, Figure 1.1 (page 10). Compile the program and run it on your system so that you understand the process. If you feel you understand the program, make modifications (add new variables, define new constants, and so on), and try to compile it again.

ANSWERS TO THE TEST YOUR UNDERSTANDING EXERCISES

1. Data is a specific kind of information—information that can be operated on by the computer.

2. Action consists of the processes involved in manipulating data. Data is *acted* on.

3. A *variable* is a symbolic name that represents a changeable value.

4. A *constant* is a symbolic name assigned a single value which cannot be changed.

5. `R2D2`, `MegaMillion` and `fOuR5678` are legal identifiers. `% Rate` and `Test.Time` are not legal because they use punctuation.

6. A variable or constant of a simple data type can represent only one value at a time.

7. Integers are whole numbers, such as 3, 12368, and −49. A `real` number must have a decimal point and at least one digit each to the left and right of the decimal, or alternatively, must be expressed in scientific notation.

8. The variable name, or identifier, and its data type.

9. An *expression* is the representation of a single value.

10. A Pascal *statement* is a complete description of action.

11.   A: 0   B: 19   C: 1   D: 0

12.   A: 136   B: 14.5   C: 43   D: 5566.75

13. In Pascal, the equal sign (=) is used to test for equality between two expressions. The assignment operator (:=) is used to assign the value of an expression to a variable.

14. A variable is considered to be undefined until it has been initialized.

15. Meaningful identifiers help the reader know what the program is doing.

16. Comments can be inserted anywhere in a program if they are enclosed between the symbols "{" and "}" or between the symbols "(*" and "*)".

17. A syntax check will reveal action that doesn't make sense, or that may be ambiguous or simply impossible.

CHAPTER 3

Getting Results
With Pascal

CHAPTER OBJECTIVE

To develop an algorithm specifying the steps necessary to perform a breakeven analysis, and to introduce the Pascal needed to translate the algorithm into a functional program.

CHAPTER OVERVIEW

Beginning with this chapter, we're going to take a slightly non-traditional approach to the presentation of Pascal. Many texts simply introduce a Pascal concept, then illustrate how to use it with numerous unrelated examples. Rather than this "catch-all" approach, we're going to introduce a motivating problem at the beginning of each chapter, develop an algorithm for the problem, *then* introduce those aspects of Pascal necessary to translate the algorithm into a functioning program.

Many businesses are relying on consultants to computerize their operations. You'll be in the role of a consultant, who works with key people in a business to analyze the tasks they want computerized. Once you've extracted enough information from your client, you must develop an algorithm for the task, then translate it into a Pascal program. By approaching problems in this way, you'll get a good idea of the processes involved in *systems analysis*. In each case, it will be necessary to thoroughly understand the problem before you can write a program to perform the desired task.

Your first assignment is for HighTech Corp., world-famous for its automatic integrated cleaning products. HighTech plans to introduce a new product, the "Electronic Sponge," and they want to develop a computer program to assist them in determining a selling price. This is called a *breakeven analysis*, because the goal is to analyze a number of selling prices, then determine how many units must be manufactured at a given price to cover production costs—or to *break even*.

New Pascal: this chapter introduces the concepts necessary to write a breakeven analysis program, beginning with the most fundamental rules for performing arithmetic with Pascal, then advancing to the concept of using a "loop" for performing repetitive actions. By the end of this chapter, you'll know how to write Pascal instructions to get input, perform calculations, and print results. These techniques are brought together in one program to solve the breakeven analysis problem.

This chapter has six sections:

- **The Breakeven Analysis Problem**
- **Establishing Variables and Constants**
- **Input with Pascal**
- **Output with Pascal**
- **Repetitive Action**
- **The Breakeven Analysis Program**

Section 1. The Breakeven Analysis Problem

INTRODUCTION

How should you approach the task of writing a program to perform a breakeven analysis? In Chapter 1, we said the first step in solving any problem, with or without a computer, is to make a concise statement of the problem.

A carefully phrased statement is then used as the basis for an initial algorithm. In this section we discuss techniques for analyzing problems and creating algorithms that are easily translated into Pascal programs.

This section has two parts:

- Analyzing the Problem
- The Breakeven Analysis Algorithm

ANALYZING THE PROBLEM

The first step in analyzing any problem is to learn enough to make a concise statement about it.

Mr. Arbaker, the product manager for HighTech in charge of the "Electronic Sponge" project, has contacted you. He's explained they would like a computer program to perform a breakeven analysis. This program would provide HighTech with breakeven information for many potential selling prices for the Electronic Sponge. Mr. Arbaker has indicated the breakeven analysis will be used with market research reports to establish a selling price for the Electronic Sponge, covering production costs and resulting in a good profit.

You question Mr. Arbaker further, discovering the breakeven analysis requires several simple calculations repeated for a pre-determined number of possible selling prices between a minimum and maximum selling price. The minimum number of manufactured units that cover production costs for a particular selling price is called the breakeven point.

On the day you meet Mr. Arbaker, you must ask the following questions:

1. *What information will the program start with?* The program requires the overall overhead production cost, and the cost of manufacturing one unit. These two data items are input only once for a particular product. The program must also request a minimum and maximum selling price for the product. The breakeven analysis program is valuable because it allows the program user to enter a variety of minimum and maximum prices, resulting in a wide range of breakeven points.

2. *What is the desired result?* We want to print a list of possible selling prices, with the breakeven point for each. Mr. Arbaker digs in his desk and produces a breakeven analysis for another of HighTech's products as an example of the desired output, shown in Figure 3.1.

3. *What action is necessary to accomplish the desired result?* First, a breakeven point must be calculated for each selling price between

```
SELLING PRICE          BREAKEVEN POINT

    3.95               6897.0 Units
    4.15               6061.0 Units
    4.35               5405.0 Units
    4.55               4878.0 Units
    4.75               4444.0 Units
    4.95               4082.0 Units
    5.15               3774.0 Units
    5.35               3509.0 Units
    5.55               3279.0 Units
    5.75               3077.0 Units
    5.95               2899.0 Units
```

Figure 3.1   Breakeven Analysis for Digital Squegee

the minimum and maximum. This calculation involves several steps.
For each possible selling price, the profit earned on a unit must be
determined by subtracting the cost of manufacturing the unit from
the potential selling price. Next, the breakeven point for that selling
price is calculated by dividing the unit profit into the overhead
cost. These calculations are then repeated for a predetermined
number of selling prices between the minimum and maximum.

THE BREAKEVEN ANALYSIS ALGORITHM

**The breakeven analysis algorithm lists the steps required to perform a
breakeven analysis for any product.**

With the information we extracted from Mr. Arbaker, we can now create
an initial algorithm for the breakeven analysis problem. When creating an
algorithm, it's helpful to number each step. Numbering the steps distin-
guishes each part of the problem as you refine the algorithm.

The goal for the initial algorithm: Make a very general description of the
action necessary to solve the problem.

Initial Breakeven Analysis Algorithm

1. *Get relevant information*
2. *Calculate the breakeven point for each of the evenly spaced
   selling prices from the minimum price to the maximum
   price*

Now that we've made an algorithm describing the general process involved in performing a breakeven analysis, we must begin to break down each step into increasingly precise descriptions of the action necessary to complete each step. As you recall, the process of adding detail to each step is called *stepwise refinement*.

Step #1 can be refined without difficulty. We simply need to list each separate input item.

Refinement of Step #1

1. *Get relevant information*

    1.1 *Request overhead production cost*
    1.2 *Request cost of manufacturing one unit*
    1.3 *Request minimum potential selling price*
    1.4 *Request maximum potential selling price*

Refining Step #2 requires a bit more thought. Before we can determine the breakeven point, we need to calculate a value that will be used to evenly increment the selling price. Then we can consider the breakeven point calculation.

Essentially, we'll be calculating a breakeven point for every evenly spaced selling price falling between the minimum and maximum price. Therefore, if the selling price does not *exceed* the maximum selling price, we will:

— Perform all necessary actions to calculate a breakeven point for the current selling price,
— Print the selling price and breakeven point,
— Add the price interval to the selling price,
— Repeat these steps until the selling price is greater than the maximum price.

Here's the refinement of step #2:

Refinement of Step #2

2. *Calculate the breakeven point for each of the evenly spaced selling prices from the minimum price to the maximum price*

    2.1 *Calculate the value of the selling price increment by subtracting the minimum price from the maximum price, then divide the result by the number of desired prices*

> **2.2**   *Consider the expression that calculates a breakeven point with the price set to the minimum price*
>
> **2.3**   *If the selling price is not greater than the maximum price then*
> > *evaluate the breakeven point expression,*
> > *print the selling price and breakeven point,*
> > ⟶ *add the increment to the selling price,*
> > *repeat step #2.2*

This algorithm illustrates one way to solve the breakeven analysis problem, but you should realize there are probably many alternatives. An algorithm is "correct" as long as it describes an accurate solution to a problem. Formulating a correct algorithm is an extremely important part of creating an effective Pascal program.

Now that we have a reasonably complete idea of the fundamental action performed by the program, our next step is to explore the statements needed to translate this algorithm into Pascal.

TEST YOUR UNDERSTANDING

1. What is the first step in analyzing any problem?

2. What are the three steps involved in creating a Pascal program?

Section 2. Establishing Variables and Constants

INTRODUCTION

Even though we haven't yet written any Pascal instructions for the breakeven analysis program, we can begin making up names for our variables and constants. At this point, giving literal names to data items will make the examples more meaningful.

A handy way to keep track of variables and constants is to write them in a table indicating whether they are used to represent input information, process information, or output information. The next section discusses creating and using a *Problem Table* for that purpose.

This section has four parts:

- Introducing the Problem Table
- Establishing Input Variables
- Establishing Output Variables
- Establishing Process Variables and Constants

INTRODUCING THE PROBLEM TABLE

A Problem Table can be used to keep track of the variables and constants used in a program.

A Problem Table is not a part of Pascal, but it can be very useful for keeping track of variables and constants used by a program, especially for a long and complex program.

Here's what a Problem Table looks like. Take a moment to draw your own before continuing with this chapter.

A Problem Table

INPUT	PROCESS	OUTPUT

Next, we'll begin to create variable names for our program, and write them into this table.

ESTABLISHING INPUT VARIABLES

Variables must be established to store input information.

Step #1 of our algorithm specifies the input variables necessary for the program:

Algorithm Step #1

1.   *Get relevant information*
    1.1   *Request overhead production cost*
    1.2   *Request cost of manufacturing one unit*

1.3   Request minimum potential selling price
1.4   Request maximum potential selling price

Each data item specified in this algorithm step must be represented by a separate variable.

As you name variables, recall that a major goal is to make your program easy to read and understand. Naming variables with self-descriptive identifiers is an excellent way to enhance a program's readability.

We recommend these variable identifiers to represent the four input values in the breakeven analysis program:

Input Information	Variable Identifier
Overhead production cost:	OverheadCost
Cost of manufacturing one unit:	CostPerUnit
Minimum selling price per unit:	MinimumPrice
Maximum selling price per unit:	MaximumPrice

Notice that our variable names use a mixture of upper and lower case letters (remember: *no* spaces allowed!). Capitalizing each distinct word in an identifier makes it easy to read. Pascal will accept any combination of upper- or lower-case letters in a program. The names themselves are arbitrary. Feel free to create different variable names you think are more meaningful.*

Now that we've created variable identifiers for input data items, we'll write each of them in the INPUT column of the Problem Table:

INPUT	PROCESS	OUTPUT
OverheadCost CostPerUnit MaximumPrice MinimumPrice		

Next, we must determine what output variables will be necessary.

---

*Some computers, such as the Apple II, only provide uppercase letters. We recommend using single-word identifiers on these machines. Any advantage gained from a lengthier, possibly more self-explanatory identifier is diminished because each unique word is harder to read when the identifier appears entirely in upper case letters.

ESTABLISHING OUTPUT VARIABLES

Variables must also be established to represent output items.

Algorithm step #2.3 specifies the output for the breakeven analysis:

Algorithm Step #2.3

**2.3   If the selling price is not greater than the maximum
price then
          evaluate the breakeven point expression,
      ⟶ print the selling price and breakeven point,
          add the increment to the selling price,
          repeat step #2.2**

Output variables represent values to be printed. Look at the sub-step marked with an arrow. Notice that for each selling price printed, the number of units that must be sold to break even will also be printed. Therefore, we need one variable to represent the selling price, and another to represent the number of units sold to break even—or the *breakeven point.*

Output Information	Variable Identifier
Selling price per unit:	`SellingPrice`
Number of units that must be sold to break even:	`BreakevenPoint`

Now add these variable identifiers to the Problem Table in the OUTPUT column:

INPUT	PROCESS	OUTPUT
OverheadCost CostPerUnit MaximumPrice MinimumPrice		SellingPrice BreakevenPoint

ESTABLISHING PROCESS VARIABLES AND CONSTANTS

Process variables and constants represent values used by the program that will remain essentially "invisible" to the user.

Process variables and constants are typically used in calculations or comparisons. As we learn more about Pascal and begin the process of translating an algorithm into a program, we may find that additional variables or constants are necessary.

Let's look at Step #2.3 of the algorithm again, to see if we can identify any process variables:

Algorithm Step #2.3

> *2.3*   *If the selling price is not greater than the maximum price then*
> > *evaluate the breakeven point expression,*
> > *print the selling price and breakeven point,*
> > ⟶ *add the increment to the selling price,*
> > *repeat step #2.2*

The step marked with an arrow gives us a clue. We'll be adding an increment to the selling price. This increment allows the selling price to be evenly increased each time the algorithm step is repeated, depending on how many different breakeven points are desired.

Process Information	Identifier
Increment for selling price:	`PriceInterval`

Now add the process variable to the Problem Table:

INPUT	PROCESS	OUTPUT
OverheadCost CostPerUnit MaximumPrice MinimumPrice	Variable: `PriceInterval`	SellingPrice BreakevenPoint

We have now created as many variables as we can from looking at the description of the problem and the algorithm. Notice, however, that we have neither specified *data types* (integer or real), nor have we *initialized* the variables. First we need to learn more about input and output with Pascal.

TEST YOUR UNDERSTANDING

3. True or False: It's necessary to use a Problem Table when writing a Pascal program.

4. Why does one make a distinction between INPUT, PROCESS, and OUTPUT variables in a Problem Table?

Section 3. Input With Pascal

INTRODUCTION

Now that we've created input variables, we must learn about Pascal's provisions for initializing them—in other words, how to get data into a program. We want to create statements that ask the program user to provide starting values for the input variables. Pascal offers several methods for obtaining input information. We will focus on the most common method, using a readln or read statement.

This section has two parts:

- Using readln and read for Input,
- Using readln for Multiple Input Values.

USING *READLN* AND *READ* FOR INPUT

A *readln* or *read* statement is used to input one or more values into a program.

A readln statement is used to accept an input value (usually from a terminal or punched cards), and assign that value to a specific variable. The input value is assigned to the variable listed in parentheses after readln.

Examples:

```
readln (Apples);
```
{reads in a single value and assigns it to the variable Apples}

```
readln (CostPerUnit);
```
{reads a value and assigns it to the variable CostPerUnit}

```
readln (MaximumPrice);
```
{reads a value and assigns it to the variable MaximumPrice}

Before readln makes an assignment to a variable, it checks to make sure the input value is compatible with the data type of the variable. In other words, if the variable was declared as an integer, readln will only make the assignment if the input value is of type integer.

readln and read, like input and output, are built-in procedures—similar to reserved words in that they have a special meaning to Pascal. For our purposes the difference between built-in procedures and reserved words is not important.

The read statement is used in the same way as readln.

Examples:

```
read (Apples);
```
{reads in a single value and assigns it to the variable Apples}

```
read (CostPerUnit);
```
{reads a value and assigns it to the variable CostPerUnit}

```
read (MaximumPrice);
```
{reads a value and assigns it to the variable MaximumPrice}

The difference between read and readln is subtle. For our purposes, either read or readln is suitable for accepting input data. Advanced programming applications, especially those dealing with text processing, have specific requirements for the use of read as opposed to readln. All examples in this book will make use of readln rather than read for obtaining input.

USING *READLN* FOR MULTIPLE INPUT VALUES

A single *read* or *readln* statement can be used to input more than one value at a time.

The number of variables accommodated by a single readln statement is theoretically unlimited. However, for the sake of readability, each readln statement should never take up more than one line in a program.

Examples:

```
readln (Apples, Oranges);           {reads two values, assigns the first
                                value to Apples, the second to Oranges}
readln (CostPerUnit, MinimumPrice, MaximumPrice);
                {reads three values, assigns the first to CostPerUnit, the second to
                        MinimumPrice, and the third to MaximumPrice}
```

We recommend using one `readln` statement for each input variable, instead of using a single `readln` statement for many variables. Using `readln` for multiple input increases the possibility the user may input values in an incorrect order. Another possibility is that the user may try to enter a value of an incorrect data type for one of the variables, thereby causing an error. We'll talk more about methods for avoiding input errors in a later section on prompting for input.

TEST YOUR UNDERSTANDING

5. What is the function of a `readln` statement?

6. True or False: `readln` and `read`, like `input` and `output`, are reserved words in Pascal.

Section 4. Output with Pascal

INTRODUCTION

Just as there are many ways to get input, numerous methods are available for getting output from a Pascal program. We will concentrate on the `write` and `writeln` statements in this section; they're the most commonly used.

`write` and `writeln` are complementary in their action to `read` and `readln`—in fact, they are also built-in procedures. However, `write` and `writeln` have many more aspects of concern to us than `readln`, because output can be formatted in a variety of ways.

This section discusses output with `write` and `writeln`, and the various techniques used to control the format of output information.

This section has five parts:

- The `write` and `writeln` Statements
- Printing Literal Text with `writeln`
- Prompting for Input
- Controlling Output Field Width with the Colon
- Printing `real` Numbers.

THE *WRITE* AND *WRITELN* STATEMENTS

write and *writeln* **can be used to print the values of variables or constants, or strings of "literal" text.**

To print the *value* of a variable or constant, we simply list the variable name in parentheses after the word `writeln`.

Examples:

```
write (Apples);                 {prints the current value of Apples}
writeln (BreakevenPoint);       {prints the current value of
                                              BreakevenPoint}
```

As you consider these examples, it's important to realize these statements will cause the *value* of each variable to be printed, *not* the literal words "Apples" or "BreakevenPoint." However, `write` and `writeln` can also print informative messages that explain the output. Anything printed by `write` or `writeln` that isn't the value of a variable or constant is called a *string,* or *literal text.* We'll show examples of literal text later.

Like `read` and `readln`, a single `write` or `writeln` statement can accommodate more than one variable. Simply list each output variable in parentheses, separating the name of each variable with a comma.

Examples:

```
writeln (Apples, Oranges);               {prints the current values
                                          of Apples and Oranges}
writeln (SellingPrice, BreakevenPoint);       {prints the current
                                 values of SellingPrice and BreakevenPoint}
```

The difference between `write` and `writeln` is apparent in the behavior of the cursor, or blinking prompt on the display screen, after the statement has been executed. write positions the cursor immediately to the right of the last output item that was printed. writeln, on the other hand, advances the cursor to the beginning of the next line. In other words, writeln produces the same effect as pressing the *return* key after all information has been printed.

For the following examples, assume that Apples = 10, and Oranges = 20.

Examples: The effect of write

Statements	Output:
1. write (Apples);	10 __ ◄── (cursor)
2. write (Apples, Oranges);	10 20 __ ◄── (cursor)
3. write (Apples); write (Oranges);	10 20 __ ◄── (cursor)

Notice that write never issues a carriage return after values are printed. Compare this to the behavior of writeln in the following examples:

Examples: The effect of writeln

Statements	Output:
1. writeln (Apples);	10 __ ◄── (cursor)
2. writeln (Apples, Oranges);	10 20 __ ◄── (cursor)
3. writeln (Apples); writeln (Oranges);	10 20 __ ◄── (cursor)

In these examples, you see how a writeln statement advances the cursor to the next line once the statement has been executed.

Look closely at the difference between write and writeln in these examples. Whether one uses write or writeln in a program depends on the purpose of the program, as well as personal preference for presenting output. Experiment with both to see which you prefer.

PRINTING LITERAL TEXT WITH *WRITELN*

Literal text, sometimes called a "string," is enclosed between single quotes in a *write* or *writeln* statement.

Literal text is useful for explaining or commenting on output. Literal text is enclosed between single quotes, and must be bracketed with parentheses, just as variables are. The quote marks indicate we want the string to be printed exactly as is, not interpreted as a variable name, or a calculation or anything else. The quote marks do not appear in the actual output.

Example 1:

Statement

```
writeln ('This is literal text.');
```

Output

```
This is literal text.
```

Example 2:

Statement

```
write ('Apples, Oranges');
```

Output

```
Apples, Oranges
```

Notice in the second example that, although `Apples` and `Oranges` are variable names, placing them between single quotes causes the *text* 'Apples, Oranges' to be printed, *not* the actual value of the variables. Consequently, we can use this feature to print both the name of a variable, and its value.

Example 1:

Statement

```
write ('Total number of apples is');
write (Apples );
```

Output

```
Total number of apples is      10
```

Example 2:

Statement

```
write ('Total number of oranges is');
write (Oranges);
```

Output

```
Total number of oranges is        20
```

Notice in these examples both literal text *and* the value of the variable were printed on the same line. Why? We used two write statements, and a write statement does not position the cursor on the next line after it has been executed.

We can use a single writeln statement to print literal text together with the value of a variable or constant. Just as we use a comma to separate variables in a writeln statement, it's also used to separate a string of text from a variable or constant.

Example 1:

Statement

```
writeln ('Total number of oranges is ', Oranges);
```

Output

```
Total number of oranges is        20
```

Example 2:

Statement

```
writeln ('The selling price is ', SellingPrice);
```

Output

```
The selling price is        43
```

As you see, it's quite handy being able to print both literal text and the value of variables with a single writeln statement.

PROMPTING FOR INPUT

When *readln* is used for input, a *write* statement should be used first to tell the user what information is expected.

write and readln are commonly used together. First, the program requests input with a write statement, then it gets the input value with a readln statement. Using write and readln together in this way is called *prompting for input.*

It's important to prompt for input. When a program executes a read statement, it then waits patiently for input until something is entered. If the program doesn't prompt for input, the user may not have the slightest idea what's going on —while the computer waits for input, it appears to be "just sitting there." After a standoff of several minutes courageous users may venture to press a few keys, but they may be entering information readln thinks is invalid—thereby causing an error message. The inevitable response: "It's broken!" A conscientious program design seeks to avoid potential problems like this at all costs, and prompting for input helps avoid this type of problem.

Example 1: Prompting for Input

Statements:

```
write ('How many oranges would you like? ');
readln (Oranges);
```

Output:

```
How many oranges would you like? _  ←—(cursor)
```

Example 2: Prompting for Input

Statements:

```
write ('How much does each unit cost to manufacture? ');
readln (CostPerUnit);
```

Output:

```
How much does each unit cost to manufacture? _ ←—(cursor)
```

We use the particular combination of write and readln because the write statement leaves the cursor on the same line as the text prompt. The `readln` statement then advances the cursor to the next line once it has read the desired input value.

The wording of a prompt should be as specific as possible to assure that the user doesn't enter an incorrect value. The prompt should not only tell the user what sort of information is expected (for example, the mimimum selling price, or the number of apples), but should also explicitly state the data type required, either type `integer` or type `real`.

CONTROLLING OUTPUT FIELD WIDTH WITH THE COLON

The number of spaces in which *writeln* **prints the value of a variable is called the "field width."**

`writeln` prints the value of a variable in a right-aligned slot with a default number of spaces. The default field width differs for each data type, and may also differ between versions of Pascal. An `integer` value is typically printed in a field width of ten spaces; a `real` value commonly is printed in a twenty-two space field.

The following example shows `integer` values printed in a default field width of ten spaces:

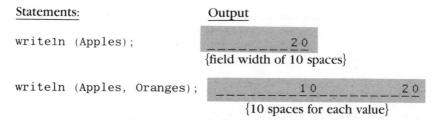

Statements: Output

`writeln (Apples);`   2 0
                                         {field width of 10 spaces}

`writeln (Apples, Oranges);`   1 0   2 0
                                         {10 spaces for each value}

The default field width can be changed to accommodate smaller or larger values, thereby making the output more readable. To change the field width in which `writeln` prints a variable, the variable identifier is followed by a colon, and a number specifying the new field width. Changing the field width is useful for creating tables of information, so numbers can all be aligned. As an example, consider the following two statements:

Statements:

```
writeln ('Total number of Macintosh apples is ', Apples);
writeln ('Total number of oranges is ', Oranges);
```

Output:

```
Total number of Macintosh apples is              10
Total number of oranges is            20
```

This output would be far easier to read if we aligned the two numbers in a column. This is easy to do; we increase the output field width for the variable Oranges. Since values are printed right-aligned in the output field, increasing the field width from the default width of 10 spaces to a new width of 19 will cause writeln to print an additional 9 blank spaces to the left of the value, aligning the value of Oranges under the value of Apples:

Statements:

```
writeln ('Total number of Macintosh apples is ', Apples);
writeln ('Total number of oranges is ', Oranges :19 );
```

Output:

```
Total number of Macintosh apples is            10
Total number of oranges is                     20
```

All these examples illustrates how values of type integer are printed with a writeln statement. Variables and constants of type real have some additional aspects to concern us.

PRINTING *REAL* NUMBERS

All *real* values in Pascal are represented in scientific notation unless the programmer requests otherwise.

Here's a table that shows the difference between scientific notation and standard decimal notation:

Scientific Notation	Standard Decimal Notation
$4.200000E+1$	4.2
$3.602000E\text{-}4$	0.0003602
$1.245367E+10$	12453670000.0

Consider the following example:

Statements:

```
SellingPrice := 4.2;
writeln (SellingPrice);
```

Output

```
4.2000000000000000000E+1
```
{default field width 22 spaces}

Notice that, even though we assigned the value 4.2 to the variable `SellingPrice`, Pascal converted it from decimal form to scientific notation when the value was printed by the `writeln` statement, with a 22 space field width.

To print `real` values in traditional decimal format, two steps are required. First, you must specify a field width whether or not you want to alter the default value. Then, you must use a *second* colon, followed by a numeral specifying the number of digits that are to be printed after the decimal point.

Example:

Statements

```
writeln ('The selling price is ', SellingPrice :8:2);
writeln('Annual finance charge is ',FinanceCharge :7:3,' %');
```

Output:

```
The selling price is 4.20
Annual finance charge is 19.625 %
```

As you can see, values printed in standard decimal format are easier to read than those in scientific notation. Notice also that we have printed a per-cent sign *after* the value has been printed. This technique is a perfectly legitimate way of further enhancing the readability of the output.

When printing a `real` value in standard decimal format, we restrict the number of digits printed after the decimal point. In doing so, we must be careful not to neglect significant digits. In the example above, if the value of `SellingPrice` had been 4.2057, the last two digits ("57") would have been thrown away. Specifying the number of digits to be printed after a decimal point tells the program to chop off the number at that point. No rounding is performed.

TEST YOUR UNDERSTANDING

7. What's the output from this program segment?

```
BreakevenPoint := 293.67;
writeln (BreakevenPoint);
```

8. What's the difference between `write` and `writeln`?

9. What is literal text?

10. How does one specify that text is to be printed literally in a `writeln` statement?

11. Why is it important to prompt for input?

12. What is "field width"?

13. How does Pascal print `real` numbers, unless told otherwise?

Section 5. Repetitive Action

INTRODUCTION

We've seen how to perform basic input and output operations in Pascal. In Chapter 2, we saw how to perform calculations. The only part of our algorithm we don't yet know how to translate into Pascal is the final statement of Step #2.3. This step says we must *repeat* an action until a particular condition is satisfied—specifically, the value of `SellingPrice` must be greater than the value of `MaximumPrice`.

Pascal provides several different ways to initiate, monitor, and terminate repetitive actions. Repeating a group of actions is usually accomplished with a *loop*. Loops are defined with a *control structure*. This section explores one of Pascal's frequently used loop control structures, the `while . . . do` statement.

This section has five parts:

• Defining a Loop Body
• The Compound Statement

- The while . . . do Loop Control Structure
- The Relational Operators
- Calculating the Price Interval

DEFINING A LOOP BODY

A *loop body* consists of related statements to be repeatedly executed a certain number of times.

Step #2.3 of the breakeven analysis algorithm lists a group of actions to be performed for each potential selling price that is considered. We can create a loop body to accommodate this action. Let's look at this algorithm step once again and attempt to translate it into Pascal.

Algorithm Step #2.3

2.3 If the selling price is not greater than the maximum price then

    ⟶ *evaluate the breakeven point expression,*
    ⟶ *print the selling price and breakeven point,*
    ⟶ *add the increment to the selling price,*
    ⟶ *repeat step #2.2*

The steps marked with arrows represent the part of the algorithm that will become repeated action in the actual program. Let's consider these steps one by one.

First action: *evaluate the breakeven point expression*

How is the breakeven point calculated? According to Mr. Arbaker, this calculation has two parts. First, the unit profit is found by subtracting the value of CostPerUnit from the value of SellingPrice. We'll create another process variable, UnitProfit, to store this value.

Next, the actual breakeven point is calculated by dividing the unit profit into the overall overhead production cost.

Translating these two calculations into Pascal is a straightforward task:

```
UnitProfit := SellingPrice - CostPerUnit;
BreakevenPoint := OverheadCost / UnitProfit;
```

Second action: *print the selling price and breakeven point*

We will use a `writeln` statement to print these values:

```
writeln (SellingPrice, BreakevenPoint);
```

Of course, we'll want to format the output—since both `SellingPrice` and `BreakevenPoint` are `real` variables—but we will worry about the details of format later.

Third action: *add the increment to the selling price*

Although we haven't yet discussed how we will calculate the increment, we have given it a name: `PriceInterval`. Adding the value of `PriceInterval` to `SellingPrice` is straightforward:

```
SellingPrice := SellingPrice + PriceInterval;
```

Fourth action: *repeat step #2.2*

Before we discuss how to control repetitive action, let's assemble the Pascal statements we've just created that make up the loop body:

```
{ begin loop body }

    UnitProfit := SellingPrice - CostPerUnit;
    BreakevenPoint := OverheadCost / UnitProfit;
    writeln (SellingPrice, BreakevenPoint);
    SellingPrice := SellingPrice + PriceInterval;

{ end loop body }
```

A very important observation: All these statements *must* be executed together to produce the effect we desire. We can coerce a group of statements to execute as a group by making them into a compound statement.

THE COMPOUND STATEMENT

A group of related statements that is always to be executed as a single group is called *compound statement.*

All four statements making up the loop body to calculate and print the breakeven point must be executed each time to produce the desired effect.

We must calculate the value of the variables `UnitProfit`, the value of `BreakevenPoint`, print `SellingPrice` and `BreakevenPoint`, and increment the variable `SellingPrice` each time through the loop. Somehow we must indicate that only these statements make up the loop body, and all others are outside the loop.

The reserved words `begin` and `end` are used to *bracket* a group of statements to be executed together. This group of statements is then considered to be a *compound statement.*

```
begin {compound statement}

   UnitProfit := SellingPrice - CostPerUnit;
   BreakevenPoint := OverheadCost / UnitProfit;
   writeln (SellingPrice, BreakevenPoint);
   SellingPrice := SellingPrice + PriceInterval;

end; {compound statement}
```

The effect of using `begin` and `end` is to consolidate the four statements in the loop body into a single statement as far as Pascal is concerned.

Now that we've defined the loop body, let's look at the `while . . . do` statement, used to control the number of times the loop is executed.

THE *WHILE . . . DO* LOOP CONTROL STRUCTURE

The *while . . . do* **statement controls the number of times, if any, a loop body is executed.**

Look at Step #2.2 and the beginning clause of Step #2.3 once again.

Algorithm Steps #2.2 and 2.3

> **2.2   *Consider the expression that calculates a breakeven point with the price set to the minimum price***
>
> **2.3   *If the selling price is not greater than the maximum, price then. . .***

Step #2.2 tells us the first thing we must do is set the value of the variable `SellingPrice` equal to the value of `MinimumPrice` (which was input by the program user):

```
SellingPrice := MinimumPrice;
```

Next, we must check to see if the selling price is greater than the maximum price. It may seem silly to make this test on the first try, since we just set the value of `SellingPrice` to equal to `MinimumPrice`. However, this is how a `while` . . . do loop is initiated. Also, if for some reason the value of `MinimumPrice` were greater than `MaximumPrice`, there would be no reason to execute the loop body, so this test must be made.

The `while`. . . do statement tests to decide whether the loop body should be executed. Here's a general outline of the `while`. . . do statement:

Outline of the *while*. . . *do* **Statement**

while *condition is true* **do**

{perform loop body . . .}

The `while` . . . do statement tests a *condition.* If the condition is *true,* the loop body is executed. If the condition is *false,* the loop body is skipped and program execution resumes at the first statement after the loop body.

What is a *condition?* It's usually the result of a comparison between two values. A condition might be a test to see if the value of one variable is greater than another. Or, a condition might be a test to see if the value of a variable equals the value of a constant. In a `while` . . . do statement, the condition *must* be true for the loop body to be executed.

How can we apply the `while` . . . do statement to the breakeven analysis program? We can use the clause *"selling price is not greater than the maximum price"* as the condition. Rephrasing "not greater than" into more common language suggests the following loop control condition:

while `SellingPrice` *is less than or equal to* `MaximumPrice` **do**

{perform loop body . . .}

To further refine this step, we must know how to translate "less than or equal to" into Pascal. "Less than or equal to" ($<=$) is one of Pascal's *relational operators.*

THE RELATIONAL OPERATORS

Pascal's relational operators are essentially the same as those of algebra.

The relational operators compare two values. Due to the limitations of most computer keyboards, Pascal's relational operators sometimes look different that those of algebra.

The Relational Operators

Algebra	*Pascal*
<	<
>	>
≤	<=
≥	>=
≠	<>

Any of these relational operators may be used to evaluate a loop control condition. Now we can establish "SellingPrice <= MaximumPrice" as the condition to be tested by the while. . .do statement before the loop body is executed.

Returning to our algorithm, we can now make a final translation into Pascal:

Final Breakeven Point Loop

```
while SellingPrice <= MaximumPrice do

  begin {loop body}

    UnitProfit := SellingPrice - CostPerUnit;
    BreakevenPoint := OverheadCost / UnitProfit;
    writeln ( SellingPrice, BreakevenPoint );
    SellingPrice := SellingPrice + PriceInterval;

  end; {loop body}
```

The last statement in the loop body now requires our attention. We need to figure out how to determine a price interval to print 10 evenly spaced selling prices between any minimum and maximum prices input by the program user.

CALCULATING THE PRICE INTERVAL

Our goal is to have the *while ... do* loop print 10 evenly distributed breakeven points between the minimum and maximum selling prices.

To accomplish this, we must calculate a price interval that can be added to the value of the variable SellingPrice each time the loop is executed.

We have already created a variable named `PriceInterval` to represent this value. The value of `PriceInterval` is calculated once by subtracting the minimum price from the maximum, then dividing that result by the number of prices to be considered. HighTech feels that 10 prices between the minimum and maximum is a reasonable number.

Here's the calculation:

```
PriceInterval := (MaximumPrice - MinimumPrice) / 10;
```

Let's use some sample data to illustrate how this calculation will accomplish the desired results. Say the user inputs $10.00 as the minimum price, and $20.00 as the maximum price. Subtracting the minimum price from the maximum price yields $10.00. Dividing this by 10 yields the price interval, or $1.00.

Now use this data to enter the while . . . do loop. The initial value of `SellingPrice` is set to `MinimumPrice` ($10.00). Each time the loop is executed, the price interval ($1.00) is added to the value of `SellingPrice`. When the loop begins its eleventh cycle, the value of `SellingPrice` becomes $21.00, thereby causing the loop control condition to become false, so the loop is exited.

Try substituting your own values for `MinimumPrice` and `MaximumPrice`, then calculate `PriceInterval` and plug these values into the loop to see how this process works.

TEST YOUR UNDERSTANDING

14. What is a compound statement?

15. Is it possible for the body of a while. . . do loop to be skipped altogether?

Section 6. The Breakeven Analysis Program

INTRODUCTION

We're now ready to translate our algorithm into a complete Pascal program. We will assemble the final program part by part.

This section has five parts:

- The Program Heading
- The Definition Part
- The Declaration Part
- The Statement Part
- The Breakeven Analysis Program

THE PROGRAM HEADING

All Pascal programs must begin with a program heading.

Creating a program heading is easy. As you recall, the program heading consists of the reserved word `program`, the name of the program (the program identifier), followed by the words `input` and `output` in parentheses. We will name our program *BreakAnalysis*. Why not "Breakeven Analysis"? We have already created a variable Breakeven Point. As you recall, the first eight characters of every identifier in a program must be unique, so we cannot use the word "Breakeven" again.

```
program BreakAnalysis (input, output);
```

In most cases, the only unique part of a program heading from one program to another is the program identifier. In more advanced programs, `input` and `output` might be replaced by programmer-defined input/output processes.

THE DEFINITION PART

All constants to be used in a program must be defined immediately after the program heading.

The only place a constant might be used to enhance the readability of this program is in the calculation to determine the price interval.

Recall the calculation:

```
PriceInterval := (MaximumPrice - MinimumPrice) / 10;
```

Since HighTech feels that 10 prices is a reasonable number, we can define a constant named `NumberOfIntervals` to be used in the calculation instead of the actual number "10."*

---

*Due to some interesting quirks in the binary arithmetic performed when this constant is used in the price interval calculation, you may end up with 11 price intervals rather than 10, depending on how your computer performs the calculation.

A constant definition consists of the reserved word const followed by the constant identifier, an equals sign, and the numeric value of the constant.

The Definition Part

```
const

    NumberOfIntervals = 9;
```

THE DECLARATION PART

All variables used by a program must be declared immediately after the constant definition part.

Recall that Pascal requires you to explicitly declare all variables before they can be used. This declaration must also specify the data type of each variable. By referring to our Problem Table, we can be sure we declare all variables the program will use.

Breakeven Analysis Problem Table

INPUT	PROCESS	OUTPUT
OverheadCost CostPerUnit MaximumPrice MinimumPrice	Variables: PriceInterval UnitProfit Constant: NumberofIntervals	SellingPrice BreakevenPoint

The Problem Table reminds us of all the variables used in a program so we won't forget to declare any.

The Variable Declaration Part

```
var
    OverheadCost, CostPerUnit, UnitProfit      : real;
    SellingPrice, MinimumPrice, MaximumPrice   : real;
    PriceInterval, BreakevenPoint              : real;
```

Notice we have declared all of the variables used in this program as type real. We made three separate declarations for the sake of readability. Instead, we could have used a single lengthy declaration, but then the data type of each variable would not have been as obvious.

THE STATEMENT PART

The statement part is a complete list of Pascal instructions describing the *action* to be performed by a program.

We have already completed a major portion of the statement part of this program by defining the while. . . do loop. All that remains is to get input information, initialize process variables, and print a heading for the output.

The program must request the values for four variables: OverheadCost, CostPerUnit, MinimumPrice, and MaximumPrice. We will use a write statement to prompt for each value, and a readln statement to accept the input for each variable.

Here are the statements necessary to get input information for the program:

```
write ('What is the overhead cost of production? ');
readln (OverheadCost);
write ('What is the cost of manufacturing one unit? ');
readln (CostPerUnit);
write ('What is the minimum selling price per unit? ');
readln (MinimumPrice);
write ('What is the maximum selling price per unit? ');
readln (MaximumPrice);
```

The next step is to initialize the process variables. The variable PriceInterval is initialized by making the calculation we discussed in Section 5. The initial value of SellingPrice will be the minimum selling price per unit, or MinimumPrice:

```
PriceInterval := (MaximumPrice - MinimumPrice) /
                    NumberOfIntervals;
SellingPrice := MinimumPrice;
```

The output from the breakeven analysis program is a table of of selling prices and their breakeven points. A common practice in printing tables of any sort is labeling the columns, so anyone reading the table will know what values are represented. Labeling output is especially important for users who don't know how a program works, and may not know what the output represents.

We can title our table by using a single `writeln` statement to print the phrases "Selling Price" and "Breakeven Point." This statement must be executed *before* the loop body. If it were part of the loop body, the program would print a label each time the loop was executed—not the effect we want. Here is the `writeln` statement that will print the title:

```
writeln ('Selling Price            Breakeven Point');
```

Notice that this `writeln` statement prints the literal text "Selling Price" and "Breakeven Point," *not* the values of the variables with similar names.

All that remains of the statement part is the `while . . . do` loop, which we've already defined. However, there's one detail we haven't attended to yet—formatting the output of the `real` variables `SellingPrice` and `BreakevenPoint`. This is how we'll format the output:

```
writeln ('$',SellingPrice:8:2, BreakevenPoint:17:1, '0 Units');
```

Let's look at all the parts of this statement. First, we print a dollar sign. This will precede the value of `SellingPrice`, leaving no doubt that the value is a dollar amount. The field width is 8 spaces, and we've indicated we only want two digits after the decimal point.

Next, we print the value of `BreakevenPoint`. We have requested a field width of 17 spaces so that the value will be printed underneath the title of the table. We also requested only one digit be printed after the decimal point. This is somewhat unrealistic, because the number of manufactured units will always a whole number. Advanced features of Pascal allow the programmer to request that a `real` variable be *rounded;* however, rounding a `real` value essentially turns the variable into an `integer`, and the programmer must beware that the value never exceeds the maximum allowable `integer` value.

Finally, the literal text "Units" is printed after each breakeven point.

We can now assemble the entire program. Recall that the statement part of a program must be bracketed with the reserved words `begin` and `end`. The final end in a program is always followed by a period. The period indicates that the program is complete.

Finally note the use of indentation and blank lines to separate the parts of the program. Although Pascal doesn't pay any attention to spaces, blank lines, or tabs, a program is easier to read if related statements (such as the loop body controlled by the `while. . .` do statement) are indented by the same number of spaces.

Deliberate indentation is a useful way to visually show that statements are related. As always, we encourage you to experiment with format and presentation to fit your own style. The only rule: make it readable!

The Breakeven Analysis Program

```pascal
program BreakAnalysis (input, output);


const
    NumberOfIntervals = 10; {Number of Selling Price's Printed}


var
    OverheadCost, CostPerUnit, UnitProfit       : real;
    SellingPrice, MinimumPrice, MaximumPrice    : real;
    PriceInterval, BreakevenPoint               : real;

begin {statement part}
    write ('What is the overhead cost of production? ');
    readln (OverheadCost);
    write ('What is the cost of manufacturing one unit? ');
    readln (CostPerUnit);
    write ('What is the minimum selling price per unit? ');
    readln (MinimumPrice);
    write ('What is the maximum selling price per unit? ');
    readln (MaximumPrice);


    PriceInterval := (MaximumPrice - MinimumPrice) /
                        NumberOfIntervals;
    SellingPrice := MinimumPrice;
    writeln ('Selling Price        Breakeven Point');


    while SellingPrice <= MaximumPrice do
      begin {loop body}
        UnitProfit := SellingPrice - CostPerUnit;
        BreakevenPoint := OverheadCost / UnitProfit;
        writeln ('$', SellingPrice:8:2, BreakevenPoint:17:1, '0 Units');
        SellingPrice := SellingPrice + PriceInterval;
      end; {loop body}
end. {Program BreakAnalysis}
```

PROGRAMMING EXERCISES

Programming Exercise 1:

Change the "number of intervals" constant to a variable, so the user can determine how many price intervals are examined. Be sure to prompt for input.

Programming Exercise 2:

HighTech would like the output to be fancier, so they can include it in their corporate report. Add statements that print HighTech's name, a title describing the purpose of the program, and the name of the product (The Electronic Sponge). Then format the output so that it's centered on a screen or page.

ANSWERS TO THE TEST YOUR UNDERSTANDING EXERCISES

1. Understanding the problem completely, and describing the problem in a concise statement.

2. Analyzing the problem, writing a complete algorithm, and translating the algorithm into a Pascal program.

3. False. A Problem Table can be useful for keeping track of variables and constants, but it is not necessary to use one.

4. To differentiate between the functions of variables used in a program.

5. readln gathers input data for a program.

6. False. read, readln, input, and output are not reserved words—they are built-in procedures having a special meaning to Pascal.

7. 2.0367000000000000E + 2. The field width was not changed, and decimal format was not requested.

8. write does not advance the cursor to the next line after executing; writeln does advance to the next line.

9. Literal text is printed exactly as it appears in a writeln statement.

10. Literal text is specified by placing it between single quotes.

11. Prompting for input is important so the user knows what type of input is expected.

12. Field width is the number of spaces in which a variable is printed by `writeln`.

13. Standard decimal format is specified as follows:

```
writeln (VariableName : 8    : 2 )
        {field width     ↑    ↑ decimal format, 2 spaces after the
                               decimal.}
```

14. A compound statement is a group of statements, bracketed by the reserved words `begin` and `end`, considered a single statement by Pascal.

15. Yes, if the loop control condition is false before the loop is executed the first time.

CHAPTER 4

Structured Programming Techniques

Chapter Objective

To discuss the fundamentals of structured programming, focusing on the use of *procedures*.

Chapter Overview

Your success with the breakeven analysis program for the HighTech Corp. has become well-known. Now the Vango Art Mart wants you to computerize their weekly payroll process. Vango uses the standard payroll calculation, involving several distinct processes: Information for each employee is collected, the gross pay calculated, the net pay determined, and finally a pay form is generated and a paycheck is issued to the employee.

New Pascal: This chapter introduces the *procedure*, used to group related actions into a distinct entity to perform a specific task. Procedures are usually designed to be autonomous "black boxes" of Pascal instructions that function independently of one another. For example, one procedure can be designed to compute the gross pay. Others will gather input data, or compute the net pay, and so on. To assure independence, carefully regulated routes of communication are established between procedures and the main program.

We also discuss another control structure that can influence the action in a program: the *if...then...else* statement.

This chapter has five sections:

- **Preparing the Weekly Payroll**
- **Structured Programming**
- **Communication Between Program and Procedures**
- **Decision Making**
- **The Payroll Program**

Section 1. Preparing the Weekly Payroll

INTRODUCTION

The technique of analyzing a problem, creating an algorithm, and translating that algorithm into a Pascal program worked beautifully in your dealings with the HighTech Corp. Therefore, we'll use the same approach to computerizing the payroll process at the Vango Art Mart.

This section has two parts:

- The Payroll Problem
- The Payroll Algorithm

THE PAYROLL PROBLEM

The first step in the problem solving process is to learn as much as possible about the problem.

Ms. O'Keefe, Vango's chief accountant, has invited you to the company's corporate headquarters. She has described the process Vango currently uses to prepare the weekly payroll for its 75 employees. At the end of each pay period, the accounting office prepares a pay form for each employee according to the following process:

First, the payroll accountant gathers the employee identification number, pay rate, and number of hours worked.

Next, the accountant calculates the gross pay. At this step, the accountant must first determine if the employee has worked overtime by comparing total number of hours worked to the standard work week of 40 hours. If there are extra hours, overtime pay is calculated for those hours at 1.5 times the regular hourly pay rate. Then regular pay is calculated as the pay rate times the standard work week. However, if there are no overtime hours, overtime pay defaults to zero and regular pay is calculated by multiplying the hourly pay rate by the number of hours worked. Then regular pay is added to overtime pay to arrive at gross pay.

Next, net pay is computed, also a two-step process. First, deductions are calculated by multiplying the FICA rate (currently 6.7%) times the gross pay. Then deductions are subtracted from the gross pay to yield net pay.

Finally, the pay form is generated by printing the employee's identification number, gross pay, deductions, and net pay.

Ms. O'Keefe explains Vango is taking a revolutionary view toward deducting income taxes from their employee's pay—they simply don't. While you may not believe this is a sound business principle, it will simplify the job of creating the algorithm and program for Vango's payroll.

THE PAYROLL ALGORITHM

The payroll algorithm describes the four distinct parts of processing the weekly payroll.

Before creating the algorithm, recall the goals of the top-down problem solving process:

— Break the problem into smaller parts to reduce its complexity.
— Begin with an algorithm that's as general as possible, and progressively *refine* it.

Let's keep these goals in mind as we extract the initial algorithm from the payroll problem. We'll make one step for each process Ms. O'Keefe described.

Initial Payroll Algorithm

1. *Collect relevant information*
2. *Compute gross pay*
3. *Compute net pay*
4. *Print the pay form*

As you see, the initial algorithm is an extremely general outline of the steps required to perform the weekly payroll. We haven't detailed the algorithm yet. But look closely at the way we've expressed the algorithm steps. Each step is a skeletal description of a group of actions that perform a single task, such as computing gross pay, or printing the pay form.

We're going to introduce a new goal to keep in mind when forming an initial algorithm. This goal is to express each algorithm step as a concise statement describing a distinct group of related actions.

Why is this desirable? As we said in the chapter overview, algorithm steps describing a group of related actions can be expressed as a Pascal *procedure.* Designing an algorithm so that each step is stated as a distinct group of actions facilitates the translation into a Pascal procedure. Procedures provide a powerful and controlled means of performing related actions. They are used commonly in Pascal programs.

Now that we have an initial algorithm for the payroll problem, our next step is to refine it, describing in greater detail the *action* that each algorithm step performs.

To refine Step #1, *Collect relevant information,* we must determine what input information is required. The relevant information for the payroll problem is:

— The employee ID number
— The hourly pay rate
— The number of hours worked

We can refine Step #1 simply by listing these three items:

Refinement of Step #1

1.   *Collect relevant information*
    1.1   *Request employee identification number*
    1.2   *Request employee pay rate*
    1.3   *Request hours worked*

Step #2 of the algorithm calls for computing the gross pay. Ms. O'Keefe's description of the gross pay calculation can be refined into two additional algorithm steps:

Refinement of Step #2

2.   *Compute gross pay*
    2.1   *If there is overtime, compute overtime pay and regular pay, otherwise compute regular pay and notice that overtime pay is zero*

> **2.2 Calculate gross pay as the sum of regular pay and overtime pay**

Step #3 is refined by expressing the actions necessary to calculate net pay. Net pay is calculated by subtracting deductions from the gross pay:

Refinement of Step #3

3. **Compute net pay**
    3.1 Calculate deductions as FICA percentage of gross pay
    3.2 Calculate net pay as gross pay less deductions

To refine Step #4, we must decide what information is necessary in a payroll report. The employee ID, the gross pay, the deduction amount, and the net pay are surely necessary. Any additional information—such as a breakdown of overtime hours and overtime pay—will be optional.

Refinement of Step #4

4. **Print the pay form**
    4.1 Print employee identification number
    4.2 Print gross pay
    4.3 Print deductions
    4.4 Print net pay

We cannot refine the payroll algorithm any further. Here is the complete algorithm for the payroll problem:

Completely Refined Payroll Algorithm

1. **Collect relevant information**
    1.1 Request employee identification number
    1.2 Request employee pay rate
    1.3 Request hours worked
2. **Compute gross pay**
    2.1 If there is overtime, compute overtime pay and regular pay, otherwise compute regular pay and notice that overtime pay is zero
    2.2 Calculate gross pay as the sum of regular pay and overtime pay
3. **Compute net pay**
    3.1 Calculate deductions as FICA percentage of gross pay
    3.2 Calculate net pay as gross pay less deductions

    4.   Print the pay form
        4.1   Print employee identification number
        4.2   Print gross pay
        4.3   Print deductions
        4.4   Print net pay

Our goal now: To transform each algorithm step into a specific group of Pascal actions that will function as an independent *procedure.*

As we did last chapter, let's create the variables our program will use for input and output. We won't create any process variables for the main program, because as you'll see the procedures we create will handle process data.

Variable Purpose	Variable Identifier
Employee identification #	`EmployeeID`
Hourly rate of pay	`PayRate`
Number of hours worked	`HoursWorked`
Gross pay for week	`GrossPay`
Total deduction amount	`Deductions`
Net pay	`NetPay`

And, just to keep track of these variables, we'll put them into a Problem Table:

Payroll Problem Table

INPUT	PROCESS	OUTPUT

`EmployeeID`
`PayRate`
`HoursWorked`
		`GrossPay`
		`Deductions`
		`NetPay`

TEST YOUR UNDERSTANDING

1. Why should one express each algorithm step as a statement of a distinct group describing related actions?

Section 2. Structured Programming

INTRODUCTION

In the late 1960's, Professor Niklaus Wirth developed Pascal as a tool for teaching computer science emphasizing a careful approach to problem solving and a disciplined, structured approach to programming. Other programming languages available at that time, such as FORTRAN and BASIC, allowed a lassiez-faire, free-form approach to problem solving and programming. Although this was useful for professional programmers, Wirth felt that programming should be initially taught as a disciplined, structured activity.

What is "structure" in a Pascal program? We have already encountered structure in the rules for declaring variables. When a variable is declared, it's "structured" by the compiler so it can represent only one kind of data.

In addition to structures for representing data, there are also structures for grouping action. This chapter focuses on grouping logically related action into structured *procedures*.

This section has five parts:

- What are Procedures?
- Translating Algorithm Steps into Procedures
- Declaring Procedures
- Calling Procedures
- The Scope of Variables and Constants.

WHAT ARE PROCEDURES?

A *procedure* is a group of Pascal statements that performs a specific task.

As we said in the chapter overview, a procedure is used to group related actions into a distinct entity that performs a specific task. Procedures should be autonomous "black boxes" of Pascal instructions that function independently of one another. Procedures are essentially "mini-programs"—they're even structured like programs.

There are several advantages to grouping related action into a procedure. First, because procedures are designed to function as independent units of action, they're relatively easy to change without worrying about the effect on the rest of the program. As an example, let's say we wanted to add some new ingredients to the mushroom soup algorithm we developed in Chapter 1. Recall the algorithm:

Mushroom Soup Algorithm

1. **Gather the Ingredients**
    1.1 **Get milk and mushrooms from the refrigerator**
    1.2 **Get flour and spices from the cupboard**
    1.3 **Get a pan out of the dishwasher**
2. **Mix the Ingredients Together**
    2.1 **Pour the milk into the pan**
    2.2 **Add the mushrooms, flour, and spices**
3. **Cook the Meal**
    3.1 **Turn on the stove**
    3.2 **Put the pan on the stove**
    3.3 **If the soup is done**
        then remove the pan
            or else repeat:
                3.3.1 **Stir the soup**
                3.3.2 **If the soup needs thickening, add flour**
                Until the soup is done
4. **Serve the Meal**

If each algorithm step were translated into a procedure, there would be no difficulties in adding new ingredients because we need only change instructions in Steps #1 and 2. We would change Step #1.3 to read: *Get flour, spices, anchovy paste, and champagne from the cupboard,* and Step #2.2 to read: *Add the mushrooms, flour, spices, anchovy paste, and champagne.* We wouldn't change any other part of the program; only those two procedures would be affected by the addition of the new ingredients.

Programs designed with procedures are relatively easy to test and debug. Instead of searching through an entire program to find a "bug," procedures can be tested and debugged independently, so errors are easier to spot.

Also, if related action is grouped into a procedure, programs are easier to read and understand. Readability is a significant advantage in programs used by more than one person.

Let's look once again at the four major steps of the payroll algorithm. Each represents a specific, unique task—therefore, we can create a procedure for each step.

Payroll Algorithm

1. **Collect relevant information**
2. **Compute gross pay**
3. **Compute net pay**
4. **Print the pay form**

Let's begin the translation from algorithm step to procedure by naming our procedures. A procedure—like a variable, program, or constant—is referred to by its *identifier.*

Algorithm Step	Procedure Identifier
1. Collect relevant information	`CollectInfo`
2. Compute gross pay	`ComputeGrossPay`
3. Compute net pay	`ComputeNetPay`
4. Print the pay form	`PrintPayForm`

TRANSLATING ALGORITHM STEPS INTO PROCEDURES

Procedures are structured like "mini-programs," with a heading, definition part, declaration part, and statement part.

The Parts of a Procedure

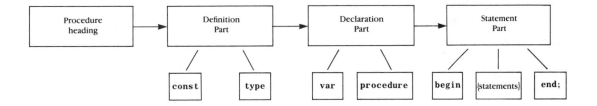

As you see, with the exception of the heading, a procedure is structured just like a complete program. To illustrate how a procedure is created, we'll translate Step #1 of our algorithm into a procedure:

Algorithm Step #1

1. *Collect relevant information*
    1.1 *Request employee identification number*
    1.2 *Request employee pay rate*
    1.3 *Request hours worked*

Translating this algorithm step into Pascal is a relatively straightforward task. As we did when we requested input information in the breakeven analysis program, we'll use a combination of `write` statements (to prompt for input values), and `readln` statements (to assign input values to specific variables):

```
write ('What is the employee ID number? ');
readln (EmployeeID);
write ('Total number of hours worked this week? ');
readln (HoursWorked);
write ('What is the hourly pay rate? ');
readln (PayRate);
```

To complete this procedure, we add a procedure heading, and the reserved words begin and end to bracket the statement part. We'll assume the variables `EmployeeID`, `HoursWorked`, and `PayRate` have already been declared—therefore, no definition or declaration part is needed for this procedure.

Final *CollectInfo* Procedure

```
procedure CollectInfo;
    begin
        write ('What is the employee ID number? ');
        readln (EmployeeID);
        write ('Total number of hours worked this week? ');
        readln (HoursWorked);
        write ('What is the hourly pay rate? ');
        readln (PayRate);
    end;
```

Notice the semi-colon after the reserved word end. We used it to separate the end from the next statement in the program. The terminating period follows only the final end of a program. Other uses of end in a program are followed by a semi-colon.

Notice also that this procedure looks rather like a compound statement. Compound statements and procedures differ in their potential to be used more than once with ease. As we'll see, once we have written a procedure we can use it repeatedly in a program, simply by using its name. A compound statement, on the other hand, must be completely written out each time it's used.

We'll use a similar process to translate algorithm Step #4, *Print the pay form,* into a procedure.

Algorithm Step #4

4. ***Print the pay form***
    - 4.1 ***Print employee identification number***
    - 4.2 ***Print gross pay***
    - 4.3 ***Print deductions***
    - 4.4 ***Print net pay***

We have decided on the name `PrintPayForm` for this procedure. Again, we assume that the variables `EmployeeID`, `GrossPay`, `Deductions`, and `NetPay` have already been declared in the `var` part of the program. Here's the complete translation of this algorithm step into a procedure.

Final *PrintPayForm* Procedure

```
procedure PrintPayForm;
    begin
        writeln ('Employee # ', EmployeeID :2);
        writeln ('Gross Pay is         $ ', GrossPay :8:2);
        writeln ('Total Deductions     $ ', Deductions :8:2);
        writeln ('Net pay for week is $ ', NetPay :8:2);
    end;
```

The first statement of this procedure prints "Employee #", then prints the value of the variable `EmployeeID`. We have specified a 2-digit field width because Vango has only 75 employees; therefore only two digits are necessary.

The next three `writeln` statement print the values of the `real` variables `GrossPay`, `Deductions`, and `NetPay`, in an eight-digit field width. Notice how we have vertically aligned the dollar signs ($) in the literal text part of each statement, to make the output more readable. And, of course, since the values are dollar amounts, we requested that `writeln` print only two digits after each decimal point.

DECLARING PROCEDURES

Procedures must be *declared* in the declaration part of a program.

The proper place for a procedure is in the declaration part of the program. All statements that make up the procedure are then associated with a single *procedure identifier.* Procedures are declared immediately after the var declaration in a program, and before the statement part of the program.

Here is an incomplete version of the Payroll program to show where procedures are declared:

Incomplete Payroll Program

```
program Payroll  (input,  output);  {  incomplete  example  to
                                     show  where  procedures
                                          are declared }

var
    EmployeeID : integer;
    PayRate, HoursWorked, GrossPay, Deductions, NetPay : real;

procedure CollectInfo;
    begin

        write ('What is the employee ID number? ');
        readln (EmployeeID);
        write ('Total number of hours worked this week? ');
        readln (HoursWorked);
        write ('What is the hourly pay rate? ');
        readln (PayRate);
    end;

procedure PrintPayForm;
    begin
        writeln ('Employee # ', EmployeeID :2);
        writeln ('Gross Pay is        $ ' , GrossPay :8:2);
        writeln ('Total Deductions    $ ' , Deductions :8:2);
        writeln ('Net pay for week is $ ' , NetPay :8:2);
    end;

begin

    { Statements... }
end.
```

In this example, we have declared two completely functional procedures. However, we've said nothing yet about how the procedures will be used. What we'll do next is set up a "main" program to orchestrate the use of these and other procedures. This is how we add structure to a program. A well designed program will have a statement part, or "main program," consisting primarily of a series of procedure *calls.*

CALLING PROCEDURES

A procedure is invoked, or *called,* by the main program when the *procedure identifier* is used as a statement.

When you call a procedure by name (identifier) in a program, control of the program is turned over to the procedure. The procedure is executed, then control returns to the statement immediately following the procedure call in the main program.

We will illustrate how procedures are called by adding more statements to the initial version of the payroll program. We will declare the procedures CollectInfo and PrintPayForm, then have the main program call them. At this point, we'll also add incomplete procedure declarations and calls for the two other procedures, ComputeGrossPay and ComputeNetPay, so you can begin to get a sense of how things will be arranged in the final program. Remember: This is an extremely incomplete program—it is only used to demonstrate how procedures are declared and called.

Skeletal Payroll Program

```
program Payroll (input, output);  { Illustrates procedure
                                    declaration and calls }
var
    EmployeeID : integer;
    PayRate, HoursWorked, GrossPay, Deductions, NetPay : real;

procedure CollectInfo;  { Complete procedure declaration }
    begin
        write ('What is the employee ID number? ');
        readln (EmployeeID);
        write ('Total number of hours worked this week? ');
        readln (HoursWorked);
        write ('What is the hourly pay rate? ');
        readln (PayRate);
    end;
```

```
procedure ComputeGrossPay; { Incomplete procedure declaration }

procedure ComputeNetPay;   { Incomplete procedure declaration }

procedure PrintPayForm; { Complete declaration }
    begin
        writeln ('Employee # ',  EmployeeID :2);
        writeln ('Gross Pay is         $ ' , GrossPay :8:2);
        writeln ('Total Deductions     $ ' , Deductions :8:2);
        writeln ('Net pay for week is $ ' , NetPay :8:2);
    end;

begin { Main Program }

    CollectInfo;        { Call to procedure CollectInfo }
    ComputeGrossPay;    { Call to procedure ComputeGrossPay }
    ComputeNetPay;      { Call to procedure ComputeNetPay }
    PrintPayForm;       { Call to procedure PrintPayForm }
end. { Main Program }
```

Like variables, procedures must be declared before they can be used. A potential source of confusion comes in thinking that, because the statement part of a procedure appears before the statement part of the main program, the procedure is executed first. This is not true. Even though procedures must be declared before the statement part of a program, they cannot be executed until *called* by the main program, or by another procedure that has been called by the main program.

Once again, careful attention to the indentation used in a program should help avoid confusion. Traditionally, the statement part of a procedure is indented more than the statement part of the main program.

A primary goal of procedure design is to make each procedure function as an independent unit of action. Variables needed only in a procedure and nowhere else should be declared in the declaration part of the procedure, not in the declaration part of the main program. Next we discuss methods for limiting the effect of variables and constants.

THE SCOPE OF VARIABLES AND CONSTANTS

Variables and constants are only effective in the part of the program where they are declared or defined.

The *scope* of a variable or constant determines where it can be used in a program. A variable or constant's scope is determined solely by where it is declared or defined in a program.

A variable has a *global* scope if it's declared in the var part of the *main program*. Global variables can be used anywhere in the program: in the statement part of the main program, or in any procedure.

A variable has a *local* scope if it's declared within a *procedure*. Local variables are restricted to the procedure in which they are declared, and cannot be directly used outside that procedure. The definitions of global and local scope apply also to constants.

The following illustration is a schematic of a program that uses variables with both global and local scope.

The Scope of Variables and Constants

```
program  Universal (input, output);
    var  Worldly;         { Global variable }
  const  Cosmopolitan;    { Global constant }

              procedure X;
                  var Native; { Local }



              procedure Y;
                  var Hick; { Local }


                      procedure Z;
```

Variable	Can be used by:
Worldly	Main Program, Procedures X, Y, Z
Native	Procedure X Only
Hick	Procedure Y and Z

Any variable used by more than one procedure must be declared in the declaration part of the main program, so that it will have global scope. If, on the other hand, a variable is used solely by one procedure, it should be declared locally within that procedure.

TEST YOUR UNDERSTANDING

2. What design feature does Pascal have that is not shared by BASIC or FORTRAN?

3. What are the four parts of a procedure declaration?

4. Where are procedures declared in a program?

5. How does a program call a procedure?

6. What's the difference between *global* and *local* scope?

Section 3. Communication Between Program and Procedures

INTRODUCTION

Since one goal of procedure design is to make a procedure function as an independent unit of action, communication between the procedure and the main program should be carefully regulated. In other words, we need rules describing how global variables may be used or changed by procedures. We must make a distinction between allowing a procedure to merely *use* the value of a global variable, and allowing it to *change* the value of a global variable.

Think of a procedure as a castle with high walls around it, the only entrance or exit being a very large gate. Variables should only be allowed into a procedure, or to leave the procedure, through the gate.

Routes of communication are set up between procedures and program via *parameters*. The two kinds of parameters we'll be discussing are *value* parameters, which pass the value of a global variable into a procedure, and *variable* parameters, which allow a procedure to change the value of a global variable.

This section has four parts:

- Passing Data Between Program and Procedure
- The Parameter List
- Value and Variable Parameters
- Formal and Actual Parameters

PASSING DATA BETWEEN PROGRAM AND PROCEDURE

Data is passed between a program and procedures via *parameters*.

A parameter is a value used by both the main program and a procedure. A parameter can pass the value of a global variable *to* a procedure from the main program, or it can return a value *from* a procedure to the main program. Parameters serve as a gateway between program and procedure.

The built-in procedures input and output used in a program heading are parameters that provide input and output capabilities for a program. For an interactive program, input is usually entered via the keyboard and output usually sent to a video display terminal.

Similarly, procedure parameters provide input and output capabilities between procedures and the main program. Procedure parameters, like input and output in the program heading, are listed in parentheses after the procedure identifier in a procedure heading.

To illustrate the use of parameters, we'll translate algorithm Step #3, *Compute net pay,* into a Pascal procedure. First we'll concentrate on developing the statement part of the procedure to see what input and output parameters are required. Then we'll create the parameters themselves.

Let's look at the actual algorithm step again:

Algorithm Step #3

3. *Compute net pay*
    3.1 *Calculate deductions as FICA percentage of gross pay*
    3.2 *Calculate net pay as gross pay less deductions*

Translating Step #3.1 into Pascal requires that we first define a constant to represent the FICA percentage, 6.67%. Then we must multiply the value of GrossPay by FICA to get the total deduction.

Step #3.2 is a single calculation: The program subtracts the value of Deductions from the value of GrossPay to arrive at NetPay.

Here is the procedure ComputeNetPay without parameters:

Preliminary *ComputeNetPay* Procedure

```
procedure ComputeNetPay (          );  { Needs parameters ... }
    const
       FICA = 0.067;

    begin
       Deductions := GrossPay * FICA;
       NetPay := GrossPay - Deductions;
    end;
```

Let's take a close look at this procedure to determine what parameters will be needed. This procedure will require two types of parameter—one type provides *input from* the main program, and the other provides *output to* the main program.

The first calculation in the statement part of ComputeNetPay uses the *value* of the global variable GrossPay. GrossPay is used as part of a calculation to determine a value for the global *variable* Deductions—not directly, but via a parameter. Therefore, this statement requires the value of GrossPay as an *input* parameter, and needs an *output* parameter to return the value of Deductions to the main program.

The second statement uses the value of Deductions and subtracts it from the value of GrossPay. These two values are already "in" the procedure, so they don't require additional parameters. However, we want the result of this calculation to be assigned to the global variable NetPay—therefore, we need another *output* parameter to return the value of NetPay to the main program.

In summary, we need three parameters for this procedure: one to provide the *value* of GrossPay to the procedure, and two to return values to the global *variables* Deductions and NetPay. We create procedure parameters by listing them in parentheses after the identifier in the procedure heading. This list is called, appropriately, a *parameter list,* and is our next subject.

THE PARAMETER LIST

All parameters to be used by a procedure must be declared in the parameter list.

The parameter list creates identifiers (names) for our parameters. Parameters are declared like variables, by specifying their name and data type in the parameter list. Here's a declaration of our *input* parameter, GrossPay, for the procedure ComputeNetPay:

```
procedure ComputeNetPay (GrossPay : real);

   begin
        { Statements....}
   end;
```

This example creates the parameter GrossPay, which will accept a value from an as yet unidentified global variable (the program will provide that information later). Once it has received the value from the main program, the parameter GrossPay will act as a local variable within the procedure ComputeNetPay.

The parameter GrossPay can only *accept* a value from a global variable. It cannot return anything to the main program. In other words, a *value* parameter can only provide input to the procedure.

Parameters can also be declared so that they exist primarily to provide output for a procedure, meaning they can change the value of a global variable. In this case, the parameter must be declared as a *variable* parameter. Variable parameters are also declared in the parameter list, but are preceded by the reserved word var. Here's a declaration of one of our *output* parameters, NetPay, for the procedure ComputeNetPay:

```
procedure ComputeNetPay ( var NetPay : real );

   begin
        { Statements....}
   end.
```

In this example, we are declaring NetPay as a variable parameter that will *return* the value of NetPay to a global variable (also as yet unknown) in the main program. Variable parameters provide output from a procedure to the main program.

That's all there is to creating a parameter list. We have demonstrated how to declare a *value* parameter for input purposes, and a *variable* parameter for output purposes. Next, we discuss the difference between value and variable parameters.

VALUE AND VARIABLE PARAMETERS

A parameter can be declared in one of two ways: As a *value* parameter to provide *input* to a procedure, or as a *variable* parameter to provide *output* from a procedure to the main program.

A *value* parameter can only provide input to a procedure. It cannot be used to change the value of the global variable that provided input. Passing a value to a procedure as a value parameter is a way of "shielding," or protecting, the global variable from everything the procedure may do with the value.

Why should we shield the global variable? Because the value of GrossPay is only calculated once for each employee, and then it should not change. Although we don't want to change GrossPay, we nonetheless must use its value to compute the FICA deduction. A value parameter allows the procedure to use the value of the global variable without any risk of changing it.

Variable parameters, on the other hand, are used specifically to *return* a value to the main program—in other words, to change the value of a global variable. We *do* want to change,—or, more precisely, *initialize*—the global variables NetPay and Deductions based on the action performed by the procedure. Therefore, we will declare NetPay and Deductions as variable parameters.

This diagram illustrates the action that will occur when the procedure ComputeNetPay is called by the main program:

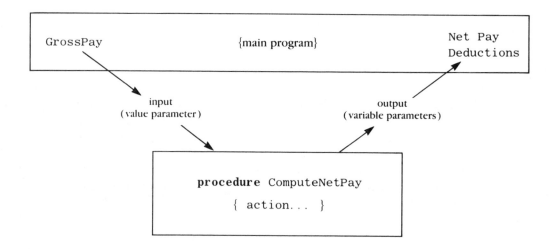

This table summarizes the key differences between value and variable parameters:

Value Parameters	Variable Parameters
Provide input only	Provide output
Become a "local" variable for the procedure	Used to change the value of a global variable

Value and variable parameters are declared at the same time in the parameter list of a procedure heading. Whether you declare value parameters first or variable parameters first makes no difference. However, we strongly advise that you adopt a consistent order for creating a parameter list—for example, declare all value parameters first, then variable parameters. By adopting a routine, you will never inadvertently declare a value parameter as a variable parameter.

Here's the final ComputeNetPay procedure declaration. In this declaration, we've indicated that *input* will be provided by the parameter GrossPay, and *output* will be provided by the variable parameters Deductions and NetPay. We declared the value parameter GrossPay first, followed by the variable parameters Deductions and NetPay.

Final *ComputeNetPay* Procedure

```
procedure ComputeNetPay (GrossPay : real;
                         var Deductions, NetPay : real);
    const
       FICA = 0.067;

    begin
       Deductions := GrossPay * FICA;
       NetPay := GrossPay - Deductions;
    end;
```

Remember, the whole point of parameters is to set up a regulated method of communication between procedure and program. As you study this procedure declaration, it's important to realize a parameter is a separate and distinct entity from a global variable. We'll clarify the distinction between global variables and parameters in a later section.

So far, we have dealt only with one end of the communication link between program and procedure, by creating a parameter list for the procedure. The second, equally important aspect of using parameters is to have the main program specify which global variables are to be used to provide values for the parameters, or to receive information from the procedure.

FORMAL AND ACTUAL PARAMETERS

A *parameter list* consists of *formal* parameters. A *procedure call* specifies the *actual* parameters (global variables) a procedure will use.

Looking at this key idea, you might be thinking there are many many kinds of parameters: input and output, variable and value, actual and formal, and on and on. Actually, we've only been dealing with two types, using different words to describe their function.

We have provided a communication channel for the procedure to communicate with the main program. We have given the procedure a way to receive input, with a value parameter, or produce output, with a variable parameter. We have told the procedure nothing yet about the actual values the program will provide, or expect in return, once the procedure is called. The parameter list specifies *formal* parameters; the program itself must provide the *actual* parameters to be used when the procedure is called.

Let's use a non-programming example to illustrate the difference between formal and actual parameters. Say that your roommate has phoned and asked you to prepare dinner for three *very* special guests. Perhaps they are "headhunters" looking for talented programmers. Or, perhaps they are treasury agents who want to ask you questions about Vango's unusual approach to the issue of deducting taxes.

In any event, you really want to make sure this dinner is successful. First, you carefully prepare a place setting for everyone at the table. In a moment of brilliant insight, you place mannequins at the table to represent your guests, so you can arrange every detail to perfection. A bit extreme, perhaps, but these are *very* important guests. Later, of course, when the guests arrive, they will take the place of the mannequins you're using to set up the arrangement of your table.

Where is this bizarre illustration leading, you ask? Well, by using mannequins to represent the unknown guests, you have essentially created formal parameters, one for each actual guest. When the guests (or actual parameters) arrive, they will replace the mannequins (formal parameters), and the action (eating dinner) will commence.

Keeping this illustration in mind, let's talk about formal parameters and actual parameters in Pascal.

A formal parameter exists only in the parameter list. A formal parameter is a "dummy" variable, or an alter-ego, designed to assume the personality of the actual parameter, and penetrate the procedure with information. In this way, the procedure gains complete control of the program at that point. Information goes in, then the procedure does its work, isolated from the rest of the program.

An actual parameter, on the other hand, is a global variable that provides a value to a procedure (if the formal parameter it replaces is a value parameter), or accepts the output from a procedure (if the corresponding formal parameter is a variable parameter). An actual parameter must be a variable that has been declared in the declaration part of the main program. Actual parameters are listed in parentheses after a procedure call.

Every formal parameter in a procedure's parameter list must be provided with a corresponding actual parameter. This makes sense—if a procedure expects input, or wants someplace to send output, the main program had better be accommodating if successful communication is to occur.

Another point to remember is that formal parameters must be listed *in the same order* in the parameter list as the actual parameters listed in the procedure call. Another skeletal version of the payroll program shows the correspondence between the formal parameters in the NetPay procedure parameter list, and the actual parameters in the procedure call:

Skeletal Payroll Program #2

```
program Payroll (input, output);  { Illustrates procedure
                                         declaration and calls }
var
     EmployeeID : integer;
     PayRate, HoursWorked, GrossPay, Deductions, NetPay : real;

procedure CollectInfo;        { Incomplete procedure declaration }

procedure ComputeGrossPay;  { Incomplete procedure declaration }

procedure ComputeNetPay (GrossPay : real;
                    var Deductions, NetPay : real);
                         { Complete procedure declaration }
     const
        FICA = 0.067;
     begin
        Deductions := GrossPay * FICA;
        NetPay := GrossPay - Deductions;
     end;
```

```
procedure PrintPayForm;      { Incomplete declaration}
begin  { Main Program }
    CollectInfo;                  { Procedure calls ... }
    ComputeGrossPay;
    ComputeNetPay (GrossPay, Deductions, NetPay);
    PrintPayForm;
end.  { Main Program }
```

A formal parameter can use the same name as an actual parameter, or a completely different name. Actual parameters, however, *must* be the names of global variables already declared in the var part of the main program. Conversely, formal parameters, which appear in a procedure's parameter list, can be given any identifier you please. Whether actual and formal parameters use the same or different names is really a matter of personal taste. Some people like to use different names, so that, once a variable gets shoved into a procedure, anyone reading a program knows it's now local to the procedure.

TEST YOUR UNDERSTANDING

7. What is a *value* parameter?

8. What is a *variable* parameter?

9. Where are value and variable parameters declared?

10. What is a formal parameter?

11. What is an actual parameter?

12. What is the relationship between formal and actual parameters?

Section 4. Decision Making

INTRODUCTION

The course a program follows, or the *program flow,* often depends on the result of a decision. Decisions are commonly made when the program compares one value to another, and chooses to perform one action or another. The components of Pascal used to make decisions are called *control structures.*

Up to this point, we have only used one of Pascal's control structures, the `while...do` loop. This control structure is ideal for controlling repetitive actions, but it doesn't help us decide between two distinct courses of action that aren't necessarily repetitive in nature.

The last part of the payroll algorithm will become a Pascal procedure to calculate the gross pay. Gross pay is regular pay plus overtime pay (if there is any). Since not all employees work overtime, our algorithm makes a test to decide if an employee has worked overtime, then calculates the appropriate pay based on the result of this decision.

Pascal's `if...then...else` control structure allows us to test for overtime hours, then perform one activity if there are overtime hours, and one or more alternative activities if there are not.

This section has one part:

- The `if...then...else` Control Structure.

THE IF...THEN...ELSE CONTROL STRUCTURE

The *if . . . then . . . else* **control structure is used to make conditional decisions in programs.**

We have already used a species of the `if...then...else` structure in developing the algorithm for the payroll problem. Let's recall Step #2 of the algorithm:

Algorithm Step #2

2. *Compute gross pay*
   2.1 *If there is overtime, compute overtime pay and regular pay, otherwise compute regular pay and notice that overtime pay is zero*
   2.2 *Calculate gross pay as the sum of regular pay and overtime pay*

In Step #2.1, we test for overtime hours. *If* there is overtime, *then* we calculate overtime pay and regular pay. If *not,* then we simply calculate regular pay and note there is no overtime pay.

Pascal's `if...then...else` structure allows us to test the truth of a *condition,* similarly to the `while...do` statement. Here's a general outline of the `if...then...else` statement:

Outline of the *if . . . then . . . else* **Statement**

```
if condition is true then
    perform action "A"
else
    perform action "B";
```

As in the `while...do` statement, a *condition* is usually a comparison between two values. For example, consider a situation where we want to test to determine which of two variables has the greater value. We can use the `if...then...else` statement to evaluate the condition, then print a message telling which is the larger.

Example:

```
if Apples > Oranges then
    writeln ('There are more apples than oranges.')
else
    writeln ('There are more oranges than apples.');
```

Notice this example shows a *single* `if...then...else` statement. Since only one action can be selected (the first action if the condition is true, or the `else` part if false), the two `writeln` expressions are considered to be part of the `if...then...else` statement. Therefore, only one semi-colon separates it from the rest of the program.

The `else` part of an `if...then...else` statement is optional. It can be omitted if no alternative action is to be performed when the `if...then` condition is false.

In the Payroll program, we want to test if the condition "there are overtime hours" is true. This test can easily be made if we first create a constant to represent the number of hours in a standard workweek. Then we can compare it to the number of hours actually worked by the employee in that week. If the number of hours worked is greater than the standard workweek, there is overtime, and overtime pay is calculated. If not, there is no overtime, and the `else` action can be executed instead.

Later, we'll create value parameters to provide this procedure with the employee's hourly rate of pay and the total number of hours worked, and a variable parameter to return the final `GrossPay` value to the main program. First, to complete the procedure itself, we must create some local variables to represent the potential extra hours and overtime pay, as well as regular pay. This is a perfect example of an instance where a Problem Table can be of tremendous value in keeping straight the function of variables.

Problem Table for *ComputeGrossPay* Procedure

INPUT	PROCESS		OUTPUT
HoursWorked PayRate	Constant: Variables:	StandardWorkWeek ExtraHours RegularPay OvertimePay	GrossPay

This Problem Table provides us with a tremendous amount of information. First, it tells us that the constant StandardWorkWeek and the variables ExtraHours, RegularPay, and OvertimePay will be local to the procedure. They are listed in the PROCESS column, meaning they don't have any input or output requirements.

The Problem Table also tells us the main program will be sending HoursWorked and PayRate as actual value parameters to the procedure, and that the main program expects a value to be returned to the global variable GrossPay once the procedure has executed.

Given this information, let's translate algorithm Step #2 into Pascal. We'll use different names for the formal parameters than the names indicated for the actual parameters in the Problem Table, just to illustrate that it can be done. We will name the formal parameters for the procedure: TotalHours and HourlyRate, and TotalPay. Here is how they match:

Actual Parameter   **Formal Parameter**
(main program)   **(procedure)**

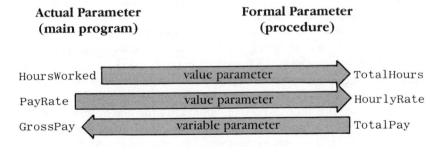

HoursWorked   value parameter   TotalHours

PayRate   value parameter   HourlyRate

GrossPay   variable parameter   TotalPay

Here's the final declaration for procedure ComputeGrossPay:

Procedure *ComputeGrossPay*

```
procedure ComputeGrossPay (TotalHours, HourlyRate : real;
                               var TotalPay : real);
    const
        StandardWorkweek = 40.0;
    var
        ExtraHours, RegularPay, OvertimePay : real;
    begin
        OvertimePay := 0.0;
        if TotalHours > StandardWorkweek then
            begin
                ExtraHours := TotalHours - StandardWorkweek;
                OvertimePay := ExtraHours * (HourlyRate * 1.5);
                RegularPay := StandardWorkweek * HourlyRate;
            end
        else
            RegularPay := TotalHours * HourlyRate;
            TotalPay := OvertimePay + RegularPay;
    end;
```

Several parts of this translation require explanation. Notice first that we initialize the variable OvertimePay to Ø.Ø *before* we test for overtime hours. If there are overtime hours, the first part of the if...then statement will assign the correct value to OvertimePay. However, if there is no overtime pay, the variable OvertimePay must still have been initialized before it can be used in the GrossPay calculation.

Second, notice we have used a compound statement as the action for the first part of the if...then statement. All three calculations making up the compound statement are important; therefore, we must bracket the action between the reserved words begin and end. Otherwise, only the first statement—ExtraHours := TotalHours - StandardWorkweek —would be executed. The if...then...else statement only executes one action: We make sure everything necessary is performed by making that action a compound statement.

Finally, notice that there is no semi-colon after the end in this compound statement. This compound statement is itself part of a single if...then...else statement, so a semi-colon is only used after the final

else clause. The semi-colons separating the statements within the compound statement are still necessary, however, to assure that each part of the
compound statement is executed correctly.

TEST YOUR UNDERSTANDING

13. Correct the errors in the following `if`...`then`...`else` statement:

```
if Apples < Oranges then do
   Total = Total + 1;
else;
   Total := 0;
```

Section 5. The Payroll Program

To complete the payroll program, we must declare all global variables.
Here's the Problem Table for the program once again:

Payroll Problem Table

INPUT	PROCESS	OUTPUT
EmployeeID PayRate HoursWorked		GrossPay Deductions NetPay

Using this table for reference, we'll declare all of the global variables for
the program:

```
var
    EmployeeID : integer;
    PayRate, HoursWorked, GrossPay, Deductions, NetPay : real;
```

Next, we must list the procedure declarations immediately after the variable declaration. Finally, we must write the statement part of the main program, consisting entirely of calls to the four procedures that do the work of the program. Each procedure *call* will supply the *actual* parameters to be used by the procedure.

Recall there must be a one-to-one match between actual and formal parameters. This means that not only must there be an equal number of actual and formal parameters, but that actual parameters must be listed *in the same order* as formal parameters.

The actual parameters for the ComputeGrossPay procedure will be the global variables HoursWorked, PayRate, and GrossPay. The actual parameters for the ComputeNetPay procedure will be the global variables GrossPay, Deductions, and NetPay.

We don't use parameters for the procedures CollectInfo and Print-PayForm because both procedures directly manipulate global variables anyway. Using parameters for procedures that handle input and output for the entire program is unnecessary, and can clutter the procedures.

Here's the statement part of the Payroll program:

Payroll Program Statement Part

```
begin    { Payroll program statement part }

    CollectInfo;
    ComputeGrossPay (HoursWorked, PayRate, GrossPay);
    ComputeNetPay (GrossPay, Deductions, NetPay);
    PrintResults;

end.    { Payroll program statement part }
```

Now we can bring it all together!

The Payroll Program

```
program Payroll (input, output);

var
    EmployeeID : integer;
    PayRate, HoursWorked, GrossPay, Deductions, NetPay : real;
```

```pascal
procedure CollectInfo;

    begin
        write ('What is the employee ID number? ');
        readln (EmployeeID);
        write ('Total number of hours worked this week? ');
        readln (HoursWorked);
        write ('What is the hourly pay rate? ');
        readln (PayRate);
    end;


procedure ComputeGrossPay (TotalHours, HourlyRate : real;
                                 var TotalPay : real);
    const
        StandardWorkweek = 40.0;
    var
        ExtraHours, RegularPay, OvertimePay : real;

    begin            { Statement part of ComputeGrossPay }
        OvertimePay := 0.0;
        if TotalHours > StandardWorkweek then
            begin               { Overtime pay calculation }
                ExtraHours := TotalHours - StandardWorkweek;
                OvertimePay := ExtraHours * (HourlyRate * 1.5);
                RegularPay := StandardWorkweek * HourlyRate;
            end               { Overtime pay calculation }
        else
            RegularPay := TotalHours * HourlyRate;
        TotalPay := OvertimePay + RegularPay;
    end;                      { procedure ComputeGrossPay }


procedure ComputeNetPay (GrossPay : real;
                               var Deductions, NetPay : real);
    const
        FICA = 0.067;

    begin
        Deductions := GrossPay * FICA;
        NetPay := GrossPay - Deductions;
    end;
```

```
procedure PrintPayForm;

    begin
        writeln ('Employee # ', EmployeeID :2);
        writeln ('Gross Pay is        $ ', GrossPay :8:2);
        writeln ('Total Deductions    $ ', Deductions :8:2);
        writeln ('Net pay for week is $ ', NetPay :8:2);
    end;

begin   { Main Program }

    CollectInfo;
    ComputeGrossPay (HoursWorked, PayRate, GrossPay);
    ComputeNetPay (GrossPay, Deductions, NetPay);
    PrintPayForm;
end.    { Payroll Program }
```

PROGRAMMING EXERCISES

Programming Exercise 1:

Insert a computation that will add a $50.00 bonus to the net pay if an employee has worked 50 or more hours in a week.

Programming Exercise 2:

Mr. Caffery, Vango's new chief accountant, has called you to say that Ms. O'Keefe has been imprisoned for tax evasion. He has requested that you add federal, state, and city tax deductions to the net pay calculation.

The federal and state tax percentages must be input by the user depending on the employee's income level. The city tax is 1.3% for every employee, regardless of income level. The pay form procedure should also be modified to list the amount of tax deducted from each category, and a total of all deductions.

ANSWERS TO THE TEST YOUR UNDERSTANDING EXERCISES

1. To facilitate the translation of the algorithm step into a Pascal procedure.
2. Pascal provides *structured programming* techniques such as the ability to specify variable data types, create procedures, and so on, not found in many other programming languages.

3. The four parts of a procedure declaration are:

    — The procedure heading,
    — The definition part,
    — The declaration part,
    — The statement part.

4. Procedures are declared in the declaration part of the main program, immediately after the variable declarations.

5. A procedure is called when its name is used as a statement.

6. Global scope means that a variable can be used anywhere in a program. Local scope means that a variable is restricted to the procedure that it was declared within.

7. A value parameter passes the *value* of a global variable into a procedure.

8. A variable parameter allows a procedure to change the value of a global variable.

9. Value and variable parameters are declared in the parameter list of the procedure heading.

10. Formal parameters are the value and variable parameters declared in a procedure heading.

11. Actual parameters are the names of global variables that will take the place of formal parameters when a procedure is called.

12. For every formal parameter declared in a parameter list, the program must supply an actual parameter when the procedure is called.

13. Original (incorrect) statement:

No "do" in an if...then statement

```
if Apples < Oranges then do
    Total      Total + 1;
else;
    Total := 0;
```

Incorrect use of semicolon

Should be assignment operator (:=)

Corrected statement:

```
if Apples < Oranges then
    Total = Total + 1
else
    Total := 0;
```

CHAPTER 5

Decision Making

CHAPTER OBJECTIVE

To discuss techniques for developing algorithms for complex problems, and to features of Pascal that help reduce the complexity of programs.

CHAPTER OVERVIEW

As we said in Chapter 1, the two fundamental operations performed by all computers are *calculations* and *comparisons*. Many computer programs designed for business applications consist almost entirely of comparisons between data values, with few actual calculations. As an example, consider the process used by a lending institution to determine a maximum loan amount. This process requires decisions that compare an applicant's financial situation with the lending institution's predefined standards for financial stability.

113

Coronado Savings and Loan has requested your services to create an "Electronic Loan Officer" program. The head of the lending institution, Mr. Stellmacher, has explained the process of determining a maximum loan amount. First, the lending institution determines a credit rating based on the applicant's annual income and net worth. This credit rating is then used to select the percentage factors to calculate the maximum loan amount.

Because *two* variable values (the annual income and net worth) must be compared to bank-defined standards to determine the credit rating, our problem solving process must involve many comparisons.

New Pascal: We will elaborate on the *if . . . then . . . else* statement, and introduce the *case* statement, a control structure useful for reducing the complexity of programs requiring sophisticated decision making.

We'll also discuss one of Pascal's most interesting features, allowing the programmer to *create* a data type custom tailored to a particular program.

This chapter has five sections:

- **The Loan Problem**
- **Analyzing Complex Problems**
- **Reducing the Complexity of Programs**
- **User-Defined Data Types**
- **The Loan Officer Program**

Section 1. The Loan Problem

INTRODUCTION

Before we can develop the loan officer algorithm, we must analyze the problem in detail. Your first task is to find out how the bank currently handles the loan evaluation process. Then, as with most other problems, you will write an algorithm, and translate it into Pascal.

This section has two parts:

- The Loan Problem
- The Initial Loan Algorithm

ANALYZING THE LOAN PROBLEM

To analyze the loan problem, determine the procedure used by a loan officer when working with a typical customer.

At Coronado Savings and Loan, the board of directors has established a procedure to determine the maximum amount a customer may borrow. First, a credit rating is determined based on two factors: the applicant's annual income and net worth. That credit rating is then used to select percentages of their annual income and net worth used to calculate the maximum loan amount.

Mr. Stellmacher feels this procedure is simple and straightforward, though it requires decisions about many possible options. When a prospective borrower applies for a loan, the loan officer follows these steps:

1. The loan officer requests information about the applicant's annual income and net worth. These two factors are good indicators of a customer's financial stability, and reflect ability to repay a loan.

2. The loan officer next uses a table prepared by the bank to classify the applicant's annual income. The income rating is simply a number between 1 and 4, with 1 representing what the bank considers a relatively high income, and 4 representing a low income. This rating simplifies the process of determining an appropriate maximum loan amount; it reduces a wide range of possible annual incomes to a single rating with one of four values. Coronado Savings & Loan uses this table to determine an income rating:

Annual Income	Income Rating
$ 100,000 or more	1
$ 35,000 – 99,999	2
$ 15,000 – 34,999	3
less than $ 15,000	4

Figure 5.1   Coronado S & L Income Rating Table

Using such a table is a particularly arbitrary way of rating an annual income. As you can see, a person with a $99,999 income will be assigned an income rating of "2," even though most people would feel this amount is close enough to deserve a "1." A human loan officer would probably take this into consideration when assigning an income rating. Unfortunately, our program will not be able to weigh such factors as "It's really close. . ."

3. Using the same technique of reducing a wide range of possible values to a single rating, a "letter grade" credit rating is determined using the applicant's net worth and the income rating.

   The table in Figure 5.2 is used to determine the credit rating. The loan officer first locates the applicant's net worth along the left side, which determines the horizontal row from which the credit rating will be selected. Then he finds the appropriate income rating column at the top of the table, and moves vertically down that column to the appropriate row. The credit rating is found at the intersection of the appropriate row and column.

		Income Rating			
		1	*2*	*3*	*4*
Net Worth	> 150,000	A	A	B	C
	≥ 50,000	A	B	C	D
	≥ 20,000	B	C	C	D
	< 20,000	C	D	D	D

Figure 5.2   Coronado S & L Credit Rating Table

   As an example, consider an applicant who has an income rating of "3" and a net worth of $75,000. Following the process just described, the loan officer would use the second row and third column, and assign this applicant a credit rating of "C."

4. Finally, the maximum authorized loan amount is computed from a predetermined formula. This formula calculates a loan amount equal to a certain percentage of the applicant's annual income added to a certain percentage of net worth. The credit rating determines the percentages used; an "A" rating allows a higher percentage to be used than a "D" rating, thereby allowing a larger loan amount. The percentages used by Coronado to determine a maximum loan amount are summarized in the table in Figure 5.3.

Credit Rating	Maximum Loan Amount
A	(20% of annual income) + (25% of net worth)
B	(20% of annual income) + (20% of net worth)
C	(15% of annual income) + (20% of net worth)
D	(10% of annual income) + (15% of net worth)

Figure 5.3   Loan Amount Percentage Table

According to this table, a person with an "A" credit rating is eligible for a maximum loan amount of up to 20 percent of annual income plus 25 percent of net worth, whereas a person with a "D" rating is eligible for a maximum loan amount of no more than 10 percent of annual income plus 15 percent of net worth.

THE INITIAL LOAN ALGORITHM

The initial loan algorithm will summarize the steps used to determine a maximum loan amount.

If we summarize the loan officer's four steps to determine a maximum loan amount, we end up with a very tidy initial algorithm.

Initial Loan Algorithm

1. *Get necessary information*
2. *Classify annual income*
3. *Determine credit rating*
4. *Compute maximum loan amount*

Now we can begin the stepwise refinement process for this algorithm, breaking down the individual steps of the algorithm and adding additional detail.

TEST YOUR UNDERSTANDING

1. Before going on to the next section, see if you can refine the loan algorithm based on what you already know of the problem.

INTRODUCTION

Although Mr. Stellmacher felt that the process of determining a maximum loan amount was relatively simple, you probably realize that each step must be explicitly and unambiguously described before we can translate the algorithm into a Pascal program. This section discusses how to refine an algorithm for a complex problem such as the Coronado S & L loan. In this section, we'll completely refine each step of the loan algorithm.

This section has four parts:

- Requesting Input Information
- Classifying Annual Income
- Determining a Credit Rating
- Computing the Maximum Loan Amount

REQUESTING INPUT INFORMATION

Algorithm Step #1 specifies the necessary input information.

A refinement of this step poses no difficulties. We simply need to indicate what information is necessary—in other words, what information must the user of the program provide?

According to the description of the problem, only the applicant's annual income and net worth are required as input information.

Refinement of Step #1

1. *Get necessary information*
   1.1 *Request applicant's annual income*
   1.2 *Request applicant's net worth*

CLASSIFYING ANNUAL INCOME

In refining Step #2, our goal is to classify the applicant's annual income according to a predefined standard.

Beginning with Step #2, we'll deal with a task that would pose little difficulty for most people. However, quite a bit of exposition is required to specifically describe the process and provide a basis for a computer program.

A very useful technique for refining an algorithm is to approach the task as if you were teaching a complete novice—which in a very profound sense is true if you intend to translate the algorithm into a computer program. As we describe the decision-making process involved in classifying an income, we'll refer to Figure 5.1.

Annual Income	Income Rating
$ 100,000 or more	1
$ 35,000 – 99,999	2
$ 15,000 – 34,999	3
less than $ 15,000	4

Figure 5.4   Coronado S & L Income Rating Table

The most direct approach to classifying an applicant's annual income is by comparing it to the two endpoints, or *boundary conditions,* for each income category. Ultimately, the income will fall within the range of incomes for one specific category, and the income rating can be assigned.

We can ask a series of questions to make these comparisons. Starting at the top of the table in Figure 5.4, we consider the first two boundary conditions ($100,000 to infinity) and ask: "Is the annual income greater than or equal to $100,000?" If yes, assign an income rating of "1." If no, proceed to the next lower category, and repeat the question using the boundary conditions for that category. This step can be stated as: "If the income is not greater than or equal to $100,000, is it greater than or equal to $35,000?" If yes, assign an income rating of "2." If no, continue this pattern of testing. As soon as an income rating is assigned, we can stop testing.

If we formalize the language we just used to describe this process, we can refine Step #2 of our algorithm:

Refinement of Step #2

2.   *Classify annual income*
    2.1   *If the annual income >= 100,000 then*
        assign income rating of "1"
    2.2   *If the annual income is not >= 100,000 then*
        if the annual income >= 35,000 then
        assign an income rating of "2"
    2.3   *If the annual income is not >= 35,000 then*
        if the annual income >= 15,000 then
        assign an income rating of "3"

> **2.4   If the annual income is not >= 15,000 then assign an income rating of "4"**

This is a complete refinement of Step #2; we cannot break it down any further. Every possible annual income that can be input will fall into one of these four categories.

Our next step is to refine Step #3, comparing the income rating with the net worth to assign an overall credit rating.

DETERMINING A CREDIT RATING

The net worth and income rating are used to locate the appropriate credit rating in the credit rating table.

To refine Step #3, we must describe the process a loan officer uses to look up a credit rating. This is a classic example of a process that would be very easy to *show* someone how to do; however, expressing the steps involved in English is awkward. Rather than attempting a narrative description of the process, we'll make a list describing each step, then use this list to create an algorithm. Refer to Figure 5.5 to help follow the steps.

		Income Rating			
		1	*2*	*3*	*4*
Net Worth	> 150,000	A	A	B	C
	≥ 50,000	A	B	C	D
	≥ 20,000	B	C	C	D
	< 20,000	C	D	D	D

Figure 5.5   Coronado S & L Credit Rating Table

1. Locate the row that applies to the applicant's net worth along the left side of the table.
2. Locate the column that applies to the applicant's income rating along the top of the table.
3. Find the box located at the intersection of the row and column determined in the two steps above.
4. Assign the credit rating found in that location to the applicant.

Note that this is *not* an algorithm to solve the problem; it leaves out very important information about the *decisions* required to perform these activities. This list of instructions assumes quite a bit of previous knowledge. Our algorithm must be much more specific.

The first step in this list describes a process similar to the one we used to determine the income rating. If we approach the refinement of Step #3 with a similar strategy of testing boundary values for the net worth categories, we can determine an initial "net worth rating" that allows us to determine the *row* from which we'll select a credit rating. Further refinement will then focus on additional testing to determine the *column* to be used together with the row to determine the credit rating.

Here is the first level refinement of Step #3:

Level One Refinement of Step #3

3. **Determine Credit Rating**
    3.1 If the net worth >= 150,000 then
            assign credit rating from first row of table
    3.2 If the net worth is not >= 150,000 then
            if the net worth >= 50,000 then
                assign credit rating from second row of table
    3.3 If the net worth is not >= 50,000 then
            if the net worth >= 20,000 then
                assign credit rating from third row of table
    3.4 If the net worth is not >= 20,000 then
            assign credit rating from fourth row of table

As in Step #2, we establish a *range* of values for each net worth category, and do it in such a way that only one of the four possible rows can be selected.

Let's use an example to illustrate the algorithm step. Susan Scharton has applied for a loan, and has received an income rating of "2." Her net worth is $43,000. Using this information in the level one refinement of Step #3, the first test (Step #3.1) fails, because her net worth is not greater than $100,000. The next test (Step #3.2) also fails, because her net worth is not greater than $50,000. However, the third test succeeds because her net worth does fall between the boundary values $50,000 and $20,000. Therefore, the third row is selected for further examination.

Now we must further refine Step #3 to locate the appropriate vertical column once a row has been selected, and assign a credit rating. The "level two" refinement of Step #3 creates an algorithm effectively describing the entire process followed by the loan officer to look up a credit rating. You

Susan Scharton
Income Rating = 2
NetWorth = $43,000

		Income Rating			
		1	*2*	*3*	*4*
Net Worth	> 150,000	A	A	B	C
	≥ 50,000	A	B	C	D
	≥ 20,000	B	C	C	D
	< 20,000	C	D	D	D

Figure 5.5(a)   Coronado S & L Credit Rating Table

should compare this refinement with the actual table itself to appreciate
how many steps we take for granted in performing such an activity in daily
life.

Level Two Refinement of Step #3

3. *Determine Credit Rating*

   3.1 *If the net worth >= 150,000 then
         assign credit rating from first row of table*
         3.1.1 *If income rating is "1", then
               assign credit rating of "A"*
         3.1.2 *If income rating is "2", then
               assign credit rating of "A"*
         3.1.3 *If income rating is "3", then
               assign credit rating of "B"*
         3.1.4 *If income rating is "4", then
               assign credit rating of "C"*
   3.2 *If the net worth is not >= 150,000 then
         if the net worth >= 50,000 then
         assign credit rating from second row of table*
         3.2.1 *If income rating is "1", then
               assign credit rating of "A"*
         3.2.2 *If income rating is "2", then
               assign credit rating of "B"*
         3.2.3 *If income rating is "3", then
               assign credit rating of "C"*

> ### 3.2.4 *If income rating is "4", then*
> *assign credit rating of "D"*
> ## 3.3 *If the net worth is not >= 50,000 then*
> *if the net worth >= 20,000 then*
> *assign credit rating from third row of table*
> ### 3.3.1 *If income rating is "1", then*
> *assign credit rating of "B"*
> ### 3.3.2 *If income rating is "2", then*
> *assign credit rating of "C"*
> ### 3.3.3 *If income rating is "3", then*
> *assign credit rating of "C"*
> ### 3.3.4 *If income rating is "4", then*
> *assign credit rating of "D"*
> ## 3.4 *If the net worth is not >= 20,000 then*
> *assign credit rating from fourth row of table*
> ### 3.4.1 *If income rating is "1", then*
> *assign credit rating of "C"*
> ### 3.4.2 *If income rating is "2", then*
> *assign credit rating of "D"*
> ### 3.4.3 *If income rating is "3", then*
> *assign credit rating of "D"*
> ### 3.4.4 *If income rating is "4", then*
> *assign credit rating of "D"*

Notice how we've used indentation to differentiate each level of the decision process. Even if we hadn't numbered the steps, the indentation would have associated specific sub steps with a major step.

Susan Scharton
Income Rating = 2
NetWorth = $43,000

		Income Rating			
		1	*2*	*3*	*4*
Net Worth	> 150,000	A	A	B	C
	>= 50,000	A	B	C	D
	>= 20,000	B	C	C	D
	< 20,000	C	D	D	D

Figure 5.5(b) Coronado S & L Credit Rating Table

Let's complete the credit rating for Susan. We select the second column, because her income rating is "2." Therefore, we assign the value "C," located in the box at the intersection of the third row and second column.

Now that we've refined our algorithm to determine an overall credit rating, determining the actual maximum loan amount is a relatively simple process.

COMPUTING THE MAXIMUM LOAN AMOUNT

The maximum authorized loan amount is computed from a predetermined formula.

Let's recall Mr. Stellmacher's description of the calculation to determine the maximum loan amount. The formula calculates a loan amount equal to a certain percentage of the applicant's annual income added to a certain percentage of net worth. The credit rating determines the percentages used in the calculation as shown in Figure 5.6.

Credit Rating	Maximum Loan Amount
A	(20% of annual income) + (25% of net worth)
B	(20% of annual income) + (20% of net worth)
C	(15% of annual income) + (20% of net worth)
D	(10% of annual income) + (15% of net worth)

Figure 5.6   Loan Amount Percentage Table

Translating the steps used to determine a credit rating into an algorithm is not difficult:

Algorithm Step #4

4. *Compute maximum loan amount*
    4.1 *If credit rating is "A" then maximum loan amount is (20% of annual income) + (25% of net worth)*
    4.2 *If credit rating is "B" then maximum loan amount is (20% of annual income) + (20% of net worth)*
    4.3 *If credit rating is "C" then maximum loan amount is (15% of annual income) + (20% of net worth)*
    4.4 *If credit rating is "D" then maximum loan amount is (10% of annual income) + (15% of net worth)*

We have now completely refined the algorithm to determine the maximum loan amount. As you see, the complete algorithm represents a description of a relatively complex task. The rest of the chapter discusses methods for reducing the complexity of programs created from algorithms such as the one we've just completed.

As usual, we will name our variables at this point.

Data Item	**Variable Identifier**
Applicant's annual income	Income
Applicant's net worth	NetWorth
Applicant's income rating	IncomeRating
Applicant's credit rating	CreditRating
Maximum loan amount	MaxLoanAmount

As you see, the identifiers we've chosen are not terribly original, but they convey the purpose of each variable. Here's a Problem Table including these variables:

Problem Table for Loan Officer Program

INPUT	PROCESS	OUTPUT
Income NetWorth	Variables: IncomeRating CreditRating	MaxLoanAmount

We will also create identifiers for our procedures:

Algorithm Step	**Procedure Identifier**
1. *Get necessary information*	GetInfo
2. *Classify annual income*	ClassifyIncome
3. *Determine credit rating*	EstablishCreditRating
4. *Compute maximum loan amount*	ComputeMaxLoanAmount

TEST YOUR UNDERSTANDING

2.   You've just seen how complex the description of even seemingly simple tasks can be. Write an algorithm describing a process that's probably tremendously easy for you — namely, recognizing your mother in a crowd of people. This algorithm should be detailed enough so that a complete stranger could use it to unfailingly identify your mother, even at an annual "Moms of America" convention with thousands of other mothers in attendance.

Section 3. Reducing the Complexity of Programs

INTRODUCTION

Complex decisions in algorithms tend to be expressed with an *if . . . then* construction, making the translation into Pascal easy—by using an if . . . then . . . else statement. We will show in this chapter that certain types of complex decisions—specifically those using a scalar value for comparison purposes—can benefit from another Pascal decision structure, the case statement. Rather than evaluating many (potentially) different conditions, the case statement evaluates a scalar variable, then uses this value to select a single action from a list of possible actions.

This section has three parts:

- Nested if . . . then . . . else Statements
- The case Statement

NESTED *IF . . . THEN . . . ELSE* STATEMENTS

An *if . . . then . . . else* **statement can have a second** *if . . . then . . . else* **statement** *nested* **in it as the action part of the statement.**

The loan algorithm is an example of a process requiring a number of comparisons. By comparing the applicant's annual income to a series of numbers representing income level, an income rating is determined. With a similar set of comparisons, the applicant's net worth is classified.

In the last section of Chapter 4, we used the if . . . then . . . else statement to test a condition and then perform one action or another, dependent on the result of the comparison. In this section, we'll again use the if . . . then . . . else statement to test a condition, and perform a specified action if the condition is true. However, if the condition is false, we'll check a further condition before specifying which of two actions to perform. The form of the conditional statement to accomplish this complex task is an if . . . then . . . else statement, in which the action specified in the else clause *is itself* an if . . . then . . . else statement.

For example, let's assume that Humby's Thrift and Mortgage has established a loan policy according to which all applicants from New Jersey are granted loans up to $1,000,000. Of the rest of the applicants, all those who are professional "stripping" telegram singers will be allowed loans up to $500,000. All other applicants will be denied loans. A complex if... then... else statement for this procedure might be written as:

```
if State = 'New Jersey'
then MaxLoanAmount := 1000000.0
else if Occupation = 'TelegramSinger'
     then MaxLoanAmount := 500000.0
     else MaxLoanAmount := 0.0;
```

This construction is called a *nested* if... then... else statement. The second if... then... else is "nested" within the else clause of the first.

A particularly useful application of nested if... then... else statements is the situation where a value must be compared to several fixed values to determine which range it falls into. For example, consider the policy of another lending institution, The Fetter Holding Company, who will grant million-dollar loan limits to anyone age 40 and above, half-million-dollar limits to anyone between age 30 and 40, and $100 limits to anyone else. A program segment for these criteria could read:

```
if Age >= 40
then MaxLoanAmount := 1000000.0
else if Age >= 30
     then MaxLoanAmount := 500000.0
     else MaxLoanAmount := 100.0;
```

The effect of this statement is to assign loan limits as summarized in Figure 5.7:

Age	Maximum Loan Amount
40 and above	$ 1,000,000
30–39	$ 500,000
under 30	$ 100

Figure 5.7 Fetter Holding Company Loan Limit Table

Just as we have nested a second if... then... else statement into a first if... then... else in this example, we could nest a third `if...then...else` into the `else` clause of the second. This gives us the opportunity to compare a variable to yet another value. We could add a third loan category, or we could make the criteria more varied—for example, we could add a test to the 30–39 category to check their type of employment before establishing a loan limit.

Nested `if...then...else` statements can be used to test as many conditions as necessary. However, excessive use of nested statements can make programs very difficult to read. In situations where the condition being tested is a scalar variable, such as the income rating or the credit rating, the `case` statement is preferable to nested `if...then...else` statements.

THE *CASE* STATEMENT

The *case* statement evaluates a scalar expression (usually a variable), and selects action determined by the value of the expression.

If we translated our refined algorithm into Pascal at this point, the program would consist mostly of numerous `if...then...else` statements. Instead, we can reduce the number of statements in the program by judicious use of the powerful case statement. The case statement compresses the expression of a (potentially) very long sequence of `if...then...else` statements.

The `case` statement evaluates a scalar expression, then compares the value to a *constant list*. When the value of the case expression matches a constant in the list, a specified action is performed.

Here's an outline of the `case` statement:

General Outline of the *case* Statement

```
case expression of
        constant value : action;
        constant value : action;
        constant value : action;
    end;
```

This generalized version begins with the reserved word case, followed by an expression to be evaluated, then the reserved word of. The *expression* is usually a scalar variable already assigned a specific value. Next, there's the case *constant* list, a list of the values to be compared to the case expression. Following each value is a description of the action that will occur if the constant value matches the expression.

Let's translate the general outline of the case statement into English:

"In **case** this expression is equal to
        this *constant value* : then perform the following action . . .
  (or)   this *constant value* : then perform the following action . . .
  (or)   this *constant value* : then perform the following action . . .
  end; "

Only one *constant value* can be selected each time the case statement is executed, because the case *expression* can have only one possible value.

How can we use the case statement in the Loan Officer program? Algorithm Step #4, "*Compute Maximum Loan Amount*", is perfectly suited for translation into a case statement:

Algorithm Step #4

4. ***Compute maximum loan amount***
    4.1 ***If credit rating is "A" then maximum loan amount is***
          (20% of annual income) + (25% of net worth)
    4.2 ***If credit rating is "B" then maximum loan amount is***
          (20% of annual income) + (20% of net worth)
    4.3 ***If credit rating is "C" then maximum loan amount is***
          (15% of annual income) + (20% of net worth)
    4.4 ***If credit rating is "D" then maximum loan amount is***
          (10% of annual income) + (15% of net worth)

The *if . . . then* form of the algorithm is relatively easy to translate into a case statement. Rather than writing "If credit rating is . . ." we write "case CreditRating of", then list the case constants and their actions.

Let's begin the translation of Step #4 into Pascal:

```
case CreditRating of
      'A'  :  { Compute MaxLoanAmount } ;
      'B'  :  { Compute MaxLoanAmount } ;
      'C'  :  { Compute MaxLoanAmount } ;
      'D'  :  { Compute MaxLoanAmount } ;
end;
```

In this skeletal version, the case statement evaluates the expression CreditRating (in this instance, a variable with a single value), and compares it to the case constant list. The constant list consists of the four "letter-grade" credit ratings, which are values of the scalar type char. When the case statement evaluates the value of CreditRating, the value will match one of the four case constants, and an appropriate maximum loan amount will be computed.

Notice that the reserved word end completes the case statement—one of the few instances in Pascal where an end is used without a matching begin.

In this example, we have not yet specified any action. We've used comments instead to indicate that some action will be performed for each case constant. The action performed, once a case constant has been selected, can be any Pascal statement, such as a writeln or an assignment statement. Action also can take the form of compound statements or procedure calls. We'll show examples of all these kinds of action later.

Here's a complete translation of Step #4 into Pascal:

Pascal Version of Algorithm Step #4

```
case CreditRating of
 'A': MaxLoanAmount := (Income * 0.20) + (NetWorth * 0.25);
 'B': MaxLoanAmount := (Income * 0.20) + (NetWorth * 0.20);
 'C': MaxLoanAmount := (Income * 0.15) + (NetWorth * 0.20);
 'D': MaxLoanAmount := (Income * 0.10) + (NetWorth * 0.15);
 end;
```

By the way, although the char values that we're using as case constants are perfectly valid as far as Pascal is concerned, we won't be using them in the final program; don't worry too much about the details of their use. Although this illustration represents correct Pascal, we are simply using the values "A" through "D" as case constants for the purpose of illustration.

As we said, any Pascal statement can be executed as action once a case constant has been selected. As promised, here's another case statement with a different kind of action for each different case constant. This time we use integer values as case constants, therefore the value represented by CreditRating must be of type integer.

Example:

```
case CreditRating of
    1: begin      {compound statement}
         MaxLoanAmount := (Income * 0.20) + (NetWorth * 0.25);
         writeln ('Loan approved for $', MaxLoanAmount);
       end;
    2: ComputeHighLoanAmount;      {Procedure call}
    3: if Income < NetWorth then
         MaxLoanAmount := Income * 0.10
       else MaxLoanAmount := 5000.0;
```

```
    4: writeln ('Your credit rating is too low for a loan.');
    5,6,7,8,9 : ;
end; {case CreditRating}
```

Let's discuss the action that occurs for each case constant in this example.

When CreditRating = 1, a compound statement is executed, as indicated by the reserved word begin. The first statement makes an assignment to the variable MaxLoanAmount. The second statement prints a message indicating the approved amount of loan. The compound statement is completed with the reserved word end— note that this end completes the compound statement only, not the entire case statement.

When CreditRating = 2, the procedure ComputeHighLoanAmount is called. As you see, to call a procedure as action, we simply use the procedure identifier as a statement. If necessary, we could also use value or variable parameters in such a call.

When CreditRating = 3, we perform an if...then...else test before making an assignment to MaxLoanAmount. Although this if..then...else statement looks lengthy, it is a single statement, and it's perfectly valid to include it as the action part of the case statement.

When CreditRating = 4, no assignment is made to MaxLoanAmount. Instead, we have writeln print a message that might be somewhat distressing to the applicant.

The last part of our varied case example requires some explanation. We're going to assume that the values 5 through 9 are not valid credit ratings. If somehow the variable CreditRating evaluates to a value between 5 and 9, we don't want to perform *any* action. Therefore, we'll execute an *empty statement,* separated from all other statements with a semi-colon. The empty statement is *not* the semi-colon itself; it is only separated by a semi-colon.

The empty statement won't cause the program to stop. It's just another type of action—specifically, action that does nothing! After executing the empty statement, program control is transferred to the next statement after the case statement. In an actual program, we would probably want to print an error message, but we're using the empty statement here for purposes of demonstration.

Why use an empty statement at all? If the value of the case expression does not match any of the case constants, an error condition arises. Some versions of Pascal will ignore this error, exit the case statement, and continue with the next program statement. However, other versions can't cope with a case expression that does not have a matching case constant, and the program will fail, or "crash." In either situation, the effect the case statement was designed to have is bypassed, and the program probably won't yield the desired result.

Some extended versions of Pascal provide an 'Otherwise' option for the case statement, that accommodates values not specifically listed as case constants.

The second point to notice about the last example is that values "5" through "9" all require the same action. All values that requiring the same action can be listed together. Therefore, we can list "5" through "9" together, separating each with a comma. A snobbish lending institution might use the case structure this way:

```
case CreditRating of
  1,2,3: writeln ('Your credit rating is too low for a loan.');
      4: writeln ('You must be joking!');
end;
```

We'll return to the case statement when we translate step #3 of the Loan Officer program into Pascal.

TEST YOUR UNDERSTANDING

3. What does it mean to "nest" an if...then...else statement?

4. What is a case *expression?*

5. How does the case statement work?

6. Can real values be used as case expressions or constants?

7. Why is the use of the reserved word end unusual in a case statement?

Section 4. User-Defined Data Types

INTRODUCTION

Pascal is an excellent language for developing business application programs because of its features that allow you to create readable and easily understood programs. The ability to invent meaningful identifiers, to use spaces and blank lines to format programs in an organized fashion, and to insert comments into a program are all examples of techniques to help create programs that are easy to read and understand.

Pascal allows us to go one step further in constructing readable programs. Using the `type` definition, we can create our own data type that will be just as meaningful to a program as the predefined data types `integer`, or `real`. Then we can actually define values for the data type that can clarify the meaning of variable values.

This section has two parts:

- What are User-Defined Data Types?
- Programming with User-Defined Types

WHAT ARE USER-DEFINED DATA TYPES

User-defined data types are *scalar* data types, with values specified by the programmer.

As you recall from Figure 5−2, Coronado Savings & Loan assigns credit ratings similar to letter grades. A credit rating of "A" is considered excellent, and "D" is considered poor. When reading a program using these values, most people would intuitively assume that "A" is better than "D"; however, without the addition of comments, some time would have to be spent tracing the program's action to be absolutely certain.

Imagine how readable the program would become if the variable `CreditRating` could have the values "Excellent," "Fair," "Good," or "Poor." Using these values could go a long way toward eliminating any doubts the program's reader might have about the purpose of the variable *or* its values. The action performed for an "Excellent" credit rating is clearly different than the action for "Poor".

Once again, Pascal provides us with a feature allowing us to enhance program readability. We can create a data type called RATING that includes four possible values to take the place of "A" through "D." These values will be "Excellent," "Good," "Fair" and "Poor."

User-defined data types are also called *enumerated* types, because the programmer must list (enumerate) each component that is a member of the data type. User-defined data types are specified, or *enumerated,* in the definition part of the program.

Let's create the data type called RATING which will consist of these four values:

```
type
    RATING = (Excellent, Good, Fair, Poor);
```

User-defined data type definitions always begin with the reserved word type, followed by the type identifier (the name of the data type), and a list of the valid values of the new data type enclosed in parentheses. Like constants, type identifiers are written in upper-case letters, to indicate that they represent user-defined values.

The type definition creates a new data type, called RATING, and specifies the values that can be assigned to variables of type RATING. Note in particular that RATING is not itself a variable: it's the identifier of a data type that has four values. Because we've enumerated (listed in order) the components of type RATING, the values are *scalar* in the same way as integer values. Our next step is to declare variables of type RATING.

What variables would benefit most from the ability to represent values of type RATING? We already mentioned CreditRating as a likely candidate. If we declare CreditRating as a variable of type RATING, we can assign values "Excellent", "Good", "Fair" and "Poor" to the variable. Another likely candidate is the variable IncomeRating. According to algorithm Step #2, IncomeRating is currently assigned an integer rating from 1 to 4. Instead, why not classify an annual income as "Excellent," "Good," "Fair," or "Poor"?

We declare variables of our user-defined type in the same way we would declare any other variable. However, rather than specifying type integer or type real as the data type, we declare them to be of type RATING instead.

Following is a variable declaration specifying CreditRATING and IncomeRating to be of the type RATING:

```
var
      IncomeRating, CreditRating : RATING;
```

By declaring CreditRating and IncomeRating to be variables of type RATING, it's now possible for any of the four values of type RATING to be *assigned* to those variables. In fact, the *only* values that may be assigned to these variables are of type RATING. The following table shows all the valid assignments that can be made to the variables CreditRating and IncomeRating:

Valid Assignments for Variables of type RATING

```
CreditRating := Excellent;      IncomeRating := Excellent;
CreditRating := Good;           IncomeRating := Good;
CreditRating := Fair;           IncomeRating := Fair;
CreditRating := Poor;           IncomeRating := Poor;
```

PROGRAMMING WITH USER-DEFINED DATA TYPES

Now we can use variables representing values of type *RATING* in the Loan Officer program.

Now that we've created a new data type, RATING, and declared two variables of that type, let's re-write the case statement that calculates the maximum loan amount, using the values of type RATING as case constants.

Revised *CreditRating case* Statement

```
case CreditRating of
     Excellent: MaxLoanAmount := (Income * 0.20) + (NetWorth * 0.25);
          Good: MaxLoanAmount := (Income * 0.20) + (NetWorth * 0.20);
          Fair: MaxLoanAmount := (Income * 0.15) + (NetWorth * 0.20);
          Poor: MaxLoanAmount := (Income * 0.10) + (NetWorth * 0.15);
end; { case }
```

TEST YOUR UNDERSTANDING

8. True or False: User-defined data types have scalar values.

9. What two steps are required to use a user-defined data type in a program?

Section 5. The Loan Officer Program

INTRODUCTION

This section concentrates on translating each step of the Loan Officer algorithm into Pascal, using what we've learned about the case statement and user-defined data types to construct an efficient and easy to read program.

This section has five parts:

- The GetInfo Procedure
- The ClassifyIncome Procedure
- The EstablishCreditRating Procedure
- The ComputeMaxLoanAmount Procedure
- The Loan Officer Program

THE *GETINFO* PROCEDURE

The *GetInfo* procedure collects necessary input data.

Recall Step #1 of our algorithm:

> 1. ***Get necessary information***
>   1.1 ***Request applicant's annual income***
>   1.2 ***Request applicant's net worth***

One advantage of using procedures to do such tasks as collecting input information is that they can be easily modified to work in a different program requiring a similar function. We can use the CollectInfo procedure we created for the Payroll program in Chapter 4 with just a few modifications to collect the information for the Loan Officer program:

The *GetInfo* Procedure

```
procedure GetInfo;
    begin
        write ('What is the annual income? ');
        readln (Income);
        write ('What is the net worth? ');
        readln (NetWorth);
    end;
```

That's all there is to it. We don't need any parameters since the procedure is reading input information and initializing global variables.

THE *CLASSIFYINCOME* PROCEDURE

The procedure *ClassifyIncome* compares the value of the variable *Income* to one or more constants that represent boundary conditions for each income rating category, then assigns an income rating determined by the result of the comparisons.

Recall Step #2 of the Loan Officer algorithm:

> 2. ***Classify annual income***
>   2.1 ***If the annual income >= 100,000 then***
>   ***assign income rating of "1"***
>   2.2 ***If the annual income is not >= 100,000 then***
>   ***if the annual income >= 35,000 then***
>   ***assign an income rating of "2"***

> **2.3** *If the annual income is not >= 35,000 then*
> *if the annual income >= 15,000 then*
> *assign an income rating of "3"*
> **2.4** *If the annual income is not >= 15,000 then*
> *assign an income rating of "4"*

We can make a relatively straightforward translation of this algorithm step into Pascal by using the same nested *if* structure found in the algorithm.

Each *boundary condition* used to test whether an applicant's income falls within a particular income category can be defined as a constant, to make the program easier to understand. This constant should represent each category's low boundary, because the high boundary will have already been tested as the low boundary of the previous category.

The income categories essentially represent low, middle, and high income ratings. Therefore, the constants representing the boundaries for each category should be named accordingly:

Constant Name and Value

```
HighIncome = 100000.0;
MidIncome  =  35000.0;
LowIncome  =  15000.0;
```

Let's create a Problem Table for this procedure.

Problem Table for *ClassifyIncome* Procedure

INPUT	PROCESS	OUTPUT
Income	Constants: HighIncome MidIncome LowIncome	IncomeRating

Finally, the parameters the procedure requires don't pose a mystery. The procedure requires the *value* of the global variable Income, and will return the IncomeRating to the main program. Income will be a *value* parameter, and IncomeRating will be a variable parameter. When we make the parameter list, we must remember that Income is a variable of type real, and IncomeRating is a variable of type RATING.

Here is the final ClassifyIncome Procedure:

Procedure *ClassifyIncome*

```
procedure ClassifyIncome (Income : real; var IncomeRating : RATING);

    const

        HighIncome = 100000.0;
        MidIncome = 35000.0;
        LowIncome = 15000.0;

    begin { ClassifyIncome }
        if Income >= HighIncome then
            IncomeRating := Excellent
        else if Income >= MidIncome then
                IncomeRating := Good
        else if Income >= LowIncome then
                IncomeRating := Fair
        else
            IncomeRating := Poor;
    end; { Procedure ClassifyIncome}
```

THE *ESTABLISHCREDITRATING* PROCEDURE

The procedure to establish a credit rating will use the *case* statement and the *if...then...else* statement to compare data of different types.

Let's recall Step #3 of our algorithm. This version of the algorithm uses values of our new data type RATING to represent income ratings and credit ratings:

   3. Determine Credit Rating

       3.1   If the net worth >= 150,000 then
              3.1.1   If income rating is "Excellent," then
                      assign credit rating of "Excellent"
              3.1.2   If income rating is "Good," then
                      assign credit rating of "Excellent"

> *3.1.3   If income rating is "Fair," then*
> *assign credit rating of "Good"*
> *3.1.4   If income rating is "Poor," then*
> *assign credit rating of "Fair"*

> *3.2   If the net worth is not $>=$ 150,000 then*
> *if the net worth $>=$ 50,000 then*
> *3.2.1 If income rating is "Excellent," then*
> *assign credit rating of "Excellent"*
> *3.2.2 If income rating is "Good," then*
> *assign credit rating of "Good"*
> *3.2.3 If income rating is "Fair," then*
> *assign credit rating of "Fair"*
> *3.2.4 If income rating is "Poor," then*
> *assign credit rating of "Poor"*

> *3.3   If the net worth is not $>=$ 50,000 then*
> *if the net worth $>=$ 20,000 then*
> *3.3.1 If income rating is "Excellent," then*
> *assign credit rating of "Good"*
> *3.3.2 If income rating is "Good," then*
> *assign credit rating of "Fair"*
> *3.3.3 If income rating is "Fair," then*
> *assign credit rating of "Fair"*
> *3.3.4 If income rating is "Poor," then*
> *assign credit rating of "Poor"*

> *3.4   If the net worth is not $>=$ 20,000 then*
> *3.4.1   If income rating is "Excellent," then*
> *assign credit rating of "Fair"*
> *3.4.2   If income rating is "Good," then*
> *assign credit rating of "Poor"*
> *3.4.3   If income rating is "Fair," then*
> *assign credit rating of "Poor"*
> *3.4.4   If income rating is "Poor," then*
> *assign credit rating of "Poor"*

This algorithm step could be translated into Pascal using the same nested *if . . . then* constructions employed by the algorithm. However, we can significantly reduce our program's complexity by taking advantage of a particular similarity in each of the innermost steps. Each step makes essentially the same general test: "If *income rating* is *value,* then assign credit rating of *X.*" In fact, there are four identical tests for the condition "income rating is Excellent," four identical tests for "income rating is Good" and so on. If we can figure out a way to utilize this similarity, we can surely reduce the complexity of the program.

How can we take advantage of this similarity? What if we used the **case** statement to first evaluate the scalar variable IncomeRating, then perform a series of if...then...else tests to evaluate the net worth and assign a value to CreditRating? This inversion of our algorithm will certainly reduce the complexity of our program.

Here's a pseudocode outline of this process:

```
case IncomeRating of

Excellent : { determine the net worth category with an
              if...then...else test, and assign a credit rating}

    Good : { determine the net worth category with an
              if...then...else test, and assign a credit rating}

    Fair : { determine the net worth category with an
              if...then...else test, and assign a credit rating}

    Poor : { determine the net worth category with an
              if...then...else test, and assign a credit rating}
end;
```

Just as we established constants to represent the low boundary condition for each income category in the ClassifyIncome procedure, we can also create constants to represent a low, middle, and high net worth category:

Constant Name and Value

```
HighNetWorth = 150000.0;
MidNetWorth  =  50000.0;
LowNetWorth  =  20000.0;
```

Creating a Problem Table will help determine the parameters needed for this procedure.

Problem Table for *EstablishCreditRating* Procedure

INPUT	PROCESS	OUTPUT
IncomeRating NetWorth	Constants: HighNetWorth MidNetWorth LowNetWorth	CreditRating

The values of IncomeRating and NetWorth must be provided to the procedure, and the value of CreditRating will be returned to the main program. Therefore, IncomeRating and NetWorth will be declared as value parameters, and CreditRating will be a variable parameter. Here is the complete procedure:

Procedure *EstablishCredit Rating*

```
procedure EstablishCreditRating (IncomeRating : RATING;
                                 NetWorth : real;
                                 var CreditRating : RATING);
    const
        HighNetWorth = 150000.0;
        MidNetWorth  = 50000.0;
        LowNetWorth  = 20000.0;
    begin { Procedure EstablishCreditRating }
        case IncomeRating of
            Excellent : begin
                        if NetWorth >= MidNetWorth then
                            CreditRating := Excellent
                        else if NetWorth >= LowNetWorth then
                                CreditRating := Good
                        else
                            CreditRating := Fair;
                        end; { IncomeRating of Excellent }
                Good : begin
                        if NetWorth > HighNetWorth then
                            CreditRating := Excellent
                        else if NetWorth >= MidNetWorth then
                                CreditRating := Good
                        else if NetWorth >= LowNetWorth then
                                CreditRating := Fair
```

```
                else
                    CreditRating := Poor;
                end; { IncomeRating of Good }
        Fair : begin
                if NetWorth >= HighNetWorth then
                    CreditRating := Good
                else if NetWorth >= LowNetWorth then
                        CreditRating := Fair
                else
                    CreditRating := Poor;
                end; { IncomeRating of Fair }
        Poor : begin
                if NetWorth >= HighNetWorth then
                    CreditRating := Fair
                else
                    CreditRating := Poor;
                end; { Income Rating of Poor }
        end; { case IncomeRating }
end; { Procedure EstablishCreditRating }
```

Notice that we consolidated some of the algorithm steps when we made this translation into Pascal. Some credit ratings are assigned to two or more net worth categories. For instance, with an "Excellent" IncomeRating, any net worth above the MidNetWorth boundary will be assigned a CreditRating of "Excellent." This also reduces the complexity of our program.

THE *COMPUTEMAXLOANAMOUNT* PROCEDURE

The final procedure in our Loan Officer program computes the maximum loan amount.

As you recall, we've already created the case statement to determine the maximum loan amount:

```
case CreditRating of

    Excellent: MaxLoanAmount := (Income * 0.20) + (NetWorth * 0.25);
         Good: MaxLoanAmount := (Income * 0.20) + (NetWorth * 0.20);
         Fair: MaxLoanAmount := (Income * 0.15) + (NetWorth * 0.20);
         Poor: MaxLoanAmount := (Income * 0.10) + (NetWorth + 0.15);

end; { case }
```

All that is required to complete this procedure is to add a writeln statement that prints the value of MaxLoanAmount, and to determine the parameters for the procedure. Once again, we'll create a Problem Table to help us.

Problem Table for *ComputeMaxLoanAmount* Procedure

INPUT	PROCESS	OUTPUT
Income NetWorth CreditRating		

The Problem Table indicates that Income, NetWorth, and CreditRating will become value parameters. This procedure is not returning any values to the main program—therefore, we don't need any variable parameters. Here's the final procedure:

Procedure *ComputeMaxLoanAmount*

```
procedure ComputeMaxLoanAmount (Income, NetWorth : real;
                                CreditRating : RATING );

  begin  { Procedure ComputeMaxLoanAmount }

    case CreditRating of

    Excellent: MaxLoanAmount := (Income * 0.20) + (NetWorth * 0.25);
         Good: MaxLoanAmount := (Income * 0.20) + (NetWorth * 0.20);
         Fair: MaxLoanAmount := (Income * 0.15) + (NetWorth * 0.20);
         Poor: MaxLoanAmount := (Income * 0.10) + (NetWorth * 0.15);

    end;  { case CreditRating }

    writeln ('Maximum loan amount is $', MaxLoanAmount :8:2);

  end;  { Procedure ComputeMaxLoanAmount }
```

THE LOAN OFFICER PROGRAM

The main program consists of a series of procedure calls.

Once again we've created a program where procedures do all the work. The main program simply makes procedure calls that supply appropriate actual parameters.

Don't forget to include the definition of the new data type RATING in the main program, or the declaration of global variables.

Here's the final program:

The Loan Officer Program

```pascal
program LoanOfficer (input, output);

type
    RATING = (Excellent, Good, Fair, Poor);

var
    Income, NetWorth, MaxLoanAmount : real;
    IncomeRating, CreditRating : RATING;

procedure GetInfo;

    begin
        write ('What is the annual income? ');
        readln (Income);
        write ('What is the net worth? ');
        readln (NetWorth);
    end;

procedure ClassifyIncome (Income : real;
                            var IncomeRating : RATING);

    const
        HighIncome = 100000.0;
        MidIncome  =  35000.0;
        LowIncome  =  15000.0;

    begin { ClassifyIncome }
        if Income >= HighIncome then
            IncomeRating := Excellent
```

```
      else if Income >= MidIncome then
          IncomeRating := Good
      else if Income >= LowIncome then
          IncomeRating := Fair
      else
          IncomeRating := Poor;
   end; { Procedure ClassifyIncome}


procedure EstablishCreditRating (IncomeRating :
                                 RATING; NetWorth : real;
                                 var CreditRating : RATING);

const

    HighNetWorth = 150000.0;
    MidNetWorth  =  50000.0;
    LowNetWorth  =  20000.0;


begin { Procedure EstablishCreditRating }
    case IncomeRating of
Excellent : begin
            if NetWorth >= MidNetWorth then
                CreditRating := Excellent
            else if NetWorth >= LowNetWorth then
                CreditRating := Good
            else
                 CreditRating := Fair;
            end; { IncomeRating of Excellent }

    Good : begin
            if NetWorth > HighNetWorth then
                CreditRating := Excellent
            else if NetWorth >= MidNetWorth then
                CreditRating := Good
            else if NetWorth >= LowNetWorth then
                CreditRating := Fair
            else
                CreditRating := Poor;
            end; { IncomeRating of Good }
    Fair : begin
            if NetWorth >= HighNetWorth then
                CreditRating := Good
            else if NetWorth >= LowNetWorth then
                    CreditRating := Fair
```

```
                        else
                            CreditRating := Poor;
                        end; { IncomeRating of Fair }
                Poor : begin
                        if NetWorth >= HighNetWorth then
                            CreditRating := Fair
                        else
                            CreditRating := Poor;
                        end; { IncomeRating of Poor }
            end; { case IncomeRating }
        end; { Procedure EstablishCreditRating }


procedure ComputeMaxLoanAmount (Income, NetWorth : real;
                                CreditRating : RATING);

    begin { Procedure ComputeMaxLoanAmount }

        case CreditRating of

            Excellent: MaxLoanAmount := (Income * 0.20) + (NetWorth * 0.25);
                 Good: MaxLoanAmount := (Income * 0.20) + (NetWorth * 0.20);
                 Fair: MaxLoanAmount := (Income * 0.15) + (NetWorth * 0.20);
                 Poor: MaxLoanAmount := (Income * 0.10) + (NetWorth * 0.15);
        end; { case CreditRating }
        writeln ('Maximum loan amount is $', MaxLoanAmount :8:2);
    end; { Procedure ComputeMaxLoanAmount }

begin { LoanOfficer main program }
GetInfo;
ClassifyIncome (Income, IncomeRating);
EstablishCreditRating (IncomeRating, NetWorth, CreditRating);
ComputeMaxLoanAmount (Income, NetWorth, CreditRating );
end. { LoanOfficer main program }
```

PROGRAMMING EXERCISES

Programming Exercise 1:

Coronado's board of directors has decided to deny loans to any applicants whose annual income is less than $5,000, regardless of their net worth. Modify the Loan Officer program accordingly.

Programming Exercise 2:

Later, the board of directors has decided that a low income is acceptable, but a net worth less than $10,000 disqualifies an applicant from a loan, unless the income rating is Excellent. Modify the program accordingly. The credit rating table now looks like this:

	Income Rating			
	Excellent	*Good*	*Fair*	*Poor*
> 150,000	Excellent	Excellent	Good	Fair
≥ 50,000	Excellent	Good	Fair	Poor
≥ 20,000	Good	Fair	Fair	Poor
≥ 10,000	Fair	Poor	Poor	Poor
< 10,000	Poor	Terrible	Terrible	Terrible

ANSWERS TO THE TEST YOUR UNDERSTANDING EXERCISES

1. How close was your refinement to ours?
2. Initial algorithm to describe mother:

If human is female then
   If female is 5'4" tall then
      If haircolor is red then
         If eyes are green then
            If birthmark appears on right ankle then
               If name is Merlene then...

As you can see, the levels of refinement necessary here to pinpoint a particular mother are quite extensive. Write your algorithm in as much detail as possible. To test the effectiveness of your algorithm, give it to a stranger to see if he or she can locate your mom in a crowd.

3. A nested if...then...else statement is the action specified by the else clause of a previous if...then...else statement.
4. The case expression is a value which is matched to a case constant to select appropriate action.

5. The case statement evaluates a scalar expression (usually a variable) and chooses an action by comparing the value to a list of constants and matching the value of the expression to a constant.

6. A real value cannot be used as case expression because the case constant list would have to be nearly infinite to accommodate all possible values a real expression could assume.

7. The word end in the case statement is unusual because it is used without a matching begin.

8. True. User-defined data types have scalar values.

9. The two steps are:
   1. Define a data type by creating a type identifier and listing the values that can be assigned to variables of that type.
   2. Declare variables of that type.

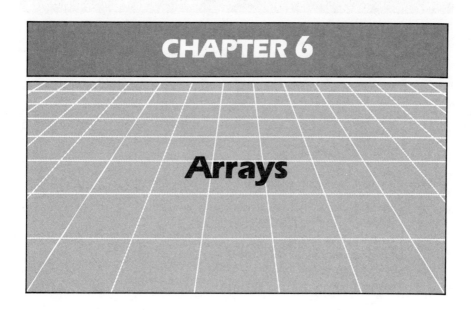

CHAPTER 6

Arrays

CHAPTER OBJECTIVE

To introduce one of Pascal's most commonly used *structures* for representing data—the *array*.

CHAPTER OVERVIEW

Your consulting talents have become notorious. Now, even large national businesses are seeking your services. Most recently Trans-Galactic Communications, an overnight delivery firm, has made you a rather lucrative proposal. Trans-Galactic plans to open new offices in various cities around the country, where they would like to automate the process of determining delivery charges for packages. This would replace the current procedure whereby a clerk looks up rates from a rate table.

New Pascal: Up to this point, we have been primarily concerned with the forms of *action* in Pascal. This chapter introduces Pascal's structures for representing *data,* focusing on the *array.* The array structure, used frequently in Pascal programs, is ideally suited for representing a table of related values, such as the rate table mentioned above.

We will also discuss another loop control structure, the f or loop, often used in conjunction with arrays.

This chapter has six sections:

- **The Delivery Charge Problem**
- **Introduction to Data Structures**
- **Creating an Array**
- **Using an Array**
- **Error Trapping**
- **The Delivery Charge Program**

Section 1. The Delivery Charge Problem

INTRODUCTION

As usual, the approach to the Delivery Charge Problem begins with an analysis of the problem. You'll meet with Mr. McClure, Trans-Galactic's Automated Systems Specialist, to learn as much as possible about their current system. Then you must form an algorithm and translate it into Pascal.

This section has two parts:

- Analyzing the Problem
- The Delivery Charge Algorithm

ANALYZING THE PROBLEM

To analyze the Delivery Charge problem, determine the steps necessary to create and use a delivery charge table.

As you sit in Trans-Galactic's plush headquarters, Mr. McClure explains the process they want you to automate. From any given city, 10 delivery zones represent different areas of the country. When a new office is established, its staff first creates the rate table listing the delivery charge per pound for each of the 10 zones.

As an example, he shows you the rate table from the Cucamonga office.

Zone	1	2	3	4	5	6	7	8	9	10
Rate per pound	$1.50	2.00	2.50	3.00	3.50	4.00	4.50	5.00	5.50	6.00

Figure 6–1   Rate Table for Cucamonga Office

When a package comes in for shipment, the charge clerk first weighs it, then determines the destination delivery zone.

The clerk computes the weight charge by multiplying the rate per pound for that zone times the package weight. Then the clerk checks the weight charge against a fixed minimum charge. If the weight charge is less than the minimum, the actual delivery charge assessed is the minimum charge. Otherwise the weight charge is used as the delivery charge.

Last of all, the clerk prepares a shipping label, and the package is shipped.

As you listen to this explanation, several different ways of solving this problem become apparent—one similar to the approach used to determine a credit rating in Chapter 5. A series of nested if...then...else statements could be used to determine an appropriate per-pound rate, then the necessary delivery charge calculation could be made.

However, a preferable approach would be to represent the entire rate table as a *data structure,* then have the program select, or "look up," the appropriate rate from the table. We'll create our initial algorithm along these lines, then demonstrate how to represent the rate table as an *array.*

THE DELIVERY CHARGE ALGORITHM

The Delivery Charge algorithm describes both the *action* necessary to solve the problem, and a *data structure* used to represent delivery rates.

Summarizing the steps described by Mr. McClure, we'll create an initial algorithm for this problem:

Initial Delivery Charge Algorithm

1. *Create rate table*
2. *Collect necessary information*

3. *Compute delivery charge*
4. *Print shipping label*

To refine Step #1 of the algorithm, we simply describe the steps involved in creating a rate table. It doesn't matter that we haven't yet discussed how this rate table will be implemented as a Pascal data structure. As always, our algorithm should describe solution steps independently of the computer.

First, we must create the structure of the table itself. Then we'll put values into the table. Our first refinement of this algorithm step should describe what this table looks like—its physical dimensions. Since there are 10 destination zones from each city, the table will consist of 10 boxes that can each hold a single value. Here is the refinement of Step #1:

Level One Refinement of Step #1

1. *Create rate table*
    1.1 *Draw table with 10 boxes numbered from 1 through and including 10*
    1.2 *Fill in the table with the rates specified by Trans-Galactic for each zone*

Now that we know what the table will look like, all we need to do is specify the per-pound rates for each zone. Refering to Figure 6–1, you see the rate for Zone #1 is $1.50 per pound. The rate for each successive zone is $0.50 greater than the previous zone. Using this information, we can complete the refinement of Step #1:

Level Two Refinement of Step #1

1. *Create rate table*
    1.1 *Draw table with 10 boxes numbered from 1 through and including 10*
    1.2 *Fill in the table with the rates specified by Trans-Galactic for each zone*
        1.2.1 *Put $1.50 in the box for zone 1*
        1.2.2 *Fill in the rest of the table by adding $0.50 to the previous rate for each successive zone*

Step #1 is now completely refined.

To refine Step #2, we must specify the input information necessary to calculate the delivery charge: the weight of the package and the destination delivery zone.

Refinement of Step #2

2.   *Collect necessary information*
     2.1   *Request weight of package*
     2.2   *Request destination delivery zone*

To refine Step #3, we must specify how the delivery charge is calculated. First, a weight charge is determined by looking up the charge per pound for the destination delivery zone and multiplying that charge by the package weight. The weight charge is then compared to a pre-determined minimum charge of $5.00. If the weight charge is less, the $5.00 minimum charge is used. Otherwise, the calculated weight charge is used.

Refinement of Step #3

3.   *Compute delivery charge*
     3.1   *Calculate weight charge by looking up per-pound rate for the destination delivery zone, then multiply it by the weight of the package*
     3.2   *If weight charge is less than minimum charge then delivery charge equals minimum charge otherwise, delivery charge equals weight charge*

The refinement of Step #4 simply lists the information to be printed on the shipping label:

Refinement of Step #4

4.   *Print shipping label*
     4.1   *Print destination zone number*
     4.2   *Print per-pound rate for destination zone*
     4.3   *Print package weight*
     4.4   *Print delivery charge*

Our Delivery Charge algorithm is completely refined. Translating this algorithm into Pascal should not be difficult. The next three sections focus on creating the *data structure* to represent the rate table, and how to use it.

TEST YOUR UNDERSTANDING

1.   The Delivery Charge problem is similar in many ways to the Loan Officer problem in Chapter 5. How do the two *algorithms* differ?

Section 2. Introduction to Data Structures

INTRODUCTION

So far, our programming tasks have not required sophisticated methods for representing data. As a result, we have only used the *simple* variable to store information. In Chapter 2 we said that a simple variable has a single memory location, and is named by an *identifier.* A simple variable can represent only one single value of a specific data type.

The simple variable is quite adequate for representing many kinds of data items. Sometimes, however, it is desirable to associate more than one value with a single identifier. Pascal provides several *data structures* that allow us to do this. Variables created with data structures are appropriately known as *structured* variables.

Pascal has four data structures: the *array,* the *record,* the *set,* and the *file.* Each data structure uses a unique method of organizing data—each represents data in a different way, and each is useful for a specific purpose.

The study of data structures could take up an entire book. We will focus on an introduction to the *array* structure, and use it to create a computerized rate table for the Delivery Charge problem.

This section has two parts:

- Introduction to Data Structures
- The Array

INTRODUCTION TO DATA STRUCTURES

"Algorithms + Data Structures = Programs."—Title of book by Niklaus Wirth, the "father" of Pascal.

We have already spent much time learning how to develop algorithms. Now we'll devote our energy to discussing the other part of Dr. Wirth's equation for successful programs.

One of Pascal's most distinctive features provides the ability to structure data based on algorithm requirements, rather than programming language requirements. Data structures allow the programmer to represent data in a meaningful and logical fashion. As an example, we'll create a data structure for the Delivery Charge program that conceptually will be nearly identical to a printed rate table.

Why use data structures? If all data is structured logically, our program has automatically become organized. Then we can spend our time concentrating on the program's action. Data structures are also absolutely necessary for certain programs requiring long-term data storage.

Data structures tend to be abstract—only truly existing in the computer's innermost depths. We're going to apply for a poetic license now, and take the scenic route in this introduction. What follows is a series of fanciful comparisons. Our intention is to help you develop techniques for *visualizing* data structures. If you can get an idea of what a data structure "looks like" in your mind's eye, then you'll be able to use them in programs far more effectively.

We'll begin with a visit to the small, rather obscure village of Walker, Switzerland, where the town council recently adopted a somewhat unusual approach to community government. In particular, all the town's zoning regulations will be based on the Pascal programming language.

The council has made some specific declarations and definitions, especially concerning private residences. Every room in a house will now have the same status as a simple variable. Therefore, a room can contain at most only one person (value) at any time. Any number of people may use the room, but never more than one person at a time.

Of course, each room must have a unique identifier, such as `Bedroom`, `Kitchen`, `Bathroom`, and so on. If Tess is in the bedroom, we say "`Bedroom` contains Tess," or "the contents of `Bedroom` is Tess," or "Tess is assigned to `Bedroom`", or even "the value of `Bedroom` is Tess." Symbolically, we write "`Bedroom := Tess`."

Assume that Tess has been assigned to the bedroom (`Bedroom := Tess`). Later, perhaps, Lauralee is assigned to the bedroom. Then `Bedroom := Lauralee`. However, when Lauralee goes into the bedroom, Tess gets pushed out.

Now imagine a house with many rooms. According to the town's new, rather restrictive zoning regulations, each room can at most hold one person at any given time.

If we wanted to visualize where all the people were staying in the house, we could draw a floor plan.

Floorplan of the Pascal House

Bedroom	Kitchen	Bedroom	Sauna	Dining Room	Den
Lauralee	Jack	Mary	Dick	Beverly	Rod

It's now apparent from our floorplan that House, as a collection of rooms, is a *structure*. House can therefore be considered as a *structured variable;* it can hold six people (values), one in each room, yet is still named by a single identifier, House. Each room (memory location) in House still has an independent existence. Now, however, we must use a two-part identifier to make assignments to House: the identifier House *together with* the name of the room each person will inhabit. Therefore, if we assigned Lauralee to the bedroom we would write: House[Bedroom] := Lauralee.

We run into a problem very quickly, however. As you see from the floorplan, both Mary and Lauralee are assigned to a bedroom—but according to the zoning regulations, all rooms (variables) must have a unique identifier. Therefore, two rooms cannot have the same identifier, Bedroom.

We solve this problem by *numbering* each room. Then we could legitimately assign Lauralee to Room 1 and Mary to Room 3 with no conflict— then House[Room1] := Lauralee, and House[Room3] := Mary.

Now for the tie-in with reality that you've so patiently waited for. The *array* structure resembles House, in that it is a collection of memory locations, each of which can contain at most one value at a time. The values stored in the cells are called *elements* of the array. The structure of the array organizes the elements of the array, just as knowing who's in each room organizes the people in our house.

THE ARRAY

An array is a structure having a single identifier to represent one or more values of a single data type.

The word "array" originates in mathematics. The array is a matrix, or a table of related values, occurring in a specific order. Arrays can be one-dimensional—that is, a single "row" of values—or they can be multi-dimensional, with rows and columns of values.

The House floor plan is a good representation of a one-dimensional array. This kind of array "looks" like a row of pigeon holes, or of mailboxes.

In Pascal, an array has a more specific definition: an array is a group of memory locations all associated with a single identifier. Unlike a simple variable, which has a single identifier and one memory location, an array uses one identifier to name a number of memory locations adjacent to one another, as shown in the illustration at the top of the next page:

Identifier   **Memory Location**

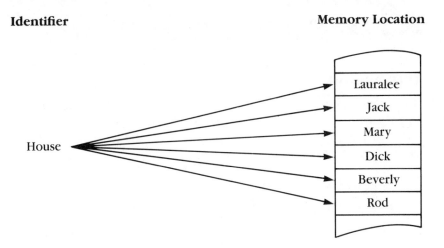

Memory locations store individual data items, or values, called the array *elements.* All array elements must be of the same *data type.* In the House example, each element's value was a person, so we could consider the data type of the elements to be type PEOPLE.

As another example, think of a baseball team as an array of players. To describe the batting order for the baseball team, we refer to each player by his position in the lineup. Batter 1 is first, followed by Batter 2, Batter 3, and so on. Each player is unique, but when the team is represented as a batting order, each player is referred to by the same identifier, namely "Batter." Notice that the identifier "Batter" is used in conjunction with the player's *position,* or location, in the batting lineup. This is a common way to refer to an array element: by its position.

Next, we discuss how to create an array, and how to use the individual elements of the array.

TEST YOUR UNDERSTANDING

2. Why is House considered a structured variable?
3. Why is it necessary to refer to a room as "House[room]"?
4. True or False: An array is a group of adjacent memory locations associated with a single identifier.
5. What are array elements?
6. How are array elements referenced?

Section 3. Creating an Array

INTRODUCTION

This section explains in detail how to create an array. First, we talk about *array variables* —variables structured as an array. Then we talk about *array subscripts,* used with an array identifier to name the location of individual array elements.

This section has two parts:

- Array Variables
- Array Subscripts

ARRAY VARIABLES

Array variables are structured by the programmer to hold a specific number of elements.

As we mentioned in Chapter 4, simple variables are *structured* to represent exactly one value of a specific data type. Array variables, on the other hand, are structured to hold a number of values of a specific data type.

Three parts make up an array variable declaration.

The Parts of An Array Variable Declaration

1. As with all variables, you must decide on an *identifier* for the array variable.
2. You must decide how many *elements*, or values, the array variable will store.
3. You must determine the *data type* of the array *elements.*

Here's an outline of an array variable declaration, with each of the three parts indicated:

```
var
   Identifier : array {number of elements} of {data type of elements};
```

Let's recall the floorplan from our Pascal House, then formally declare House as an array variable.

Floorplan of the Pascal House

Room 1	Room 2	Room 3	Room 4	Room 5	Room 6
Lauralee	Jack	Mary	Dick	Beverly	Rod

Since the *elements* in the Pascal House are people, with the values "Lauralee," "Mary," "Dick," and so on, we must first define our own data type containing those values:

```
type
    PEOPLE = (Lauralee, Jack, Mary, Dick, Beverly, Rod);
```

Note that the elements of House are *not* the rooms—the rooms are locations that store elements. Now, to declare House as an array variable, let's list the three parts that will make a complete declaration:

1. *Array variable identifier:* House
2. *Number of elements:* 6
3. *Data type of elements:* PEOPLE

Using this information, we can make a complete declaration of the array variable House:

```
var
    House : array [ 1..6 ] of PEOPLE;
```

The number of elements stored by the array variable is called the array *dimension.* As you see, the array dimension for House is enclosed between square brackets immediately after the reserved word array. In this example, the array dimension uses a special symbol we haven't encountered yet. Two dots (..) is Pascal's symbol meaning "through and including." Therefore, the array dimension [1..6] sets aside 6 unique memory locations, "1 through and including 6." Soon we'll see how these integer values "1 through and including 6" can be used to name individual elements of the array.

Using the "through and including" symbol (..) specifies that our array dimension is a *subrange* of type integer. That is, the values "1 through and including 6" are only part of the complete range of integers, typically ±32,767 on most computers. An array dimension must be of a scalar type, usually a subrange of type integer, as we have shown above, or of type char or `boolean`. However, dimensioning an array with anything other than a subrange of type integer is beyond the scope of this text.

An array must be dimensioned to ensure each element is assigned a specific memory location. A dimension that's too small may cause a program error because too few memory spaces will be reserved. A dimension that's too large, on the other hand, allocates too many memory locations, making the program inefficient.

ARRAY SUBSCRIPTS

Subscripts serve as an *index* for the elements in an array variable.

"Subscript" is another term borrowed from mathematics. Consider a problem where one wants to refer to the sides of a square. Any one side can be referred to with the variable "S," with an integer indicating which side we're talking about. For example, the third side would be referred to as S_3.

Similarly, the elements of an array variable can be referred to by their location in the array. However, since we cannot indicate a true subscript on a computer keyboard, we use square brackets around the subscript value instead. Therefore, the third element of the array variable House would be referred to as House[3]. Array subscripts, or *subscripted variables,* allow us to "look-up" the value of an element stored in a particular memory location of the array variable.

Don't confuse the *value* of an element with its *subscript.* As you recall, the values of each element of the array variable House must be of type PEOPLE. Therefore, House[3] does not equal "3"; House[3] references (subscripts) the third element of House, and, according to our floorplan, House[3] contains the value "Mary".

Refer again to the Pascal House floorplan. Let's list the value of each element in the array variable House.

Array Element	Contents
House[1]	Lauralee
House[2]	Jack
House[3]	Mary
House[4]	Dick
House[5]	Beverly
House[6]	Rod

To reference an element, we must use both the array variable identifier *and* an integer subscript indicating the position of the element we are referencing. Notice that subscript values don't include the word *"room,"* even though that's what they represent. Instead, each subscript is an integer value representing a room's *position* in the variable House. When we dimensioned the array, we specified there would be six elements associated with the identifier House. Each element is referred to by its position in the array, from 1 through and including 6.

Let's start translating the Delivery Charge algorithm into Pascal, beginning with Step #1. We know we want to use an array (representing the rate table) which holds the per-pound delivery charge for each of 10 destination zones.

We'll create the array representing Trans-Galactic's delivery charge rate table following the three steps outlined previously. First: we must choose an identifier for the array variable. We will use the identifier RateTable.

Second: we must dimension the array. We know that 10 elements are necessary—one element to store the per-pound rate for each delivery zone— therefore, our dimension will consist of 10 memory locations.

Third: we must determine the data type of the elements. Each element represents a per-pound rate for that particular delivery zone. Since these rates are dollar amounts, the data type of the elements will be type real. Here's a list summarizing the information necessary to declare an array variable representing the rate table:

1. *Array variable identifier:* RateTable
2. *Number of elements:* 10
3. *Data type of elements:* real

Translating this information into a Pascal array variable declaration is a straightforward task:

```
var
    RateTable : array [1..10] of real;
```

The variable RateTable is now structured to contain 10 elements, each capable of representing a real value. Each element is referred to by its position in the array, using the identifier RateTable and the integer subscript indicating the element's position in the array. The sixth element of RateTable, which will store the per-pound cost for sending a package to destination zone #6, is referred to as RateTable[6].

TEST YOUR UNDERSTANDING

7. What are the three parts of an array declaration?

8. What does the special symbol made up of two dots (..) stand for?

9. Consider the following statement:

```
House[7] := Clare;
```

   A.   What is the value of the array element?
   B.   What is the array identifier?
   C.   What is the value of the array subscript?
   D.   What is the data type of the subscript?
   E.   What is the data type of the array element?

Section 4. Using an Array

INTRODUCTION

Now that we've declared an array variable, we must initialize the array elements, and learn how to use an element's value for various types of action.

In this section, we'll discuss two methods of initializing array elements. The first initializes each array element with a series of assignment statements. The second sets up a loop, to visit and initialize each array element in turn.

We also discuss using array elements, and creating an array type so that array variables can be used as parameters for procedures.

This section has five parts:

- Initializing Array Variables
- The for Loop
- Initializing an Array with the for Loop
- Manipulating Array Elements
- Creating an Array type

INITIALIZING ARRAY VARIABLES

Array variables, like simple variables, must be initialized before they can be used in a program.

It's important to realize that *every* element of an array variable must be initialized before the variable can be used by the program. Numerous methods exist for initializing the elements of an array variable. One method initializes each element with an assignment statement.

Recall the declaration of the array variable RateTable:

```
var
    RateTable : array [1..10] of real;
```

We structured RateTable so that it contains 10 real elements. Each element is referred to by the variable identifier RateTable together with an integer subscript between 1 and 10 indicating the position of the element in the array. Let's refer to the original Trans-Galactic rate table to see which rates are assigned to each zone:

Trans-Galactic Rate Table

Zone	1	2	3	4	5	6	7	8	9	10
Rate per #	1.50	2.00	2.50	3.00	3.50	4.00	4.50	5.00	5.50	6.00

Using this rate table, we can make the following assignments to the 10 elements of the array variable RateTable:

```
RateTable[1]   := 1.50;
RateTable[2]   := 2.00;
RateTable[3]   := 2.50;
RateTable[4]   := 3.00;
RateTable[5]   := 3.50;
RateTable[6]   := 4.00;
RateTable[7]   := 4.50;
RateTable[8]   := 5.00;
RateTable[9]   := 5.50;
RateTable[10]  := 6.00;
```

For a small array, initialization of each element with a separate assignment statement is an acceptable, but somewhat awkward technique. However, what if we had 100, or 1000 delivery zones, instead of just 10? In that case, our program would have a very lengthy list of assignment statements.

Careful examination of our rate table shows that the value of each array element is $0.50 greater than the previous element. To simplify the initialization process for the entire array, we can use a loop structure to visit and initialize each array element with an appropriate value.

THE *FOR* LOOP

The *for* loop performs a group of actions a specific number of times.

Here's an outline of the for loop:

```
for CounterVariable := BeginningValue to EndingValue do
    begin

        { loop body ... }

    end;
```

Let's examine this outline in detail. The for loop uses the value of a *counter variable* to determine whether the loop body should be executed. As long as *CounterVariable* does not exceed *EndingValue*, the loop body is executed.

Counter Variable is a scalar variable initialized by the for loop to *BeginningValue*. Then the loop body is executed. At the bottom of the loop, *CounterVariable* is *automatically* incremented, in this case by 1. In effect, an invisible "*CounterVariable* := *CounterVariable* + 1" statement is always the final statement of a for loop body controlled by an integer counter variable.

After the loop body has been executed and *CounterVariable* has been incremented, the for loop cycles back to the top and tests to see if *CounterVariable* is greater than *EndingValue*. If not, the loop body is executed again. However, once the value of *CounterVariable* is *greater than EndingValue*, the loop body is skipped, and control passes to the next statement after the loop body.

In the following example, the loop body will be executed 10 times:

Example:

```
for CounterVariable := 1 to 10 do
    begin

    { Loop body .... }

    end;
```

The for loop is very useful for *definite iteration*—that is, repeating action a specific number of times. Other uses of the for loop include a variation allowing the loop to start with a *BeginningValue greater than* the *EndingValue*, and *decrement Counter Variable* instead of incrementing it. However, our use of the for loop will be limited to initializing each element of the array variable RateTable.

INITIALIZING AN ARRAY WITH A *FOR* LOOP

In certain cases, a *for* loop can be used to initialize each element of an array variable.

Let's "fill in the blanks" of the for loop outline, and use it to initialize each element of the array variable RateTable. First, we need a *counter variable*. Since we are effectively initializing 10 "delivery zones" in RateTable, we'll declare a variable named ZoneNumber to serve as the counter variable. The array dimension specified 10 elements or "zones" for RateTable, "1 through and including 10"; therefore, ZoneNumber must be declared as type integer, to match the subscript type of each element. Ten elements must be initialized; therefore *BeginningValue* will be 1 and *EndingValue* will be 10.

Here's the control structure we've developed so far:

```
for ZoneNumber := 1 to 10 do

    begin

        { loop body .... }

    end;
```

Now we must focus on the loop body. The first time through the loop, we want to initialize RateTable[1] to $1.50. Each element thereafter will be assigned a value $0.50 greater than the previous value.

If we declare a variable that will represent the actual per-pound rate we want to assign to each element, we can initialize it to $1.50 *before* entering the loop, then increase its value by $0.50 after it has been used to assign a value to an element. Thus, we will declare a variable named ChargePerPound, of type real (since ChargePerPound will be representing dollar amounts), for this purpose.

Let's assemble the entire for loop control structure we just discussed.

For Loop to Initialize *RateTable*

```
var
    ZoneNumber : integer;                { Counter variable }
    ChargePerPound : real; { Stores the current per-pound
                                          delivery charge }

begin
    ChargePerPound := 1.50 { Start at $1.50 }
    for ZoneNumber := 1 to 10 do
      begin
          RateTable[ZoneNumber] := ChargePerPound;
                  { Assign ChargePerPound to current element }
      ChargePerPound := ChargePerPound + 0.50;
                               { Increment ChargePerPound }
              { "invisible" ZoneNumber := ZoneNumber +1; }

      end;   { for loop }

  end;
```

Notice that we use the *value* of ZoneNumber as the array subscript each time an assignment is made to an element of RateTable. In this way the value of ZoneNumber can serve a dual function, both by acting as the counter variable and representing the subscript value of each array element in turn. This is possible because the for loop increases the value of ZoneNumber by 1 each time the loop body is executed.

We are able to use a for loop to initialize each element of the array variable RateTable because each element is exactly $0.50 greater in value than its predecessor. We would not be able to use the for loop to initialize this array if the cost per pound for each zone were not evenly distributed.

MANIPULATING ARRAY ELEMENTS

The value of individual array elements can be used or modified.

We have already seen how to make an assignment directly to an array variable element with the assignment statement. The following statements each make assignments to specific elements of the array variable RateTable:

```
RateTable[4] := 15.95;        { Assign '15.95' to element 4 }

RateTable[2..6]:= 3.00;   { Assign '3.00' to elements 2
                                through and including 6 }

RateTable[Zonenumber] := 6.35; { Assign '6.35' to the ele-
                                ment whose subscript has
                                has the same value as
                                ZoneNumber }
```

In addition to assigning values to array elements, we can also print the value of an array element. For example, if we wanted to print the per-pound rate for a particular zone (that is, the value of an array element), we would use a `writeln` statement:

Statements	Output
`writeln (House[6]);`	Rod
`writeln (RateTable[3]);`	2.500000000000E+1

We can also change the value of array elements. We don't need to know the value of an element to change it—we need only know its position, or subscript value. For example, we can add $0.23 to the per-pound rate for a zone with the following statements:

```
RateTable[5] := RateTable[5] + 0.23;

RateTable[ZoneNumber] := RateTable[ZoneNumber] + 0.23;
```

Remember: it's extremely important that you not confuse the *value* of an element with its *subscript.* In each example above we're adding 0.23 to the value of the element referenced by a particular subscript value. We are not changing the subscript itself. In other words, we are changing the *value* found at a certain memory location, not the *position* of the memory location.

We have now seen how to manipulate array variables and their elements. We have built a `for` loop to initialize each element of the array variable `RateTable`. In effect, we have nearly completed the translation of algorithm Step #1 into Pascal. All that remains is to put the `for` loop into a procedure, and decide on parameters for the procedure.

CREATING AN ARRAY TYPE

An array can be defined once as a *type,* then variables can be declared of that type.

If we intend to use a procedure to initialize each array variable element, we must pass that variable to the procedure via a parameter. What would happen if we tried to pass `RateTable` as a parameter now? Consider the following procedure heading:

```
procedure InitializeRateTable (var RateTable : array [1..10]
                                          of real);
                              {Invalid parameter list }

    begin

      { Statements.... }

    end;
```

Can you determine the parameter's type from this declaration? Neither can Pascal. This is not an acceptable format in a parameter list. How do you pass an array variable as a parameter?

First, create a data type for the array. Then, declare variables of that type (note they will be array variables), and use them as parameters for the procedure.

Although this two-step process may seem like a lot of work, once an array type has been defined, variable declarations are a snap—a significant advantage in programs using dozens or hundreds of arrays.

The array-type definition looks very similar to an array variable declaration, but with two differences. First, an array type definition begins with the reserved word `type`, followed by the type identifier. Second, an equal sign follows the identifier, rather than the colon used in variable declarations.

We will use the array-type identifier RATEARY, so we can still use the identifier `RateTable` we originally chose for our array variable. (We abbreviate "ARY" to avoid confusion with the reserved word `array`).

Here's the complete array-type definition of RATEARY:

```
type

    RATEARY = array [1..10] of real;
```

Now that we have a array type, the declaration of `RateTable` as an array variable of that type is very easy indeed:

var

        RateTable : RATEARY;

Now a procedure heading and parameter list can be completed:

procedure InitializeRateTable (**var** RateTable : RATEARY);

In addition to being able to pass `RateTable` as a parameter to a procedure, we can easily create a number of similar arrays in a program. For example, if we want to store 10 or a hundred different rate tables with a similar array structure, say the rate tables for different cities, all we need do is create identifiers for each array variable, and declare them to be of type RATEARY:

var

        KenoshaRates, MinneapolisRates, SanDiegoRates : RATEARY;

This variable declaration saves us a lot of repetitious typing. All three variables have been structured similarly—as arrays with ten elements of type real.

TEST YOUR UNDERSTANDING

10. What's the fundamental difference between a `while. . .do` loop and a `for` loop?

11. True or False: It is necessary to include a statement in a `for` loop body to increment the counter variable.

12. Give two reasons for creating an array type in a program.

Section 5. Error Trapping

INTRODUCTION

Every Pascal programmer experiences a particular revelation at some point in their career. This revelation is usually prompted by an increased awareness of that mythical beast, the *program user.* The revelation isn't a happy or pretty one—but every programmer usually finds the inner resources to cope with its implications, and carry on with the business of writing effective programs.

What is this revelation? Simply this (paraphrased from Murphy): That a program user will discover any and every possible way to screw up your program. You must develop the foresight to anticipate, or *trap* errors, preventing even the most determined efforts to make your program fail.

This section has two parts:

- What is Error Trapping?
- The `repeat...until` Statement

WHAT IS ERROR TRAPPING?

Some statements and procedures in a program should be devoted to recognizing and coping with errors.

There are many kinds of errors, so there are many kinds of error trapping. Explicit prompts for input can help program users avoid some errors. However, if the user ignores a prompt and inputs an incorrect value, your program should be *robust* enough to recognize that the data is incorrect, ignore it, and persist with a request for a correct value.

Other types of error trapping focus on internal processes. For example, it is occasionally desirable to test the result of a calculation for validity before continuing action.

In the Delivery Charge program, the user must enter a number representing a valid destination zone for the program to function correctly. Trying to enter a destination zone of 11 or −7 or 32767 will cause a program error, because there are only 10 destination zones. We must make sure that the user inputs a destination zone between 1 and 10. We can use the `repeat...until` statement to repeat a prompt for input until the user enters a valid destination zone.

THE *REPEAT . . . UNTIL* STATEMENT

The *repeat . . . until* **statement repeats action until a *condition*** *is true.*

Here is an outline of the `repeat...until` statement:

```
repeat

    { Statements .... }

until condition is true;
```

Notice the repeat. . . until statement is a *loop control structure* similar to the while. . . do loop. There is a significant difference between them: The while. . . do structure tests a condition *before* the loop body is executed. If the condition is true, the loop body may never be executed. On the other hand, the loop body controlled by the repeat. . . until structure is *always* executed at least once, and then the condition is evaluated. The while. . . do statement is preferable to control most conditional action; however, for our current needs we must get an input value before we can see if it is valid or not, so the repeat. . . until structure is called for.

Here is a repeat. . . until structure that checks for a valid destination zone:

```
repeat

    write ('What is the destination zone? ');
    readln (DestinationZone);
until DestinationZone <= 10;
```

Although this program segment will persist in requesting a destination zone until a valid entry is made, it doesn't give the user a clue as to *why* it's repeating a prompt when incorrect values are entered. We should also print an error message if the prompt is to be repeated. An if. . . then statement can determine whether DestinationZone is too large, and print a message if it is:

```
if DestinationZone > 10 then
    write ('Sorry, that is an invalid zone.');
```

Bringing this all together:

```
repeat
    write ('What is the destination zone? ');
    readln (DestinationZone);
    if DestinationZone > 10 then
        write ('Sorry, that is an invalid zone.');
until DestinationZone <= 10;
```

This is an effective error trap, because it won't allow a user to continue with the program until they input a valid positive integer. Note, however, that we have not trapped negative values, nor have we made any provisions for handling input information other than type `integer`. An error will certainly occur if a user tries to input "6" as "six", because "six" is not a value of type `integer`.

As you progress with programming, error trapping will take on a more significant role in your programs. Some advanced business application programs consist almost entirely of error trapping, with very little actual calculation.

TEST YOUR UNDERSTANDING

13. Why is error trapping important?

14. True or False: The action specified by a `repeat...until` structure will always be executed at least once.

15. What is the fundamental difference between the `while...do` and the `repeat...until` loop control structures?

Section 6. The Delivery Charge Program

INTRODUCTION

We are ready now to translate the entire Delivery Charge algorithm into Pascal. Let's create some names for our procedures:

Algorithm Step	Procedure Identifier
1. Create rate table	`CreateRateTable`
2. Collect necessary information	`CollectInfo`
3. Compute delivery charge	`CalculateCharge`
4. Print shipping label	`PrintShippingLabel`

This section has five parts:

- The `CreateRateTable` Procedure
- The `CollectInfo` Procedure
- The `CalculateCharge` Procedure
- The `PrintShippingLabel` Procedure
- The Delivery Charge Program

THE *CREATERATETABLE* PROCEDURE

The *CreateRateTable* **procedure will initialize each element of the array variable** *RateTable.*

We already created the body of this procedure when we developed the for loop that visits and initializes each array element. Also, since we created an array type RATEARY, we can now use the array variable RateTable as a parameter for the procedure.

The idea that you can pass an entire array as a parameter to a procedure may seem difficult to accept at first, especially if the array is large. No difference really exists between using a simple variable or an array variable as a parameter for a procedure.

Array variables can be passed as either value parameters, or as variable parameters, depending on whether you want to change the value of any elements. As with simple variables, you must indicate whether a parameter is a value parameter or variable parameter in the procedure heading parameter list.

We must pass the array variable RateTable as a *variable* parameter of type RATEARY; once the array is initialized by the procedure, we want the rest of the program to have access to it.

Here is the final CreateRateTable procedure:

Procedure *CreateRateTable*

```
procedure CreateRateTable (var RateTable : RATEARY );
   var
     ZoneNumber : integer;
     ChargePerPound : real;
   begin
     ChargePerPound := 1.50;
     for ZoneNumber := 1 to 10 do
        begin
           RateTable[ZoneNumber] := ChargePerPound;
           ChargePerPound := ChargePerPound + 0.50;
        end; { loop body }
     end; { procedure CreateRateTable}
```

THE *COLLECTINFO* PROCEDURE

The *Collectinfo* procedure is similar to our other *Collectinfo* procedures, but includes some error trapping features.

Algorithm Step #2

Our program requires two input items: The zone number to which a package will be delivered, and the package's shipping weight. Both data items will be declared as global variables in the main program, because they will be used by other procedures in the program. We will also add the repeat...until construct to the procedure to assure that a destination zone entered by the user is in a correct range of values.

Procedure *CollectInfo*

```
procedure CollectInfo;
   begin
      repeat then
         write ('What is the destination zone? ');
         readln ( DestinationZone );
         if DestinationZone > 10
         writeln ('Sorry. That is an invalid zone. ');
      until DestinationZone <= 10;
      write ('What is the weight of the package in pounds? ');
      readln (ShippingWeight);
   end;
```

THE *CALCULATECHARGE* PROCEDURE

This procedure calculates the actual delivery charge.

Let's look at algorithm Step #3 again:

Algorithm Step #3

3. *Compute delivery charge*
    *3.1 Calculate weight charge by looking up per-pound rate
          for the destination delivery zone, then multiply it by
          the weight of the package*

3.2   *If weight charge is less than minimum charge then delivery charge equals minimum charge otherwise, delivery charge equals weight charge*

Step #3.1 says that we must first look up the per-pound rate for the destination delivery zone. This is very easy —we simply use the value of DestinationZone as the subscript for the array variable RateTable. Then we can multiply this value by the value of ShippingWeight.

Step #3.2 can be translated almost without change into Pascal, substituting symbols for words.

A Problem Table for the CalculateCharge procedure will help us determine which variables must be used as parameters:

Problem Table for Procedure *CalculateCharge*

INPUT	PROCESS	OUTPUT
DestinationZone ShippingWeight RateTable	Constant: MinimumCharge	DeliveryCharge

Three value parameters are necessary: we'll pass the values of DestinationZone, ShippingWeight, and RateTable into the procedure. DeliveryCharge will be returned to the main program, so it will be declared as a variable parameter. And, since the value of MinimumCharge is only needed within the procedure, it will be defined locally.

Here's the final procedure:

Procedure *CalculateCharge*

```
procedure CalculateCharge (RateTable : RATEARY;
                           ShippingWeight : real;
                           DestinationZone : integer;
                           var DeliveryCharge : real);
   const
     MinimumCharge = 5.00;
```

```
begin
   DeliveryCharge := ShippingWeight * RateTable[DestinationZone];
   if DeliveryCharge < MinimumCharge then
      DeliveryCharge := MinimumCharge;
end; {procedure CalculateCharge}
```

THE *PrintShippingLabel* PROCEDURE

The final procedure prints the shipping label for the customer.

Step #4 of the algorithm tells us what must be printed on the shipping label:

Algorithm Step #4

4. ***Print shipping label***
    4.1   ***Print destination zone number***
    4.2   ***Print per-pound rate for destination zone***
    4.3   ***Print package weight***
    4.4   ***Print delivery charge***

No parameters are needed for this procedure because all variables to be printed are global. The translation is straightforward:

Procedure *PrintShippingLabel*

```
procedure PrintShippingLabel;
   begin
      write ('The rate for zone ', DestinationZone :2);
      writeln ('is $', RateTable[DestinationZone] :4:2);
      write ('Delivery charge for ', ShippingWeight :6:1 );
      writeln (' pound package is $ ', DeliveryCharge :6:2);
   end; {procedure PrintShippingLabel}
```

Notice our use of write and writeln to split two lines of output in the *program*. When this program runs, there will only be two lines of output that will look something like this:

```
The rate for zone 4 is $ 3.00
Delivery charge for 10 pound package is $30.00
```

All that remains is to include our array-type definition, declare our global variables, and make a list of procedure calls, and the program is complete.

THE DELIVERY CHARGE PROGRAM

```pascal
program DeliveryCharge (input, output);


type
    RATEARY = array[1..10] of real;


var
    RateTable : RATEARY;
    ShippingWeight, DeliveryCharge : real;
    DestinationZone : integer;


procedure CreateRateTable (var RateTable : RATEARY);
    var
        ZoneNumber : integer;
        ChargePerPound : real;
    begin
        ChargePerPound := 1.50;
        for ZoneNumber := 1 to 10 do
            begin
                RateTable[ZoneNumber] := ChargePerPound;
                ChargePerPound := ChargePerPound + 0.50;
            end; { loop body }
    end; { Procedure CreateRateTable}


procedure CollectInfo;
    begin
    repeat
        write ('What is the destination zone? ');
        readln ( DestinationZone );
        if DestinationZone > 10 then
            writeln ('Sorry. That is an invalid zone. ');
    until DestinationZone <= 10;
      write ('What is the weight of the package in pounds? ');
      readln (ShippingWeight);
    end; {procedure CollectInfo}
```

```
procedure CalculateCharge (RateTable : RATEARY;
                           ShippingWeight : real;
                           DestinationZone : integer;
                           var DeliveryCharge : real);
   const
     MinimumCharge = 5.00;

   begin
     DeliveryCharge := ShippingWeight * RateTable[DestinationZone];
     if DeliveryCharge < MinimumCharge then
        DeliveryCharge := MinimumCharge;
   end; {procedure CalculateCharge}

procedure PrintShippingLabel;
   begin
     write ('The rate for zone ', DestinationZone :2);
     writeln ('is $', RateTable[DestinationZone] :4:2);
     write ('Delivery charge for ', ShippingWeight :6:1 );
     writeln (' pound package is $ ', DeliveryCharge :6:2);
   end; { procedure PrintShippingLabel }

begin
   CreateRateTable (RateTable);
   CollectInfo;
   CalculateCharge (RateTable, ShippingWeight, DestinationZone,
   DeliveryCharge); PrintShippingLabel;
end.
```

PROGRAMMING EXERCISES

Programming Exercise 1: Trans-Galactic has added five new destination zones. Zones 1 - 10 remain at the same rate; however, the rates for zones 11 through 15 are incremented by $0.75, rather than $0.50. In other words, the rate for zone 11 is now $6.75, for zone 12 $7.50, and so on. Add a new for loop to the CreateRateTable procedure to initialize zones 11 - 15.

Programming Exercise 2: Trans-Galactic is now offering reduced rates for customers who do not need overnight service. The rates for 2 day delivery are exactly half of the rates for 1 day delivery. Create a second array to store these rates. Your program must now ask the user what kind of service they desire.

ANSWERS TO THE TEST YOUR UNDERSTANDING EXERCISES

1. The Loan Officer algorithm makes a series of decisions to determine a value; the Delivery Charge algorithm *looks up* a value from an existing table of values. The values represented in the Loan Officer program could be put into an array—in fact, this would make the program more efficient—but the "rating" tables require a *two-dimensional* array, which is beyond the scope of this text.

2. House is a structured variable because its single identifier refers to many locations, or rooms.

3. House [room] is the name of a single room. House is the name of a structure with many rooms.

4. True. An array is a group of adjacent memory locations associated with a single identifier.

5. Array elements are the individual values, or data items, stored in an array.

6. Array elements are referenced by their position in an array.

7. The three parts of an array declaration are:
   — The array *identifier*
   — The *number of elements,* or dimension of the array
   — The *data type* of the elements

8. The special symbol (..) is read "through and including."

9.   A.   Value of array element: Clare
     B.   Array identifier: House
     C.   Value of array subscript: 7
     D.   Data type of subscript: integer
     E.   Data type of array element: PEOPLE

10. The while. . . do loop loop body will only be executed as long as a *condition* is true. The for loop will be executed a predetermined number of times, as specified by the *counter variable.*

11. False. The counter variable is automatically incremented after each execution of the loop body.

12. Two reasons for creating an array type in a program:
    — Array variables with a similar structure are easier to declare
    — Array variables can be passed as parameters to a procedure.

13. Error trapping is important to prevent program failures or *crashes.*

14. True. The loop body of a repeat. . . until structure is always executed at least once.

15. The while. . . do loop tests a condition before the loop body is executed, and will not execute the loop if the condition is *false.* The repeat. . . until structure tests a condition after executing the loop body, and will always execute the loop at least once.

The Elements of BASIC

A Problem Solving Approach for Business

by

Steven L. Holder

and

Chris Sherman

Interactive Technologies Corporation

Publisher: Gary Carlson
Editor: Matt Danielson
Managing Editor: Lorie Rothstein
Technical Editors: Steven Levy
                   Lew Hollerbach
Product Manager: Bill Rosen

Printed in the United States of America

IBM, and IBM PC are trademarks of International Business Machines, Inc.

Apple, is a trademark of Apple Computer, Inc.

Library of Congress Cataloging in Publication Data

Holder, Steven L.
    The elements of BASIC.

    Includes index.
    1. Basic (Computer program language)   2. Business—
Data processing.   I. Sherman, Chris.   II. Title.
III. Title: The elements of B.A.S.I.C.
HF5548.5.B3H65 1984   001.64′24   84-3679
ISBN 0-471-80653-6

This book is dedicated to Nancy Holder
with loving appreciation for her tremendous support.

S.H.

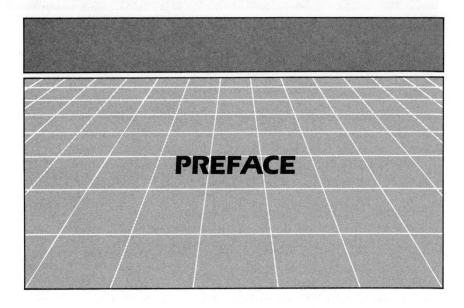

PREFACE

The Elements of BASIC is an introductory programming text emphasizing the principles of problem solving, and the fundamentals of writing solutions in the form of a BASIC program. For the student with no previous computer experience, this text establishes a firm foundation of problem solving skills that can be generalized to any programming language.

The Elements of BASIC is a concise introduction to problem solving with BASIC. Using common business examples, we present a variety of techniques for developing solutions that can be translated into computer programs. Although the emphasis is on microcomputers, the concepts covered apply to all kinds of computers, from large mainframes to lap-sized portables.

Features

The Elements of BASIC has several unique features not found in other programming texts:

Motivating Problem. Each chapter begins with a motivating problem designed to stimulate the student's interest. We systematically introduce the concepts and programming fundamentals needed to solve the problem, making the student a partner in the development of a solution. At the end of the chapter, all new concepts are combined in a BASIC program that solves the motivating problem.

Highlighted Key Ideas.   Each new concept begins with a concise statement of the key idea, highlighted for emphasis. The key idea is followed by detailed explanation, with abundant examples illustrating its uses and application. After three or four new key ideas have been introduced, questions and exercises are provided for the student to test their understanding.

Software Supplement.   Free to adopter's of this text, the software supplement contains the programming solutions to the motivating problems. Also on the diskette are the authors' solutions to the exercises found at the end of the programming chapters. The instructor is encouraged to copy these programs for student use. The software supplement is formatted for both the IBM PC and the Apple II/IIe microcomputers.

Overview

Because it is short and inexpensive, *The Elements of BASIC* is a perfect companion text to any data processing or information science text book, or it may be used independently of any other text. The writing is clear and conversational, with each chapter introducing essential concepts in a logical sequence.

Chapter 1 sets the scene: a small company has purchased a new computer. The student is placed in the position of managing the computer, and developing programming solutions that satisfy the company's needs. This chapter introduces the fundamental concepts of computer operation, and the relationship between the computer and programs. With this knowledge, the student is prepared to approach the computer with confidence derived from understanding.

Chapter 2 supposes that the student has chosen the BASIC programming language for solving company problems—and problems there are. The managers of several departments have already asked for help in using the computer for specific tasks. To accomplish these tasks, the student must learn how the BASIC language is structured, and how programs are written, stored, retrieved, and executed.

In Chapters 3 through 6, the student faces one business problem after another, from the Marketing Department to the Shipping Department. Of course, the solution to each problem introduces the student to new BASIC statements and techniques. Examples throughout each chapter demonstrate BASIC applications in a great variety of business situations. The program at the end ties together all concepts presented in the chapter.

In short, *The Elements of BASIC* is an ideal introduction to problem solving and the BASIC programming language for any student.

To the Student

Each chapter in *The Elements of BASIC* is divided into sections. Each section in turn is divided into several parts. Each part introduces a new "key idea" in a shaded box.

Example: A Key Idea

THE PRINT STRING STATEMENT

> When PRINT is followed by a string enclosed in quotes, the computer prints the characters appearing between the quotes.

At first, the key idea serves as an introduction to a new concept by briefly summarizing the following paragraphs. Later, you should use shaded key ideas as a "quick reference" when reviewing. Each key idea heading is listed in the Table of Contents, making it easy for you to find the material you wish to study.

All BASIC programs and program segments appear in this special COMPUTER PRINTOUT TYPESTYLE. BASIC commands that you can enter at a keyboard are printed in **BOLD FACE**. Results printed by the computer are in the same typeface, but not in boldface. All examples used in this book can be run on a computer. You are encouraged to use and modify these programs as you learn.

Acknowledgements

We thank the many people who have contributed to this project—such as Matt Danielson, Gary Carlson, and Lorie Rothstein at Wiley for their unflagging efforts to bring this text to print—Rick Grunsky, Patrick Mahoney, Marilyn Correa, and George Gintowt for their reviews and suggestions—and especially Dr. Charlotte Chell of Carthage College for her insight, dedication and enthusiasm, which unquestionably improved the final product.

For their encouragement and support, we also thank Dr. Richard A. Walker, Tom Fetter, Jack Spiegelberg, Lauralee Butler, Mary Breach, Rod Daynes, and Beverly Butler at Interactive Technologies Corporation; and Karen Sharpe, Dion Aquino, Clayton Becker, Sheila Gillam and Carl Miller at the Microcomputer Center, San Diego City College.

Steven L. Holder
Chris Sherman
February 29, 1984

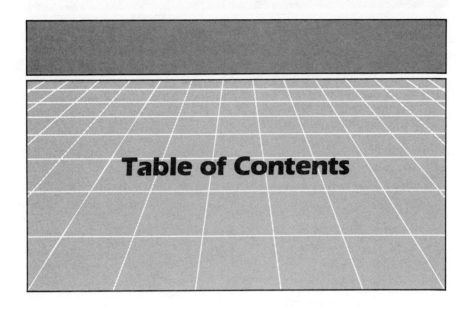

Table of Contents

CHAPTER 3. — GETTING RESULTS WITH BASIC   57

SECTION 1. — The Rules for Making Calculations   58

- The Arithmetic Operators   59
- The Hierarchy of Operations   60
- Using Parentheses to Alter the Order of Operations   62

SECTION 2. — Getting Immediate Results from the Computer   65

- The PRINT arithmetic Statement   65
- The PRINT string Statement   66
- Using the Semicolon in a PRINT Statement   67

SECTION 3. — Getting Results from a Computer Program   68

- The PRINT variable Statement   69
- Using the Comma in a PRINT Statement   70
- PRINTing a Blank Line   72

SECTION 4. — Formatting Numeric Output   73

- The INT Function   74
- Rounding Off Whole Numbers   75
- Rounding Dollar Values   76

SECTION 5. — Getting Data into a Program   78

- The INPUT Statement   79
- INPUT with Prompt   82

SECTION 6. — Performing Repetitive Calculations   84

- The FOR. . . NEXT Loop   85
- The STEP   88

SECTION 7. — The Breakeven Analysis Program   92

- Developing an Algorithm   92
- Writing a BASIC Program   93
- The Breakeven Analysis Program   96

CHAPTER 4. — FUNDAMENTAL PROGRAMMING TECHNIQUES   101

SECTION 1. — Using Loops to Repeat Instructions   102

- The GOTO Statement   103
- The Endless Loop   104

CHAPTER 1

Computers and Computer Programs

CHAPTER OBJECTIVE

To explain the fundamental concepts of computer operation and the nature of computer programs.

PROBLEM

The company you work for has just acquired a small computer, and you've been placed in charge. It's your job to learn how to use the computer to solve problems for your company.

CHAPTER OVERVIEW

This chapter describes in non-technical terms the components of a computer, the purpose and use of programming languages, the relationship of computers and computer programs, and the life cycle of a computer program. This background knowledge will prepare you to approach a computer with the confidence necessary to use it effectively.

This chapter has four sections:

- **The Computer System**
- **The Need for Programming Languages**
- **The Purpose of Computer Programs**
- **The Life Cycle of a Computer Program**

Section 1. The Computer System

INTRODUCTION

A computer is an electronic device that can perform calculations using instructions stored in its memory. The ability to store instructions is what separates a computer from a simple calculator.

The memory of the computer is only one of five principal components of a computer system. In this section, we discuss these five components, their function, and the relationship of one component to another.

This section has five parts:

- The Central Processing Unit
- The Memory
- Input Devices
- Output Devices
- Auxiliary Storage Devices

THE CENTRAL PROCESSING UNIT

The central processing unit, also known as the CPU, is the electronic brain of the computer. It contains the electronic circuits necessary to carry out the instructions stored in memory.

Under the control of instructions stored in memory, the CPU performs five basic functions:

1. The CPU can copy two numbers from memory, perform a calculation, and store the result back in memory.
2. The CPU can copy two values from memory, compare them, and determine which is larger or whether they are equal. The result of this comparison can be used to determine which instruction the computer will execute next.
3. The CPU can copy a value from one memory location to another.
4. The CPU can receive data from an input device or an auxiliary storage device and store the data in memory.
5. The CPU can transmit data stored in memory to an output device or an auxiliary storage device.

THE MEMORY

The memory consists of electronic circuits that store electrical charges. In various combinations of "on" and "off," these charges create codes representing data.

The unit of memory in which an electrical charge is stored is called a *bit*. If the charge is present, the bit is considered "on"; if not present, the bit is considered "off." As humans, we represent these on and off states as 1s and 0s; this is how the word bit was derived, from *BInary digiTs*.

Bits are organized into groups of eight, and each group is called a *byte*. Because there are 256 possible arrangements of 1s and 0s in a byte, we have 256 "codes" for representing letters of the alphabet (upper and lower case), digits, and special symbols. Thus, any character can be stored in one byte of memory.

The size of the computer's memory is very often measured in Ks, such as 64K. A K represents 1024 bytes of memory, so a computer with 64K bytes of memory is capable of storing something over 65,000 characters.

The memory and the CPU together are sometimes referred to as "the computer."

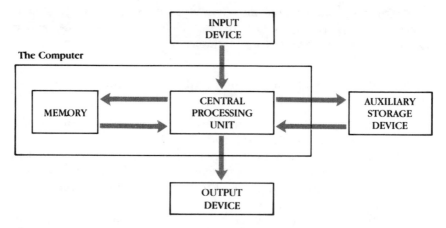

INPUT DEVICES

Input devices allow humans to enter instructions and data to be transmitted to the computer.

The most common input device is a keyboard. When a key is pressed, the code for that character is sent to the CPU which stores the code in memory. When giving instructions to the computer, we type a series of characters to form specific words the computer has been programmed to recognize. The computer however, has no way of determining when we finish typing an instruction unless we give it a signal. For this we use the ENTER key.

Depending on the computer, the ENTER key may be marked ENTER, RETURN, XMIT, TRANSMIT, or some similar word or symbol. Regardless of this key's marking, every keyboard has one, and it serves the same purpose for every computer—signaling the computer to act on the instruction we just typed. In this text, we will always refer to it as the ENTER key.

OUTPUT DEVICES

Output devices allow the computer to transmit results and messages to humans. The most common output devices are a printer and a video monitor.

The video monitor is a television-like screen sometimes referred to as a CRT (Cathode Ray Tube). It's the primary output device for most micro-

computer systems. Results can be displayed on the monitor almost immediately, but it's not a permanent form of output.

When a more permanent form of output is needed, the computer can be
directed to transmit results to a printer. Printer output is often referred to
as *hardcopy*. Although the output is more permanent, the printer works
much more slowly than the monitor.

AUXILIARY STORAGE DEVICES

Auxiliary storage devices are used by the computer to record the contents of its memory for future use. The electrical charges in memory can
be represented as magnetized spots on a magnetic tape or a magnetic
disk. The computer can read these magnetic spots and restore the data
in memory when needed.

The most common auxiliary storage device for a microcomputer is a disk
drive. If we insert a magnetic diskette into the disk drive, we can direct the
computer to store instructions or data on the diskette and also read instructions and data from the diskette back into its memory. Thus, an auxiliary
storage device is both an input and output device.

Auxiliary storage, also referred to as *secondary memory,* is important for
two reasons. First, data stored in the computer's memory may be erased as
a result of normal computer operation—or abnormal circumstances. As part
of normal operation, data in memory is erased when new data is stored in
its place or the computer is turned off. Abnormal circumstances, such as
programming errors and power interruptions, can also cause memory to be
erased. By purposely storing the contents of memory on a diskette, we can
prevent its loss from accidental erasure, and save instructions and data for
future use.

The second reason for auxiliary storage is that a computer's memory is
seldom large enough to store all the instructions and data it's required to
use. Auxiliary storage allows us to store large quantities of data and instructions outside the computer in a form readily transferable into memory as
needed.

TEST YOUR UNDERSTANDING

1. Instructions are stored in _____ and executed by the
_____.

2. _____ is also called secondary memory.

3. We transmit data and instructions to the computer through _____.

4. The computer transmits results and messages to humans through

_____.

Section 2. The Need for Programming Languages

INTRODUCTION

The computer is an electronic device that performs certain functions when specific sequences of 1s and 0s are received by the CPU. Entering instructions in the form of 1s and 0s, however, is arduous. Therefore, a computer is designed so that these necessary sequences of binary digits are created by typing specific words and numbers, a complete set of which we call a programming language.

In this section, we discuss two broad categories of programming languages and illustrate some of their variety.

This section has three parts:

- The Language of the Machine
- Languages That Resemble English
- The Variety of Languages

THE LANGUAGE OF THE MACHINE

The computer's electronic circuits accept and operate on a particular set of instructions, called its *machine language*.

The CPU is designed to perform certain operations when it receives specific sequences of binary digits (1s and 0s); any one such sequence is called a *machine instruction.* The complete set of machine instructions for a given CPU is its machine language. Machine instructions are the only instructions the CPU can directly execute.

To write instructions in machine language (which we won't be doing in this text), the programmer uses a set of 16 characters called *hexadecimal numbers,*—hexadecimal meaning "16." These are the numbers 0 through 9 and the letters A through F, each corresponding to a unique sequence of four binary digits. Using appropriate combinations of hexadecimal numbers, the programmer can write a series of instructions in the CPU's own language.

When stored in memory, these instructions form a machine language program to control the operation of the computer.

Most machine language programs that control the computer are *transparent*; we don't see them and we often don't realize they are there. These programs work "backstage," so to speak, acting as middleman between you (the computer user) and the CPU. They interpret the instructions we type at the keyboard and provide the CPU with the detailed machine language instructions necessary to carry out our commands.

Example

This example of instructions is written in the machine language of the IBM PC.

```
74  1F
3C  A4
77  3E
BB  12  1D
33  D1
```

Each pair of hexadecimal numbers is stored in one byte of memory as a specific sequence of binary digits, representing part of a machine instruction. The complete instruction takes two or three bytes, depending on what we instruct the computer to do.

Using machine language, the programmer can direct the computer to perform such basic operations as moving a value from one location in memory to another, adding one value to another, and comparing two values to determine which is larger or whether they are equal. By combining many of these elementary instructions, the programmer can write a program instructing the computer to read the characters you've typed and compare them to a list of valid commands. When a match is found, the program forwards the corresponding machine language instructions to the CPU which then executes your command.

LANGUAGES THAT RESEMBLE ENGLISH

Because writing instructions in machine language is not particularly easy, other languages have been created using English words and English-like statements to give instructions to the computer.

Machine language is called *low-level* because instructions are written in the *computer's* native language, not our own. Other programming languages resembling English have been created; these are called *high-level* languages.

The use of such languages is made possible by machine language programs that translate high-level language statements into machine instructions.

Writing instructions in a high-level language requires no special knowledge of the internal workings of the computer or its machine language, so we can concentrate on the solution of a problem without thinking about the particular construction of the computer we're using. High-level languages are also somewhat standardized between various computers. Whereas we can use a machine language on only one type of computer, we can use a standard high-level language on many different types of computers—if the appropriate translator program is available.

THE VARIETY OF LANGUAGES

Since the invention of the computer, hundreds of programming languages have been developed, each with its own unique set of words and statements to give instructions to the computer.

Anyone may create a programming language, and a large number of groups and organizations have. Some of the languages have become popular; they're easy to use or make it easy to solve particular types of problems. Some are not so popular, however, because they are difficult or have only limited applications. In general, each language is created for a particular purpose.

One of the early languages still being used today is FORTRAN (for FORmula TRANslator), developed for performing numerical computations. COBOL (COmmon Business Oriented Language), developed by a committee of computer industry representatives, is widely used in solving business problems and preparing business reports. Two other popular languages are Pascal (named after the French mathematician) and BASIC (Beginner's All-purpose Symbolic Instruction Code), developed by universities for use in teaching the concepts of programming.

Each language has its own set of words and statements for giving instructions to the computer, and the types of instructions given vary from language to language. Assuming we have experience with several languages, we could select one for use in a particular application, based on the type of problem or the computer's capability for that language.

Example

This example illustrates the same computer instructions written in three different programming languages: BASIC, Pascal, and COBOL.

BASIC:

```
FOR SELLINGPRICE = MINPRICE TO MAXPRICE STEP PRICEINCRMENT
   LET ITEMPROFIT = SELLINGPRICE - CSTPERITEM
   LET BREAKEVEN = OVERHEAD / ITEMPROFIT
   PRINT SELLINGPRICE, BREAKEVEN
NEXT SELLINGPRICE
```

Pascal:

```
SellingPrice := MinPrice;
WHILE SellingPrice <= MaxPrice DO
   BEGIN
      ItemProfit := SellingPrice - CostPerItem;
      BreakEven := Overhead / ItemProfit;
      WRITELN (SellingPrice :8:2, BreakEven :17:0);
      SellingPrice := SellingPrice + PriceIncrement;
   END;
```

COBOL:

```
PERFORM BREAKEVEN-CALCULATION
        VARYING SELLING-PRICE FROM MINIMUM-PRICE
        BY PRICE-INCREMENT
        UNTIL SELLING-PRICE IS GREATER THAN MAXIMUM-PRICE.

BREAKEVEN-CALCULATION.
        COMPUTE ITEM-PROFIT = SELLING-PRICE - COST-PER-ITEM.
        COMPUTE BREAKEVEN = OVERHEAD / ITEM-PROFIT.
        MOVE SELLING-PRICE TO SELLING-PRICE-PRINT-LINE.
        MOVE BREAKEVEN TO BREAKEVEN-POINT-PRINT-LINE.
        DISPLAY BREAKEVEN-PRINT-LINE.
```

TEST YOUR UNDERSTANDING

5. The native language of the CPU is its _____.

6. Machine language instructions are written using _____ while high-level language instructions are written using _____.

7. Each high-level language has its own _____ for giving instructions to the computer.

8. The use of high-level languages is made possible by _____.

Section 3. The Purpose of Computer Programs

INTRODUCTION

A computer is merely a machine requiring instructions to perform certain functions, and computer programs provide these instructions. In this section we discuss three general types of programs.

This section has four parts:

- Programs to Operate the Computer
- Programs to Translate Languages
- Programs to Solve Problems
- The Steps a Program Must Perform

PROGRAMS TO OPERATE THE COMPUTER

Operating system programs are the front-line supervisors of the computer, managing computer operating details and providing the CPU with detailed instructions for carrying out our commands.

Although a variety of programs supervise various functions of the computer, we're going to discuss two categories we call the Operating System and the Disk Operating System (DOS).

The Operating System is a program placed in a special permanent memory of the computer when it's manufactured. When the power is turned on, this program takes control of the computer. On a microcomputer, one of the first things the Operating System does is look for a diskette in the disk drive, then search it for a program called the Disk Operating System. When the DOS is located, it's transferred into memory and given control of the computer.

While the exact relationship of the DOS and the Operating System differs with various computers, we can think of the DOS as the primary supervisor of the computer and the Operating System as working for the DOS. Together, they interpret the commands we type at the keyboard, and provide the detailed instructions necessary for the CPU to carry out those commands. Since they work together, we'll refer to them under the single name of DOS.

Most of the time, we consider the DOS to be the computer itself. Depending on the computer, the DOS performs such various functions as transferring data and programs from memory to the diskette or from the diskette to memory, copying programs from one diskette to another, executing other programs, and monitoring internal functions of the computer to ensure everything's working smoothly. To determine the full extent of the DOS commands you have available, consult the reference manual for your computer.

The following is a conceptual illustration showing the DOS function within the computer system.

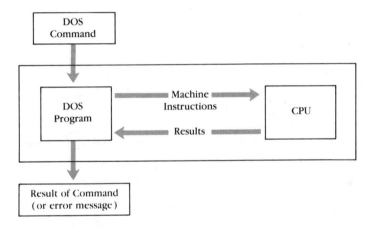

While other programs are running, the DOS remains in the background, still in control but quietly supervising and monitoring the instructions given to the CPU. If an error occurs, the DOS will interrupt the program that's running and display an error message. In most cases, it will also terminate the program and resume primary control of the computer.

PROGRAMS TO TRANSLATE LANGUAGES

Since the CPU can execute only those instructions written in its own machine language, high-level language instructions must be translated into machine language before the computer can execute them.

In this book, you'll learn to write instructions in the BASIC programming language, but for the computer to execute these instructions it must have a program called the *BASIC Interpreter*. The Interpreter translates BASIC instructions into the computer's machine language.

On some computers, you must ask the DOS for the BASIC Interpreter from the diskette, while on other models, it comes as part of the Operating System or the DOS itself. In any case, the Interpreter must be present and in control before you can give the computer BASIC instructions.

While learning to use the BASIC language, you'll probably become familiar with a variety of error messages displayed by the Interpreter when it's unable to translate an instruction. When an instruction can be interpreted, it's translated and forwarded to the CPU for execution. Since the DOS is monitoring all instructions given to the CPU, it also displays an error message if it detects that an instruction cannot be executed for some reason.

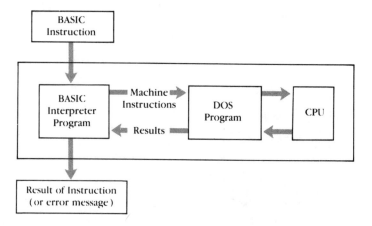

PROGRAMS TO SOLVE PROBLEMS

A program which provides the detailed instructions for solving a particular problem is called an *application program*.

Writing application programs is the subject of this text. In the coming chapters, you will see a variety of problems and the BASIC instructions we can use to solve them. For now, let's get an overview of how an application program works.

An application program must be in the computer's memory to be used. If you've just typed a list of instructions into the computer, that program is in memory. If you want to use a program previously written and stored on diskette, you must give a command to copy the program from diskette to memory. This is called "loading" the program.

Once the program is in memory, the computer is given a command to begin executing the instructions in the program; this is called "running" the program. While the program is running, it's supplying the instructions to the computer. The BASIC Interpreter translates each instruction of the program into machine language, and the DOS monitors the instruction as it's passed to the CPU. If either the BASIC Interpreter or the DOS detects an error, the application program will be stopped, and an error message will be displayed.

An application program, while running, has primary control of the computer. You're not able to give instructions or commands to the computer until the program has stopped, either because all program instructions have been executed or because of an error.

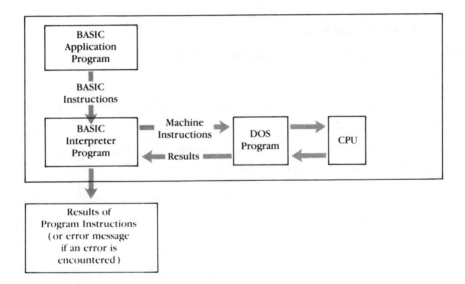

THE STEPS A PROGRAM MUST PERFORM

Application programs must perform three fundamental steps: input, process, and output.

To solve a particular problem, a program must obtain the specific data to be used, perform whatever calculations or processes are necessary to solve the problem, then display the results on an output device.

The program instructions can direct the computer to accept data from the keyboard or locate data stored on a diskette. The program can then direct the computer to perform the step-by-step calculations or other processes required to solve the problem using the data it's been given. Once the results have been produced, the program must direct the computer to display the results on an output device, such as a printer or video monitor. Results may also be stored on diskette for future use by the computer, or for later retrieval and viewing.

PROGRAM

Get the Data
Perform the Calculations
Display the Results

TEST YOUR UNDERSTANDING

9. Two programs that operate the computer are the _____ and the _____.

10. The program that translates BASIC instructions into machine instructions is the _____.

11. Before the computer can be given BASIC instructions, the _____ must be present and in control of the computer.

12. An _____ provides the instructions necessary for the solution of a particular problem.

13. The three steps a program must perform are _____, _____, and _____.

Section 4. The Life Cycle of a Computer Program

INTRODUCTION

Between its birth and ultimate retirement, a computer program passes through five distinct phases. Recognizing each phase is important in the management and use of computer programs. Creating programs to solve problems is also much easier when the steps involved in this process are clear.

This section has five parts:

- Designing the Program
- Coding the Program
- Testing the Program
- Implementing the Program
- Maintaining the Program

DESIGNING THE PROGRAM

When we decide a problem is to be solved using the computer, we must first devise a solution that can be translated into a computer program. By writing a solution in the form of an algorithm, we can outline a program to solve the problem.

To give the computer instructions necessary to solve a problem, we must first know how to solve the problem ourselves. The first task is to write down a step-by-step description of how the problem is to be solved. Such a description is called an *algorithm.*

Since there's usually more than one way to solve any problem, creating an algorithm gives us a chance to plan an approach to the problem's solution in an organized manner. Since a program must obtain data, perform calculations, and display results, we must account for these steps in the algorithm. If a series of calculations is needed, each calculation must be described. The completed algorithm represents the steps the program must perform to solve the problem.

Example

The following simple example illustrates an algorithm describing the steps of a problem's solution.

A program is required to calculate the selling price for merchandise purchased in quantities of 12 dozen and sold at a 30 percent markup. The steps required to solve this problem are described in the following algorithm:

1.   Obtain price for 12 dozen units.
2.   Divide price for 12 dozen by 144 to find cost per unit.
3.   Multiply cost per unit by .30 to find markup amount.
4.   Add markup amount to cost per unit to find selling price.
5.   Display selling price.

CODING THE PROGRAM

After the algorithm has been written and the solution to the problem is clear, the steps in the algorithm can be translated into BASIC instructions. This is called *coding* the program.

Coding is a simple process when you've written a good algorithm. The instructions are written first using a pencil and paper. When the complete program has been coded, it's double-checked to ensure the steps have been correctly translated into BASIC, and the instructions will produce the correct solution to the problem. The program is then entered into the computer for testing.

Example

This example illustrates a BASIC program that performs the steps outlined in the algorithm above. In the coming chapters, we'll discuss the meaning of these instructions, but they are presented here to illustrate the relationship between the algorithm and the program.

```
10 INPUT "WHAT IS THE PRICE FOR 12 DOZEN UNITS"; PRICE
20 LET UNITCST = PRICE / 144
30 LET MARKUP = .30 * UNITCST
40 LET SALEPRICE = UNITCST + MARKUP
50 PRINT "THE SELLING PRICE IS $"; SALEPRICE
```

TESTING THE PROGRAM

Testing is one of the most important steps in the development of a program; it ensures the program produces the correct results and the correct solution every time.

After we've entered the program into the computer's memory, we give the command to begin running the program. We then enter data for which we already know the correct results, and compare the output of the program to these results. By running the program many times using input data representing every possible combination of circumstances, we can increase our confidence that the program will perform correctly in all cases.

Most computer errors are the result of inadequate program testing. When a program has not been tested for all possible combinations of conditions, a programming error might be present—though it might not be discovered until a customer receives a bill for $3,000,000,000.00. Once a program produces the correct results for all sets of data, the program is ready to be implemented.

IMPLEMENTING THE PROGRAM

When ready to be implemented, the program and the instructions for its use are both made available to those people in the company needing it.

After the program has been tested, it's stored on a diskette, then given to those people who need it. The program alone, however, is not enough. Instructions must also be provided to explain the procedure for running the program, the type of data to be entered, and how the results are to be interpreted. These instructions are referred to as *documentation.*

Good documentation is important. Many valuable programs are never used because the documentation is so poor no one can figure out how to use the program. A program might also be abandoned if it requires a change, but the documentation is insufficient to make the change at a reasonable cost.

MAINTAINING THE PROGRAM

Programs will often remain in use for years. As changes occur in the business environment, changes will have to be made to the program.

Such changes in the business environment include new government tax rates and regulations, new prices of products and business procedures, or alterations in the format or content of output. These changes require that the program be modified so the desired output will still be correctly produced.

Maintenance of a program may also be required if we discover the program sometimes produces incorrect results. When an error is discovered in the output, the source of that error must be located and corrected immediately.

TEST YOUR UNDERSTANDING

14. In the design phase, we use an _____ to describe the steps the program must perform to solve the problem.

15. After designing a solution, the program is _____ and entered into the computer.

16. The purpose of testing a program is to ensure that it _____.

17. To implement the program, we must provide _____ and _____ to those people who need it.

18. Program maintenance may be required because of _____ or because _____ have been discovered.

ANSWERS TO "TEST YOUR UNDERSTANDING" EXERCISES

1. Memory; Central processing unit
2. Auxiliary storage
3. An input device
4. An output device
5. Machine language
6. Hexadecimal numbers; English words and English-like statements.
7. Unique set of words and statements
8. Machine language programs which translate high-level language statements into machine instructions.
9. Operating System; Disk Operating System (DOS)
10. BASIC Interpreter
11. BASIC Interpreter
12. Application program
13. Input; process; output
14. Algorithm
15. Coded
16. Produces the correct results every time it is run.
17. The program itself; instructions for its use (documentation).
18. Changes in the business environment; errors

CHAPTER 2

What You Should Know About BASIC

CHAPTER OBJECTIVE

To explain the essential elements of the BASIC language and the fundamental procedures for writing and storing programs.

PROBLEM

You have decided the BASIC programming language best suits the problem-solving needs of your company. The managers of several departments in your company have already asked you to help them apply the computer to problem-solving in their areas. Before you can assist them, however, you must learn the essential elements of the BASIC language, and the procedures for writing and storing programs.

CHAPTER OVERVIEW

The BASIC programming language is not difficult to learn when you have a clear picture of the language's elements, and know how instructions to the computer are written in BASIC. Before advancing to the actual writing of problem-solving programs, you must also understand the common procedures for entering, viewing, executing, storing, and retrieving programs.

This chapter introduces the elements and structure of the BASIC language, and many of the most commonly used commands.

This chapter has six sections:

- **Writing Instructions in BASIC**
- **Using Variable Names to Represent Data**
- **Executing Instructions in BASIC**
- **Entering a BASIC Program**
- **Saving a Program for Future Use**
- **Making Programs Understandable**

Section 1. Writing Instructions in BASIC

INTRODUCTION

The BASIC programming language uses English words and English-like statements in its instructions to the computer. The BASIC Interpreter translates these statements into machine instructions the computer can execute. The BASIC Interpreter is itself a computer program, and, to correctly translate a BASIC instruction, that instruction must conform to certain rules called the "syntax" of the language.

When a BASIC instruction does not follow the language rules, the Interpreter is unable to correctly translate it. This causes the Interpreter to send us an error message, such as SYNTAX ERROR. We can avoid syntax errors by understanding the essential elements of a BASIC instruction. This section explains the concept of reserved words and the elements of a BASIC statement.

This section has two parts:

- Some Words Are Reserved
- Making a Statement

SOME WORDS ARE RESERVED

To give instructions to the computer, we must use words it has been programmed to accept.

The BASIC language contains many words with specific meanings to the BASIC Interpreter. When we use these words, the BASIC Interpreter "recognizes" them and translates them into specific machine instructions. Words with special meanings in BASIC are called "reserved words" or "keywords."

Each keyword in the BASIC language causes the computer to perform a specific action. Some keywords represent an instruction by themselves, but others must be used together in particular combinations. Some require that additional information be supplied with them to form a complete instruction. Each keyword has its own rules of syntax describing how the word is to be used so that a statement can be correctly translated by the BASIC Interpreter.

Here are a few of the keywords in BASIC. Each has a special meaning when correctly used in a BASIC instruction.

LET	FOR	GOTO	INPUT
TO	NEXT	GOSUB	PRINT
READ	IF	OR	ON
DATA	THEN	AND	END

Since the BASIC Interpreter translates BASIC instructions into machine instructions, each computer manufacturer must write a BASIC Interpreter program specifically for its machine. This gives the manufacturer the opportunity to include additional keywords in the BASIC language for its computer. Therefore, the complete list of keywords will vary slightly among computers. Consult the BASIC Reference Manual for your computer to obtain a complete list of the keywords it uses.

Learning to use the BASIC language is a process of learning to use the BASIC keywords, one word at a time. In this chapter and those following, you will be introduced to the use of the keywords listed above. In each case, the rules for using the keyword and the function performed by the computer will be explained. While learning the use of a BASIC keyword, concentrate on the rules for its use and the function it causes the computer to perform.

With only a few exceptions, the keywords introduced in this text can be used on any computer with a Disk Operating System and a BASIC Interpreter. If an exception occurs, consult the BASIC Reference Manual for your computer to determine the proper keyword and its use for your computer.

MAKING A STATEMENT

Instructions are given to the computer by combining certain types of words and symbols to form statements.

An instruction written in the BASIC language is called a statement. There are five elements that may appear in a statement, depending on the proper syntax for that statement:

1. KEYWORDS—Each statement must include a keyword or proper combination of keywords.
2. LITERALS—A statement may include a specific number (a numeric literal), or a specific string of characters (a string literal).
3. SYMBOLS—A statement may include certain symbols used in arithmetic operations, assignment operations, and comparisons.
4. PUNCTUATION—A statement may require certain punctuation marks in order to be interpreted correctly.
5. VARIABLE NAMES—A variable name may sometimes be used in a statement in place of a number or a string of characters.

Example

The following BASIC statements illustrate the five elements that can appear in a statement.

```
LET   TAX   =   SALE   *   .06
 :     :    :     :     :    :
 :     :    :     :     :    :......Numeric Literal
 :     :    :     :     :
 :     :    :     :     :.....Symbol (for multiplication)
 :     :    :     :
 :     :    :     :.....Variable Name
 :     :    :
 :     :    :.....Symbol (for assignment of a value
 :     :              to a variable)
 :     :.....Variable Name
 :
 :......Keyword
```

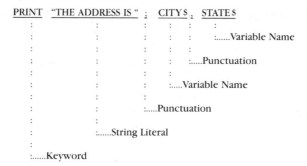

TEST YOUR UNDERSTANDING

Identify the elements in the following statements. (All keywords used in these statements have been introduced in this section.)

1. PRINT 14 * AMOUNT
2. LET AMOUNT = QTY * CST
3. INPUT "WHAT IS YOUR CHOICE"; CH$
4. FOR DIGITS = 1 TO 10
5. IF SALE > 100 THEN PRINT "DISCOUNT APPLIES"

Section 2. Using Variable Names to Represent Data

INTRODUCTION

If a friend asks you how to calculate the area of a piece of land, you might say "Area equals length times width". If you were to write this down, you might write:

$$Area = Length \times Width$$

Since you don't know the size of the land he is considering, you must use names to represent the proper values for this calculation. These names (area, length, and width) are examples of "variable names." Variable names are used to represent values when the actual values to be used are not yet known. A variable name is sometimes called simply a "variable".

Using variable names to represent values, you can give your friend the instructions for calculating the area of the land. When he finds out the length and width, he can perform the calculation.

In the same way, we give instructions to the computer. Using variable names, we tell the computer what calculations to perform. When it is time to perform the calculation, values are entered into the computer for each variable name. The computer then uses these values to perform the calculation.

This section describes two types of variable names, and the essential rules for creating and using variable names.

This section has four parts:

- Numeric Variable Names
- String Variable Names
- Rules for Creating Variable Names
- The LET... = Statement

NUMERIC VARIABLE NAMES

A numeric variable name represents a place in memory for storing a numeric value.

To humans, a numeric variable name represents an unknown number, but to the computer it represents a place in its memory where a numeric value may be stored. Think of the variable name as the name of a memory area, and think of the number as the value stored in that area. Whenever the variable name is used, the computer goes to that area and retrieves whatever value it finds there.

(Since the word "number" can be potentially confusing—is "378" one number, or is it three numbers?—we prefer to use the term "value" when referring to a number stored in memory.)

Example

Assume the value 125.99 has been stored in memory in a place called PRICE, and the value 10.50 has been stored in memory in a place called DELIVERY.

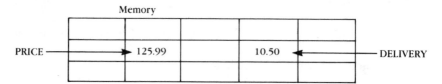

The following is a BASIC instruction we can give to the computer. (Throughout this text, we use bold print to indicate what is typed at the keyboard.)

PRINT PRICE + DELIVERY

When we instruct the computer to execute this statement, it retrieves the value stored in the place called PRICE (125.99), then retrieves the value stored in the place marked DELIVERY (10.50). It then adds these two values and prints the result, as illustrated below.

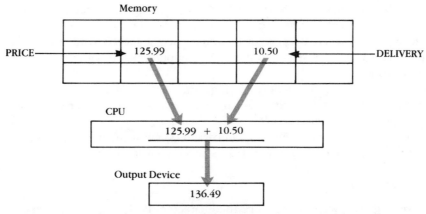

Assume now that the contents of the memory areas are changed; PRICE now contains 88.56, and DELIVERY now contains 5.00. If we instruct the computer to execute the same statement a second time, it finds 88.56 in the place marked PRICE, and 5.00 in the place marked DELIVERY. The calculation is performed using these values, and a different result is obtained.

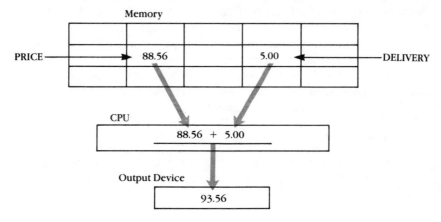

STRING VARIABLE NAMES

A string variable name represents a place in memory for storing a sequence of characters.

Numeric values are not the only values we can store in the computer's memory. We can also store words, names, or any other sequence of characters. A sequence of characters stored in memory is called a "string," and a variable name assigned to the area where a string is stored is called a "string variable name."

A place in memory reserved for storing a string of characters is very different from a place reserved for a numeric value, because a string requires more storage space. Because of this difference, a special symbol must be used with the variable name to signal the computer that this area is reserved for a string.

The symbol used to identify a string variable name is the dollar sign ($). A variable name ending with a dollar sign represents an area in memory for storing a string of characters.

To give the computer a string of characters, the string must be enclosed within double quote marks ("). This is called a "string literal."

Example 1

Let's assume we want to store the characters JOHN SMITH in memory. To identify the characters we want stored, we must enclose them in double quote marks. Thus, "JOHN SMITH" represents a string of 10 characters beginning with J and ending with H. (The 5th character is the space.)

In addition to identifying the boundaries of a string, the quote marks serve another purpose. They prevent the computer from trying to interpret the character string as an instruction. If the quote marks are omitted, the BASIC Interpreter views JOHN SMITH as two numeric variable names. This may result in a syntax error, depending on the statement in which it occurs. In any event, those characters are not stored in memory.

On the other hand, if a keyword or a variable name is unintentionally enclosed in quotes, the Interpreter does not recognize the keyword or variable name. In a sense, anything within the quotes is treated as "data."

Example 2

Assume that the string of characters "1212 13TH AVENUE" has been stored in memory under the string variable name ADDRESS$.

ADDRESS$

Memory

| | 1 | 2 | 1 | 2 | | 1 | 3 | T | H | | A | V | E | N | U | E | | |

The variable name ADDRESS$ is read as "address string." Notice the dollar sign ($) is added to the name to tell the computer this variable name represents an area of memory for storing a string. The characters stored in this area are 1212 13TH AVENUE, which we refer to as the "value" of the variable ADDRESS$.

The following BASIC statement directs the computer to print the value of the variable ADDRESS$.

PRINT ADDRESS$

When this statement is executed, the computer goes to the place in memory called ADDRESS$, and prints the string of characters stored there.

1212 13TH AVENUE

(Where this is printed depends on the output device you are using. On microcomputers, it is most often on the video monitor.)

Notice the quote marks are not stored in memory, nor are they printed. They are used only to identify the beginning and end of a character string when we give the string to the computer; they are not part of the string itself.

RULES FOR FORMING VARIABLE NAMES

To be interpreted correctly, a variable name must conform to certain rules, many of which depend on the computer being used.

When the BASIC Interpreter attempts to translate a BASIC statement, it follows certain rules regarding variable names. To write statements which the computer can interpret, we must observe these rules.

The rules that apply to most computers are listed below, but again you should check your own BASIC reference manual for the rules that apply to your computer.

1. The first character in any variable name must be a letter of the alphabet.
2. Numbers may be used in the variable name after the first character.
3. No special characters or spaces are allowed in a variable name.
4. The maximum length of a variable name depends on your computer, *however*, many computers recognize no more than the first two characters of a variable name regardless of its length.
5. Most computers will signal a syntax error if you use a variable name containing a keyword.

Example 1

The first character in a variable name must be a letter of the alphabet. Numbers may be used after the first character.

Valid Variable Name	Invalid Variable Name
A1	2B
SIDE2	6PACK
YEAR3	7UP
R2D2$	3PO$

Example 2

No special characters or spaces are allowed in a variable name.

Valid Variable Name	Invalid Variable Name
QTYSOLD	QTY SOLD
SIXPCT	SIX%TAX
CHARGE	$PERHOUR

Example 3

Many computers will recognize only the first two characters of a variable name. This will cause problems if you have more than one variable name with the same two leading characters.

Assume that the following variables have been used in a program:

SALARY	TIME	TITLE$
UNITAMOUNT	SAVINGS	UNITSALES

When these six variable names are used in a program, the computer will reserve places in memory for storing the values of these variables. This might be pictured as follows:

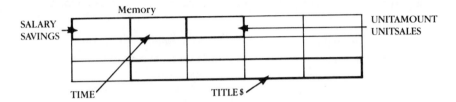

Since most computers use only the first two characters of a variable name, the names UNITAMOUNT and UNITSALES are considered the same variable (UN); only one place in memory is reserved for the value of that variable. Similarly, SALARY and SAVINGS are considered to be the same variable (SA); again, only one place in memory is reserved.

The variables TIME and TITLE$, however, are given different places in memory; one is a numeric variable, the other is a string variable. The dollar sign at the end of TITLE$ is recognized, and the computer considers these two variables to be different and unrelated, even though the first two characters are the same.

An area in memory can hold only one value at a time. If a new value is assigned to a variable, the old value is erased and the new value is stored in its place. For instance, if the value 3000 is entered into the computer for UNITSALES, the computer stores this value in the place in memory called UN. If the value 1.98 is then entered as the value of UNITAMOUNT, the computer erases 3000 from the place called UN, and stores 1.98 there instead.

A problem occurs when we try to perform a calculation using UNIT-SALES. We are expecting the value 3000 to be used in the calculation; that's what we gave the computer for UNITSALES. Instead, the computer finds the value 1.98 in UN, and uses that in the calculation—not what we intended.

We can remind ourselves of this rule and avoid such problems if we draw our memory diagrams using only two characters for the variable names.

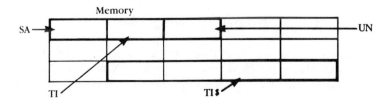

Example 4

Most computers will signal a syntax error if a variable name contains a keyword within it. The following variable names cannot be used on many computers; each contains a keyword the BASIC Interpreter recognizes.

Variable Name	Keyword Contained
COST	COS (Cosine Function)
RATE	AT
DEDUCTION	ON
INTEREST	INT (Integer Function)
INCREMENT	REM (Remark statement)
TOTAL	TO
FORCE	FOR
WORK	OR

To avoid this, we can modify a variable name so that it no longer contains the keyword, yet is still understandable.

CST	INCRMENT
RTE	TTL
DEDUCT	FRCE
NTEREST	WRK

THE LET. . . = STATEMENT

We can assign a value to an area of memory using the LET . . . = statement.

Now that we know how to create a valid variable name to represent an area in memory, how do we store a value in that area? One method is to "assign" a value to a specific variable using the LET. . . = statement. The general format of this statement is:

LET variable-name = value

"Variable-name" represents a valid variable name we have created, and "value" represents a value to be stored in memory. When the LET. . . = statement is executed, the value on the right side of the equal sign is stored in memory under the variable name that appears left of the equal sign. Typing a LET... = statement at the keyboard is not very interesting, though, since you can't see a value being stored in memory.

Example 1

Assume the following instruction is given to the computer:

```
LET  QUANTITY  =  15
```

When this instruction is executed, the computer checks to see if it has already reserved a place in memory with the name QU. If not, it reserves an area with this name and stores the value 15 in that area. If an area has already been reserved with the name QU, the computer erases the value previously stored there, and stores the value 15 in its place.

We can picture the function of the LET... = statement:

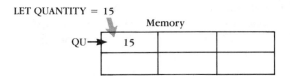

This function is referred to as "assignment." The value 15 is "assigned" to the memory area represented by QUANTITY. In this case, the equal sign does not mean "equal"; it is referred to as an "assignment operator", and it means "be assigned the value of."

Example 2

The value on the right side of the assignment operator can be a calculation, also called an "expression." When an expression is included in a LET... = statement, the expression is evaluated first, and then the result is stored under the variable name. For example:

```
LET  SALE  =  4.99  +  .30
```

In this case, the computer adds 4.99 to .30 and stores the result of 5.29 in the memory area called SA.

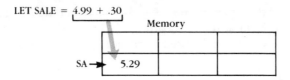

Example 3

The same variable name can appear on both sides of the assignment operator in the LET. . . = statement.

LET COUNTER = COUNTER + 1

In this example, let's assume that the value 3 has already been stored under the variable name COUNTER. When this LET. . . = statement is executed, the computer first performs the calculation on the right of the equal sign. Then it stores the result under the variable name left of the equal sign.

Since the calculation contains the variable name COUNTER, the computer retrieves the value stored under that name and uses that value in the calculation. The result is then stored back in memory as the new value of COUNTER.

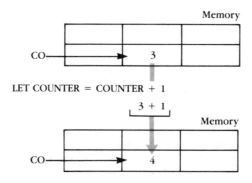

Example 4

A string of characters can be assigned to a string variable using the LET. . . = statement.

LET SCHOOL$ = "CITY COLLEGE"

When this statement is executed, the string of characters within quote marks is stored in memory under the string variable name SC$.

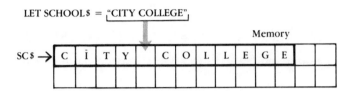

LET SCHOOL$ = "CITY COLLEGE"

Memory

SC$ →

| C | I | T | Y | | C | O | L | L | E | G | E | | |

TEST YOUR UNDERSTANDING

6. A numeric variable name represents a place in memory for storing a _____, and a string variable name represents a place in memory for storing a _____.

7. Identify each variable name below as string or numeric.

QTY	CITY$	AD$	WEIGHT	RTE
AMT	CLASS	CHOICE$	X	SIZE$

8. Which variable names below would be considered invalid on most computers?

NUMBER	2NDITEM	DESCRIP$	COUNT	MILE-PER-HOUR
UNITCST	NM1$	ACCT#1	TIME2	SALES TAX

9. Identify the keyword contained in each variable name below, then revise the variable name so that it no longer contains the keyword.

SHIFT   TOLL   LETTER$ MONTH$ SHORTAGE   STANDARD

Section 3. Executing Instructions in BASIC

INTRODUCTION

There are two ways the computer can execute a BASIC instruction. One is called the "immediate mode"; the other is the "deferred mode". This section explains the difference between these two modes, and how and why they are used.

This section has two parts:

- Instructions That Are Executed Immediately
- Instructions That Are Executed Later

INSTRUCTIONS THAT ARE EXECUTED IMMEDIATELY

In the immediate mode, an instruction is executed when it is entered.

When an instruction that does not begin with a number is typed in at the keyboard and the ENTER key is pressed, the computer attempts to execute the instruction immediately.

The immediate mode can be useful for obtaining quick results for calculations performed in one step. The immediate mode can also be useful for experimenting with instructions or variable names. If there is an error in the instruction or the variable name is improper, the computer will respond immediately with an error message.

The computer does not retain an immediate instruction in its memory. After the instruction is executed, it cannot be executed again unless it is entered again.

Example 1

If this instruction is typed at the keyboard:

```
PRINT "THE TIME IS 6:00 PM"
```

and the ENTER key is pressed, the computer immediately executes the instruction by printing:

```
THE TIME IS 6:00 PM
```

(Where this is printed depends on the output device you are using. We will assume that it is on the video monitor.)

Example 2

If this instruction is typed at the keyboard:

```
TELL ME THE TIME
```

and the ENTER key is pressed, the computer immediately responds with an error message. Depending on the computer, this may appear as

```
?SYNTAX ERROR
```

or

```
SN ERROR
```

or something similar.

In this case, the computer is unable to translate the instruction it has been given. The instruction is not a valid BASIC statement because it contains no keywords the BASIC Interpreter can recognize. In the immediate mode, an error in the instruction causes an error message to be displayed immediately.

Example 3

If this instruction is typed at the keyboard:

PRINT VIOLET$

and the ENTER key is pressed, many computers would immediately respond with:

```
0
?SYNTAX ERROR
```

In this case, the string variable name VIOLET$ contains the BASIC keyword LET. The BASIC Interpreter sees this instruction as

```
PRINT VIO LET $
```

The BASIC Interpreter views VIO as a numeric variable, so it prints the current value of VIO (in this case − 0). The BASIC Interpreter then sees LET $ as an invalid BASIC statement, and displays an error message.

If you have any doubts about whether a certain variable name is legal, use the immediate mode to test it, as in this example. If you get no error message, the variable name is acceptable.

INSTRUCTIONS THAT ARE EXECUTED LATER

By numbering the instructions we give the computer, we can create a list of instructions that will not be executed until we give the command RUN. This list of instructions is a computer program.

When a problem requires a series of steps for its solution, we must have a way of giving the computer a series of instructions that it will remember. Since we're giving the computer a list of instructions, we don't want it to start executing the instructions until the entire list is given. In this case the deferred mode is used.

To give the computer a BASIC instruction in the deferred mode, we must begin the instruction with a number. This signals the computer that the instruction is *not* to be executed immediately. Instead, when the ENTER key is pressed, the instruction is stored in the computer's memory. On most computers, the BASIC Interpreter doesn't attempt to interpret the instruction at this time. If there's an error in the instruction, the error won't be detected until the computer attempts to execute it.

By typing a series of numbered instructions and pressing the ENTER key after each one, we can store an entire list of instructions in the computer's memory. When the list is complete, we give the computer a command to begin executing the instructions in this list.

The BASIC command to execute the instructions in memory is RUN. When RUN is typed and the ENTER key is pressed, the computer will execute the instructions in memory starting with the lowest numbered instruction in the list, continuing in order, to the highest. If an error is encountered in any instruction, the computer will stop executing instructions and an error message will be displayed.

Example 1

Assume the following instruction is typed at the keyboard. (Note the number before the keyword PRINT.)

```
20 PRINT "THE TIME IS 6:00 PM"
```

When the ENTER key is pressed, nothing appears to happen. The computer only stores the instruction in memory. It doesn't attempt to execute the instruction because the number in front of the instruction signals the computer to defer execution.

If we now type the command RUN and press the ENTER key, the computer begins executing the instructions it has stored in memory. Assuming this is the only instruction in memory, it is executed as shown below.

```
RUN
THE TIME IS 6:00 PM
```

The computer has executed the instruction by printing the string literal which follows the keyword PRINT.

Example 2

Assume that a second instruction is entered at the keyboard.

```
40 TELL ME THE TIME
```

When the ENTER key is pressed, the computer stores this instruction in memory along with the previous one. By typing RUN, we direct the computer to begin executing the instructions it has stored in memory. The result might appear as follows:

```
RUN
THE TIME IS 6:00 PM
?SYNTAX ERROR IN 40
```

The computer starts with the lowest numbered instruction stored in its memory, and executes it. This instruction (20) causes the computer to print the message THE TIME IS 6:00 PM. The computer then attempts to execute the next instruction in the list (40), but discovers it cannot interpret the instruction. The computer stops executing instructions and displays an error message indicating the number of the invalid statement.

TEST YOUR UNDERSTANDING

10. What is the difference between a statement that is executed immediately, and a statement that is stored in memory?

11. What command directs the computer to begin executing the instructions stored in memory?

12. A list of instructions stored in memory is called a _____.

Section 4. Entering a BASIC Program

INTRODUCTION

After you have written a BASIC program, you will have to enter the instructions of the program into the computer. This process is simple if you understand the use of line numbers, how to get the computer to display your program to you, and how to modify the instructions in the program.

This section has three parts:

- Line Numbers
- LISTing the Program
- Inserting, Erasing, and Changing Lines

LINE NUMBERS

To enter a program into the computer's memory, we must assign a different line number to each instruction in the program.

A numbered instruction is referred to as a program "line." The number assigned to the instruction is called a "line number," which may be any whole number from 1 to approximately 64000. (On some computers, this may range from 1 to approximately 32000. Check your BASIC reference manual.)

The computer stores the lines of a program in sequence by line number. Frequently, we number the lines of a program by tens (10, 20, 30, 40, etc.) to leave room between instructions to add new instructions, if necessary. For instance, if we must add an instruction after line 10 but before line 20, we can assign the line number 15 to this new instruction. This causes the new line to be stored in memory between lines 10 and 20.

Although we can write more than one instruction on a line (by typing a colon between each instruction), this can lead to difficulties for the beginning programmer. In this book, we will write every instruction on a separate line (with one exception explained at the end of this chapter).

LISTING THE PROGRAM

To see the instructions that have been stored in memory, we use the command LIST.

After entering any statement in the program but before entering the next, we can direct the computer to display the instructions stored in memory. The BASIC command to display the instructions we have entered is LIST.

When we type the word LIST and press the ENTER key, the computer displays the instructions stored in memory, listing them in line number sequence. If no instructions are currently stored in memory, nothing is displayed.

If we wish to look only at certain lines from the program, we may specify those lines in one of two ways:

> LIST line#
> LIST line#1 − line#2

This first command causes display of only the line in memory with that specific line number. If there is no such line number in memory, nothing is displayed.

The second command causes display of all lines in memory from the first to the second line number specified. If there are no such line numbers in memory (or, on some computers, if line #1 is greater than line #2), nothing is displayed.

These two variations of the LIST command allow us to look either at one line or a small part of the program. The command LIST by itself displays the entire program.

When entering a program into the computer, we should ask for a listing every now and then. If a mistake is made—such as typing two instructions without pressing the ENTER key after each—the mistake could be apparent when the program is listed.

Example 1

The instructions in a program can be entered in any order. Let's assume that the following instructions have been typed at the keyboard and the ENTER key has been pressed after each instruction. (Notice that line 15 has been entered after line 20.)

```
10 LET QUANTITY = 40
20 PRINT SUBTTL
15 LET SUBTTL = QUANTITY + 12
```

We can display the instructions that have been stored in memory by typing the command LIST.

```
LIST
10 LET QUANTITY = 40
15 LET SUBTTL = QUANTITY + 12
20 PRINT SUBTTL
```

The computer lists the lines of this program in line-number sequence. Even though line 15 was entered after line 20, it was inserted in its proper sequence in memory. By occasionally listing the lines entered, we can ensure that the computer is receiving what we're sending.

Example 2

Assuming that the program above is still in memory, we could direct the computer to display a single line from the program—line 10, for instance.

```
LIST 10
10 LET QUANTITY = 40
```

Example 3

In one form of the LIST command, we can specify a range of lines. The computer will display all lines in the range including the lines specified. For example:

```
LIST 4-15
10 LET QUANTITY = 40
15 LET SUBTTL = QUANTITY + 12
```

Since there are only two lines in the program within the range of lines 4 to 15, these are displayed.

Example 4

If we request a listing of a line number not in the program, nothing will be displayed.

```
LIST 12

—
```

Nothing appears because no line 12 exists in the program used in this example.

If we request a listing of a range of lines not in the program, nothing will be listed.

```
LIST 16-19

—
```

There are no lines in this program with numbers from 16 to 19, so nothing is displayed.

INSERTING, ERASING, AND CHANGING LINES

Line numbers are used to control the inserting, erasing, and changing of lines.

In the process of entering a program, it may be necessary to insert a line, change or correct a line, or erase a line from the program.

We can insert an instruction into a program by assigning it a line number between two other line numbers. Since lines are stored in line-number order, the instruction will be inserted in proper sequence when the ENTER key is pressed.

To correct or change a line, simply retype the line using the same line number as before. The computer cannot have two instructions with the same line number; when a line is retyped, the computer erases the old line and stores the new line in its place.

To erase a line from a program, type the line number only and press the ENTER key. A line with no instruction on it is not saved in memory. If there is already a line in memory with that number, that line is erased.

Example 1

Assume we have entered the following instructions:

```
40 LET CITY$ = "DULUTH"
60 PRINT CITY$, ST$
```

We discover we have omitted an instruction at line 50 to assign a string value to the string variable ST$, so we now enter line 50.

```
50 LET ST$ = "MINNESOTA"
```

When this program is listed, we see that line 50 has been properly inserted after line 40 and before line 60.

```
LIST
40 LET CITY$ = "DULUTH"
50 LET ST$ = "MINNESOTA"
60 PRINT CITY$, ST$
```

Example 2

Using our previous example, let's assume that, after listing the program, we discovered a typographical error on line 40.

```
LIST
40 LET CUTY$ = "DULUTH"
50 LET ST$ = "MINNESOTA"
60 PRINT CITY$, ST$
```

This typographical error must be corrected, so we retype line 40.

40 LET CITY$ = "DULUTH"

When the program is listed again, we see the old line 40 is erased from memory, and the new line 40 stored in its place.

```
LIST
40 LET CITY$ = "DULUTH"
50 LET ST$ = "MINNESOTA"
60 PRINT CITY$, ST$
```

To avoid having to retype a line because of a typographical error, always check the line before pressing the ENTER key. It is possible to back up and correct a mistake before pressing the ENTER key. After ENTER is pressed, the instruction is stored in memory, and the only way to change it is to type the line over again.

Example 3

Let's assume that we had typed in the following program, but on line 30 we had accidentally used the letter O instead of zero for the number 30. (Note the slight difference between the letter "O" and the digit "0".)

```
10 LET PRICE = 2.59
20 LET QUANTITY = 5
30 LET SALE = PRICE * QUANTITY
40 PRINT SALE
```

After listing the program, this mistake is obvious.

```
LIST
3 O LET SALE = PRICE * QUANTITY
10 LET PRICE = 2.59
20 LET QUANTITY = 5
40 PRINT SALE
```

Because the letter O was typed instead of zero, the computer has stored the instruction as line number 3. We now have two problems. There is a line 3 to be erased, and a line 30 to be inserted. To erase line 3, we simply type 3 and press the ENTER key. If we LIST the program after doing this, we see:

```
3
LIST
10 LET PRICE = 2.59
20 LET QUANTITY = 5
40 PRINT SALE
```

Line 3 has been erased by entering only the line number. Line 30 can now be added to the program by typing it with its correct line number. After making this correction, we LIST the program to verify that it is now correct.

```
30 LET SALE = PRICE * QUANTITY
LIST
10 LET PRICE = 2.59
20 LET QUANTITY = 5
30 LET SALE = PRICE * QUANTITY
40 PRINT SALE
```

TEST YOUR UNDERSTANDING

13. What happens when you type the command LIST and press the ENTER key?

14. Write the command to display line 45 of a program. Also write the command to display lines 20 through 80 of a program.

15. Assume that the following program has been entered into the computer.

```
10 LET MILES = 700
20 LET SPD = 55
30 PRINT "MILES ="; MILES
40 PRINT "SPEED ="; SPD
50 PRINT "TRAVEL TIME ="; MILES / SPD
```

a. What would you type at the keyboard to change the instruction on line 20 to:

```
LET SPD = 60
```

b. What would you type to erase line 30?

c. What would you type to insert the following instruction between line 20 and line 30?

```
PRINT "TRAVEL TIME CALCULATOR"
```

Section 5. Saving a Program for Future Use

INTRODUCTION

It is necessary to save programs somewhere outside the computer's memory; when the computer is turned off, its memory is erased. Also, the computer will hold in its memory only one BASIC program at a time. If you transfer a program from a diskette into the computer's memory, the program that was in memory is erased and the new program takes its place.

In order to save a program for future use, we must have a way to transfer the program to a diskette, and to get the program back when we want to use it.

This section introduces the BASIC commands which direct the computer to store a program on diskette, to erase a program from memory, and to read a program from diskette back into memory.

This section has four parts:

- The SAVE Command
- The NEW Command
- The LOAD Command
- The RUN filename Command

THE SAVE COMMAND

The SAVE command causes the computer to transfer a program from memory to a diskette.

The word SAVE is a Disk Operating System (DOS) command recognized in BASIC. The general format of the SAVE command is:

SAVE filename

A program stored on a diskette is considered to be a "file"; thus, the name you give your program is a "filename." Each program saved on the diskette must be given a unique name so the computer can find it when you need it.

When you type the word SAVE followed by a name created for your program, the computer transfers to the diskette a copy of whatever BASIC program is currently in memory. The program is stored under the name given in the command.

The precise rules for forming filenames vary among computers, but typical restrictions involve maximum length, permissible first characters, and the use of special characters. Consult the BASIC reference manual for your computer to determine rules for forming filenames.

Note: On some computers, filenames must always be enclosed in quotation marks. For the purposes of illustration, this rule is assumed in the following examples.

Example

Let's assume the following command is typed at the keyboard:

SAVE "PROBLEM1"

When the ENTER key is pressed, the computer transfers to the diskette a copy of whatever BASIC program is in memory. The filename "PROBLEM1" is assigned to the program on the diskette.

If you use a filename already on the diskette, the old program on the diskette is erased, and a copy of the program in memory is stored in its place. Be careful not to use the same filename for two different programs, unless you intend to replace the old program with a new version.

Every so often you can save whatever part of the program you have entered. The program does not have to be complete to be saved. Each time you save the program (using the same filename in every case), the previous version of the program is erased and the current version is stored in its place.

It's a good idea to use the SAVE command frequently when you are entering a program. Accidents may occur to erase your program from memory. If you have already saved part of the program when this happens, you will be able to get that part back from the diskette. If you have not saved anything, you will have to retype all the instructions that were erased.

Think of this another way: if a program is accidentally erased, but you had been saving every hour, you might have an hour's worth of work to do over. If you had been saving every five minutes, you will have only five minutes worth of work to re-do.

THE NEW COMMAND

The NEW command erases whatever BASIC program is in memory.

Let's say that you have entered a program, and you have saved that program on a diskette. Since the program is now safely stored on diskette, you can erase the program from memory.

The command to erase a BASIC program from memory is NEW. When you type the word NEW and press the ENTER key, whatever BASIC program is in memory is erased. Be sure you have saved the program on diskette before erasing it from memory.

It is important to erase an old program from memory before you try to type in a new program. If you don't, the computer considers any new lines you type to be additions or changes to the old program currently in memory. You will end up with a program that is a combination of old and new program lines. To avoid this, always type NEW before you start to enter a new BASIC program.

Example

In this example, we have entered a three-line program, then listed and saved it. This sequence of events appears as follows.

```
70 LET PRICE = 17.89
80 LET DISCOUNT = PRICE * .10
90 PRINT DISCOUNT
LIST
70 LET PRICE = 17.89
80 LET DISCOUNT = PRICE * .10
```

```
90 PRINT DISCOUNT
SAVE "DISCOUNT"
```

When the program is saved, a *copy* is transferred to the diskette. The program itself is not removed from memory. We can show this by again listing the program after it has been saved.

```
LIST
70 LET PRICE = 17.89
80 LET DISCOUNT = PRICE * .10
90 PRINT DISCOUNT
```

Since a copy of the program has been stored on diskette, we can erase it from memory. After typing NEW and pressing the ENTER key, we try to list the program. Since the program has been erased from memory by the NEW command, the LIST comes up empty. There is no longer any program in memory to list.

```
NEW
LIST
```

THE LOAD COMMAND

The LOAD command causes a program to be transferred from a diskette into the computer's memory.

The word LOAD is a DOS command that is recognized in BASIC. The general format of the LOAD command is:

LOAD filename

When the LOAD command is executed, the computer locates the specified program file on the diskette, then transfers a copy of that program into memory. Whatever BASIC program is currently in memory is erased and replaced by the program being loaded.

A program can be loaded only if it has been previously saved on the diskette. If the filename in the LOAD command does not correspond exactly to the name given when the program was saved, the program file will not be found. This may cause an error message to be displayed, such as FILE NOT FOUND.

Example 1

Let's assume that we want to retrieve a program we had worked on yesterday. We saved it to the diskette using the filename "CHAP3". Now we must load it from the diskette back into memory.

LOAD "CHAP3"

The LOAD command causes the computer to search the diskette for the file "CHAP3", then transfer a copy of that file into memory.

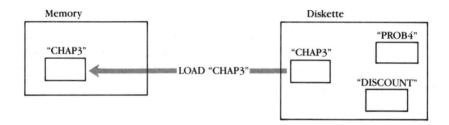

Example 2

After a program is loaded, it's in the computer's memory. In order to see the program, you must list it after it has been loaded.

```
LOAD "DISCOUNT"
LIST
70 LET PRICE = 17.89
80 LET DISCOUNT = PRICE * .10
90 PRINT DISCOUNT
```

THE RUN FILENAME COMMAND

A program can be loaded from the diskette and executed by typing the command RUN and the name of the program.

The BASIC command RUN causes the computer to begin executing the instructions of whatever BASIC program is currently in memory. A variation of the RUN command is the RUN filename command.

RUN filename

This command directs the computer to locate the specified program file on the diskette, load the program into memory, and begin executing the instructions in that program. If the specified file cannot be located on the diskette, then an error message is displayed, such as FILE NOT FOUND.

Example

The RUN filename command performs the same function as the two commands LOAD filename and RUN. For instance, the command

RUN "CHAPT3"

produces the same result as these two commands:

LOAD "CHAPT3"
RUN

TEST YOUR UNDERSTANDING

16. Assume you have written and entered a program. You now wish to save this program using the filename "SALESAVG", then begin entering a new program. What commands would you use to save the program to the diskette, then erase it from memory?

17. Write the command you would use to run a program named "MORTGAGE" currently on the diskette.

18. Write the commands you would use to load a program named "TAXRATES", list it, run it, then save it under a new name, "TAXPROG".

19. If after entering a program, you type the following commands,

    SAVE "CH3PROB"
    NEW
    SAVE "CH3PROB"

what would finally be stored on the diskette under the name "CH3PROB" ?

20. What would be the result if you typed the following commands after entering a program?

    SAVE "INTRATE1"
    SAVE "INTRATE2"

21. If the following commands are entered, what program will be executed?

```
LOAD  "DISCOUNT"
LOAD  "MORTGAGE"
LOAD  "INTRATE1"
RUN
```

Section 6. Making Programs Understandable

INTRODUCTION

Programming can be exciting; it allows us to control the power of the computer. In our headlong rush to exercise this control, however, we often overlook the cardinal rule of programming: *make programs understandable*.

It is all too easy to write a program giving the correct solution to a problem, but which cannot be understood by others. Even the person who writes the program can have difficulty understanding it after not using it for a few weeks.

Before we advance to the actual writing of programs, we must understand the essential techniques for writing programs other people can read and understand. Those techniques and their importance are presented in this section.

This section has three parts:

- The Importance of Readability
- Using Variable Names That Have Meaning
- The REM Statement

THE IMPORTANCE OF READABILITY

A readable program saves us time in testing and maintaining that program.

A program written for a business application will often remain in use for years. As changes occur in the business environment, changes must be made to the program. If that program is not easy to read and understand, such changes can be difficult and time-consuming.

Often, the person who wrote the program is no longer around when changes must be made. If the program cannot be understood by others, it may prove too difficult to modify. In this situation, the program could be abandoned; it is no longer useful as it is, and it would be too expensive to alter.

Making a program understandable also simplifies its testing. If an error exists in the program, the error will be easier to locate and correct if the program is readable. This fact alone should be enough incentive to write programs we can easily read and understand.

USING VARIABLE NAMES THAT HAVE MEANING

One technique for making a program readable is to use variable names describing what the variable represents.

The simplest technique for making programs understandable is to choose variable names with meaning. Because of all the rules for forming variable names, many people take the simple way out by using only one- and two-letter variable names. The question then arises, "What does this stand for?"

Using a name describing what the variable stands for makes it easier to follow what the program is doing. If changes must be made to the program, it is easier to locate where the changes must be made.

Similarly, a numeric constant in a program can be given a name. Whenever that value is needed in a calculation, it can be referred to by its name. This makes it easier to understand what the calculation does, and makes it easier to change the value of the constant, if necessary.

Example 1

Here we illustrate portions of two programs that perform exactly the same function. Compare these program segments and decide for yourself which is more understandable.

```
Program A    210 LET DA = 30
             220 LET T = D1 + D2 + D3
             230 LET A = T / DA
             240 PRINT A

Program B    210 LET DAYS = 30
             220 LET TTLSALES = D1SALES + D2SALES + D3SALES
             230 LET AVERAGE = TTLSALES / DAYS
             240 PRINT AVERAGE
```

Example 2

The following segment is from a program which computes the average number of units sold, the average amount of sales, and the average pay for a department with 14 salesmen. The number 14 is a literal in this program.

```
Program A   130 LET UNITAVERAGE = NMBERTTL / 14
            140 LET AMOUNTAVERAGE = SALESTTL / 14
            150 LET AVERAGEPAY = TTLPAYROLL / 14
            160 PRINT UNITAVERAGE, AMOUNTAVERAGE, AVERAGEPAY
```

This next program segment performs the same function, but the literal 14 has been assigned to a variable name. The variable name is then used in each of the calculations.

```
Program B   125 LET NUMSALESMEN = 14
            130 LET UNITAVERAGE = NMBERTTL / NUMSALESMEN
            140 LET AMOUNTAVERAGE = SALESTTL / NUMSALESMEN
            150 LET AVERAGEPAY = TTLPAYROLL / NUMSALESMEN
            160 PRINT UNITAVERAGE, AMOUNTAVERAGE, AVERAGEPAY
```

The department has just hired a new salesman, so the number changes to 15. Which of the two programs above would be easier to alter? In Program A, the literal 14 would have to be changed to 15 in three separate places. In Program B, the literal 14 needs to be changed in only one place.

Which of the two programs is easier to understand? In Program A, 14 does not tell us much about what it stands for. In Program B, the variable name tells us exactly what the number stands for. By using that name in the calculation, the purpose of the calculation is clearer. If it is necessary to change the number of salesmen, it will also be easier to find where the change must be made.

THE REM STATEMENT

We can make a program more understandable by using the REM statement to insert remarks in a program listing.

The most valuable technique for making a program understandable is to use REM statements. The keyword REM stands for *remark*. The general format of the REM statement is:

REM programmer's comments

After the keyword REM, you may write anything you wish. REM is a signal to the BASIC Interpreter to ignore what follows. Since the BASIC Interpreter ignores everything that follows the word REM, you are free to write any comments you like to explain the program.

When the program is run, all REM statements are ignored. REM statements are comments for people, not instructions for the computer. REM statements appear only in the program listing. Anyone trying to read and understand your program can see these comments in the listing.

Example 1

Compare the following programs and decide which is more understandable.

```
Program A    10 LET PRINCIPAL = 1000
             20 LET PERCENT = .06
             30 LET TIME = 20
             40 LET NTEREST = PRINCIPAL * PERCENT * TIME
             50 PRINT NTEREST
```

```
Program B    10 REM THIS PROGRAM COMPUTES THE SIMPLE INTEREST
             20 REM ON A $1000 BOND AT 6%, FOR 20 YEARS,
             30 REM USING THE FORMULA :
             40 REM INTEREST = PRINCIPAL * RATE * TIME
             50 LET PRINCIPAL = 1000
             60 LET PERCENT = .06
             70 LET TIME = 20
             80 LET NTEREST = PRINCIPAL * PERCENT * TIME
             90 PRINT NTEREST
```

Example 2

Earlier in this chapter, we mentioned that more than one instruction can be written on a single line by placing a colon (:) between the instructions. Because of the difficulties this can cause for the novice programmer, we will always place each instruction on a separate line, *with one exception*.

When useful for clarifying an instruction, a REM statement may be included on the same line as another instruction. A REM statement is a valid BASIC statement, so it must be separated from the first instruction by a colon. This use of the REM statement is illustrated below.

```
20 LET PRINCIPAL = 1000 : REM $1000 BOND
```

TEST YOUR UNDERSTANDING

22. Create variable names for storing values which represent the name of a company, the number of employees in the sales department, and the number of employees in manufacturing. Try to make these names understandable.

23. Following the examples in this chapter, write a program which assigns values to each of these variables, then prints the value of each variable. Make up your own values to use in the program. Use REM statements to explain what your program does.

24. Create your own filename and write the command to save this program onto a diskette.

25. Write the command to cause this program to be loaded from the diskette and executed.

ANSWERS TO "TEST YOUR UNDERSTANDING" EXERCISES

1. PRINT (keyword); 14 (numeric literal); * (symbol); AMOUNT (variable name).
2. LET (keyword); AMOUNT (variable name); = (symbol); QTY (variable name); * (symbol); CST (variable name).
3. INPUT (keyword); "WHAT IS YOUR CHOICE" (string literal); the semicolon (punctuation); CH$ (variable name).
4. FOR (keyword); DIGITS (variable name); = (symbol); 1 (numeric literal); TO (keyword); 10 (numeric literal).
5. IF (keyword); SALE (variable name); > (symbol); 100 (numeric literal); THEN (keyword); PRINT (keyword); "DISCOUNT APPLIES" (string literal).
6. numeric value; string (or sequence) of characters.
7. String variable names—CITY$, AD$, CHOICE$, SIZE$; numeric variable names—QTY, AMT, CLASS, WEIGHT, X, RTE.
8. Invalid on most computers—2NDITEM, ACCT#1, MILE-PER-HOUR, SALES TAX.
9. SHIFT (IF), suggest SHFT ; TOLL (TO), suggest TLL ; LETTER$ (LET), suggest LTR$; MONTH$ (ON), suggest MNTH$; SHORTAGE (OR), suggest SHRTAGE ; STANDARD (AND), suggest STNDARD.
10. A statement which is stored in memory begins with a number.
11. RUN

12. computer program
13. The computer displays all instructions currently in memory.
14. `LIST 45` ; `LIST 20-80`
15a. `20 LET SPD = 60`
15b. `30`
15c. `25 PRINT "TRAVEL TIME CALCULATOR"` (Note: any line number from 21 through 29 is correct.)
16. `SAVE "SALESAVG"`
    `NEW`
17. `RUN "MORTGAGE"`
18. `LOAD "TAXRATES"`
    `LIST`
    `RUN`
    `SAVE "TAXPROG"`
19. The program file would be on the diskette, but it would contain nothing. The NEW command erases memory, then the SAVE command saves an empty file in place of the previous one.
20. You would have the same program stored on the diskette twice; once under the filename `"INTRATE1"`, once under the filename `"INTRATE2"`.
21. The program currently in memory (i.e., the last one loaded—`"INTRATE1"`) would be executed.
22. Suggested—COMPANY$, SALESPERSNEL, MANUPERSNEL.
23. Sample solution:

```
10 REM ASSIGN VALUES TO VARIABLES
20 LET COMPANY$ = "ACME MFG. CO." : REM COMPANY NAME
30 LET SALESPERSNEL = 24 : REM SALES PERSONNEL
40 LET MANUPERSNEL = 135 : REM MANUFACTURING PERSONNEL
50 REM PRINT VALUE OF EACH VARIABLE
60 PRINT COMPANY$
70 PRINT SALESPERSNEL
80 PRINT MANUPERSNEL
```

24. Sample solution: `SAVE "SAMPLE"`
25. Sample solution: `RUN "SAMPLE"`

    or `LOAD "SAMPLE"`
        `RUN`

CHAPTER 3

Getting Results with BASIC

CHAPTER OBJECTIVE

To describe the rules and symbols used in performing calculations, and the methods for getting data into a program and obtaining results from a program.

PROBLEM

Your company is about to introduce a new product for which it must establish a selling price. In setting a price, the marketing director considers the breakeven point, which is the minimum number of units that must be sold for profits to cover overhead costs. To determine the breakeven point at a given price, first calculate the unit profit by subtracting unit cost from selling price. The breakeven point is found by dividing the unit profit into the overhead costs, which for this product total $10,000.

To help him set a price for the product, the marketing director has asked you to write a program to prepare a breakeven analysis—a list of breakeven points computed for each of several prices within a given price range.

CHAPTER OVERVIEW

Writing a program to perform a breakeven analysis requires an understanding of several elementary concepts commonly used to solve many business problems. This chapter introduces these concepts beginning with the most fundamental rules for performing arithmetic on a computer and advancing to the technique for performing repetitive calculations.

In this chapter, you will learn how to write a BASIC program to obtain data, perform calculations, and present results. These techniques are all brought together into one program that solves the breakeven analysis problem.

This chapter has seven sections:

- **The Rules for Making Calculations**
- **Getting Immediate Results from the Computer**
- **Getting Results from a Computer Program**
- **Formatting Numeric Output**
- **Getting Data Into a Program**
- **Performing Repetitive Calculations**
- **The Breakeven Analysis Program**

Section 1. The Rules for Making Calculations

INTRODUCTION

Solving problems with a computer very often involves some type of arithmetic. When the computer performs calculations, it follows a very specific set of rules called "the hierarchy of operations." It is important to understand this hierarchy of operations so that a calculation is represented correctly in a BASIC instruction. Otherwise, the computer may be instructed to make a calculation in a sequence different from what we intended.

This section has three parts:

- The Arithmetic Operators
- The Hierarchy of Operations
- Using Parentheses to Alter the Order of Operations

THE ARITHMETIC OPERATORS

The arithmetic operators are the symbols we use to instruct the computer to perform calculations.

In BASIC, five symbols are used for the arithmetic operations of addition, subtraction, multiplication, division and exponentiation. These symbols are used in writing BASIC instructions to perform calculations.

+	Addition
−	Subtraction
*	Multiplication
/	Division
∧	Exponentiation

Note: The symbol used for exponentiation may vary from computer to computer.

Example 1

The addition of two or more values can be expressed:

```
19 + 45 + 17 + 5
COUNT + 1
PRICE + TAX + DELIVERY
```

Example 2

The subtraction of one value from another can be expressed:

```
44 - 17
INVENTRY - 12
PRICE - CST
```

Example 3

The multiplication of two or more values can be expressed:

```
60 * 24 * 7 * 52
PURCHASE * .06
LNGTH * WIDTH * HEIGHT
```

Example 4

The division of one value by another can be expressed:

```
64 / 16
INCHES / 12
OVERHEAD / PROFIT
```

Example 5

Exponentiation (raising a number to a power) can be expressed:

```
5 ^ 2             (5 * 5) or (5 squared)
LNGTH ^ 3         (LNGTH * LNGTH * LNGTH)
                     or (LNGTH cubed)
NTEREST ^ YEARS   (NTEREST raised to the
                        power YEARS)
```

THE HIERARCHY OF OPERATIONS

When several arithmetic symbols are used in a single expression, the operations are performed in a specific sequence determined by the hierarchy of operations.

This hierarchy is summarized in the following rules:

RULE 1—All exponentiation (^) is performed before any other operation. When more than one exponentiation symbol is present, the computer performs each exponentiation in order from left to right.

RULE 2—All multiplication and division (*, /) are performed before addition and subtraction. These operations are considered equal in importance and are performed in order from left to right.

RULE 3—Addition and subtraction (+,−) are performed last. They are also considered equal in importance and are performed in order from left to right.

Example 1

To demonstrate the hierarchy of operations, the following expression is evaluated:

7 + 18 / 3 ^ 2 - 5

Exponentiation is performed first (Rule 1):

7 + 18 / <u>3 ^ 2</u> - 5
7 + 18 /   9   - 5

Multiplication and division are performed before addition and subtraction (Rule 2):

7 + <u>18 / 9</u> - 5
7 +   2   - 5

Addition and subtraction are performed last. They are performed in the order they appear, from left to right (Rule 3):

<u>7 + 2</u> - 5
 <u>9   - 5</u>
   4

Therefore, the value of the original expression is 4.

Example 2

The following expression is evaluated:

9 + 4 * 6 / 3 - 2

There is no exponentiation, so multiplication and division are performed in the order they appear (Rule 2):

9 + <u>4 * 6</u> / 3 - 2
9 + <u>24 / 3</u> - 2
9 +   8   - 2

Addition and subtraction are performed last (Rule 3):

$$
\begin{array}{r}
\underline{9\ +\ 8}\ -\ 2 \\
\underline{17\ -\ 2} \\
15
\end{array}
$$

Therefore, the value of the expression is 15.

Counterexample 3

Let us assume that in example 2 above, we had intended for the computer to divide 3 into $(9 + 4 * 6)$, then subtract 2. Since $(9 + 4 * 6) = 9 + 24 = 33$, then 33 divided by 3 gives us 11, and $11 - 2$ is 9. This is not the result obtained in Example 2. Because the computer strictly follows the rules of the hierarchy of operations, its result is not what we expected or intended.

USING PARENTHESES TO ALTER THE ORDER OF OPERATIONS

When we wish the operations to be performed in an order that is different from the hierarchy of operations, parentheses must be used.

An expression which contains parentheses is evaluated according to the following rules:

RULE 4—When parentheses are present in an expression, all operations inside the parentheses are performed before any others. Within parentheses, the operations are performed in the order of the hierarchy of operations (Rules 1–3).

RULE 5—When more than one set of parentheses is present in an expression, the computer evaluates the expressions inside each set of parentheses, proceeding from left to right, before performing the operations outside the parentheses.

RULE 6—When one set of parentheses is inside another set, the expression in the innermost set is evaluated first.

Example 1

We have rewritten the expression from the previous example. Now it is evaluated beginning with the operations contained in parentheses (Rule 4):

$(9\ +\ 4\ *\ 6)\ /\ 3\ -\ 2$

Inside the parentheses, the hierarchy of operations is followed (Rule 4):

```
(9  +  4 * 6)  /  3  -  2
(9  +   24   )  /  3  -  2       (Multiplication before addition—Rule 2)
        33        /   3  -  2
```

Now that all operations inside the parentheses have been performed, the remaining operations may be performed.

```
33 / 3  -  2       (Division before subtraction—Rule 2)
   11   - 2
        9
```

The value of the expression is 9.

Example 2

The following expression is evaluated beginning with the operations in the leftmost set of parentheses (Rule 5):

```
43  -   (7 + 2) *  (8  -  5)
43  -      9    *  (8  -  5)
```

Proceeding from left to right, the expression in the next set of parentheses is then evaluated (Rule 5):

```
43  - 9   *   (8  -  5)
43  - 9   *        3
```

After all expressions in parentheses have been evaluated, the remaining operations are performed:

```
43  -  9 * 3       (Multiplication before subtraction—Rule 2)
43  -   27
      16
```

The value of this expression is 16.

Example 3

This next expression is evaluated beginning with the operation contained in the innermost set of parentheses (Rule 6):

```
( (7 + 1) / 2 ) ^ 2 / 8
(    8    / 2 ) ^ 2 / 8
```

The operation inside the remaining set of parentheses is performed before any operations outside the parentheses (Rule 4):

```
( 8 / 2 ) ^ 2 / 8
    4     ^ 2 / 8
```

The remaining operations are now performed according to the hierarchy of operations:

```
4 ^ 2 / 8     (Exponentiation is performed first—Rule 1)
  16 / 8
    2
```

The value of the original expression is 2.

TEST YOUR UNDERSTANDING

1. Evaluate each of the following expressions:
   a. `(7 + 4) * (3 + 1) / 2`
   b. `7 + (4 * 3 + 1) / 2`
   c. `3 + 4 ^ 2 - 1 * 8 / 4`
   d. `(3 + 4 ^ 2 - 1) * 8 / 4`

2. Write an arithmetic expression for each of the following calculations:
   a. Multiply 6 times 5, add 2, then divide the result by 8.
   b. Subtract 5 from 7, square the result, then add the product of 3 multiplied by 5.

3. Write an arithmetic expression for each of the following calculations using variable names in place of numeric values:
   a. Add CST, DELIVERY, and MARKUP, then divide the result by QUANTITY.
   b. Multiply PARTS times TAX, add PARTS and LABOR to the result, then multiply the total by PCTDOWN.

Section 2. Getting Immediate Results from the Computer

INTRODUCTION

Now that you know how the computer handles calculations, we can demonstrate the BASIC statements that cause the computer to perform a calculation and display the result. This section introduces those statements and a method for displaying messages to accompany the results.

This section has three parts:

- The PRINT arithmetic Statement
- The PRINT string Statement
- Using the Semicolon in a PRINT Statement

THE PRINT ARITHMETIC STATEMENT

The keyword PRINT followed by an arithmetic expression causes the computer to evaluate the expression and print the result.

The word PRINT is a keyword in BASIC. When PRINT is followed by an arithmetic expression, the computer evaluates the expression and prints the result on the output device currently being used. In this text, we assume that the output device is a video monitor, and all results are printed on its screen.

NOTE: On many computers, one blank space is printed immediately before a positive numeric value. If a value is negative, the negative sign is printed in this space. This is the format in which output is shown in this text. If your computer does not print a blank space before the positive numeric value, take this into consideration when comparing your output to that in the examples.

Example 1

Assume you earn $5.20 per hour and have worked 32 hours this week. You want to know what you have earned for the week. If you type the following BASIC statement in the immediate mode (without a line number),

```
PRINT 5.20 * 32
```

and then press the ENTER key, the computer prints:

```
 166.4
```

Example 2

Assume you have just placed an order for 27 dozen personalized pencils at $6.50 per dozen and three cases of paper at $20.97 per case. You want to know the total of your order. If you type the following BASIC statement:

```
PRINT (27 * 6.50) + (3 * 20.97)
```

and then press the ENTER key, the computer prints:

```
 238.41
```

which is the value of the arithmetic expression.

THE PRINT STRING STATEMENT

When PRINT is followed by a string enclosed in quotes, the computer prints the characters appearing between the quotes.

PRINT can be used to display messages as well as the results of calculations. When the word PRINT is followed by characters enclosed in quote marks, the characters are displayed on the screen. The computer does not attempt to interpret what is inside the quotes; it merely duplicates the string on a character-by-character basis.

Example 1

When this BASIC statement is executed,

```
PRINT "BREAKEVEN ANALYSIS FOR PRODUCT X"
```

the message inside the quotation marks is duplicated on the screen:

```
BREAKEVEN ANALYSIS FOR PRODUCT X
```

Example 2

When this BASIC statement is executed,

PRINT "(27 * 6.50) + (3 * 20.97)"

the message contained in the quotes is displayed:

(27 * 6.50) + (3 * 20.97)

Notice the computer does not attempt to evaluate the expression. Since the expression is enclosed in quotation marks, it is treated as just another string of characters to be duplicated on the screen.

USING THE SEMICOLON IN A PRINT STATEMENT

We can include more than one item in a single PRINT statement, and separate the items with a semicolon. The semicolon causes the items to be printed one after the other on the same line.

Example 1

Executing the following BASIC statement,

PRINT "$"; 5.20 * 32

causes the computer to print:

$ 166.4

In this example, we have printed two items using one PRINT statement. The first item is a string containing one character, the dollar sign, inside the quote marks. The second is an arithmetic expression, 5.20 * 32, which the computer evaluates as 166.4. These two items are separated by a semi-colon in the PRINT statement, causing them to be printed one after the other. The space between the two items is the space reserved for a potential negative sign in the numeric result.

Example 2

When the following BASIC statement is executed,

PRINT "THE TOTAL IS $"; 17 * 3.99; " FOR YOUR ORDER"

the computer prints:

THE TOTAL IS $ 67.83 FOR YOUR ORDER

Three items are printed in this example. The first and last items are strings enclosed in quotes. The middle item is an arithmetic expression evaluated as 67.83. Again, each item is separated from the others by a semicolon in the PRINT statement, causing them to be printed one after the other. The space that appears between 67.83 and FOR is the first character in the second string literal.

TEST YOUR UNDERSTANDING

4. Write a PRINT statement to compute and print the average of 256, 325, 119, and 200.

5. Assume that this month you charged a total of $38.00 on your charge account, then made a payment of $27.00. The previous balance of your account was $187.00. Write a PRINT statement to compute the new balance and print the result with the accompanying message, NEW BALANCE IS $.

6. Assume you own 17 ounces of gold, the current market value of which is $512.70 per ounce. To sell this gold, you will have to pay a 3% broker's commission. Write a PRINT statement to compute the value of the gold and the amount you would have to pay the broker. The result is to be printed in the following format:

VALUE OF GOLD IS $ _____ LESS $ _____ COMMISSION

Section 3. Getting Results from a Computer Program

INTRODUCTION

The previous examples demonstrated the use of BASIC instructions in the immediate mode, in which an instruction is executed immediately after it is entered—very useful for getting quick results from simple calculations. The solution of many problems, however, requires more than a few instructions. In these cases, a program is needed.

The only difference between an instruction executed immediately and one that becomes part of a program is the presence of a line number. When a number appears at the beginning of an instruction, the computer does not execute the instruction immediately. Instead, the instruction is stored in the computer's memory. Many instructions may be written by the programmer and stored by the computer.

When the BASIC command RUN is given, the computer begins to execute the instructions currently in memory, beginning with the lowest numbered line and continuing to the highest numbered line. This section demonstrates the elementary techniques for obtaining output from a BASIC program.

This section has three parts:

- The PRINT variable Statement
- Using the Comma in a PRINT Statement
- PRINTing a Blank Line

THE PRINT VARIABLE STATEMENT

The keyword PRINT followed by a variable name causes the computer to print the value currently being stored under that variable name.

Example 1

Let's assume that the following two-line program has been entered into the computer:

```
10 LET PROFIT = 3.59 - 2.45
20 PRINT PROFIT
```

When the command RUN is typed and the ENTER key is pressed, the computer executes the instructions in the program beginning with line 10. This LET...= statement causes the computer to subtract 2.45 from 3.59 and store the result of 1.14 under the variable name PROFIT.

The next instruction in sequence, line 20, is a PRINT statement; the computer prints the value currently stored under the variable name PROFIT.

The command to begin executing the program and its output are shown below:

```
RUN
 1.14
```

Example 2

Assume the program from the previous example has been erased (using the NEW command) and a new program is entered.

```
NEW
40 LET TITLE$ = "WAR AND PEACE"
80 PRINT TITLE$
```

The first statement instructs the computer to store the characters WAR AND PEACE under the variable name TITLE$. The second statement then instructs the computer to print the value currently stored under TITLE$.

The result of running this program is:

```
RUN
WAR AND PEACE
```

USING THE COMMA IN A PRINT STATEMENT

Instead of a semicolon, we can use a comma to separate the items in a PRINT statement. This causes the items to be printed in predetermined positions in the line, referred to as "print zones."

In BASIC, an output line is divided into "print zones," the number and size of which vary from computer to computer. For discussion purposes, we shall assume that there are 5 zones in an 80-character line, and that each zone is 16 characters wide, as illustrated below.

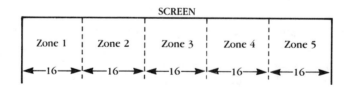

We can cause items to be printed in these zones by using a comma, instead of a semicolon, to separate the items. When the comma is encountered in a PRINT statement, the computer advances to the beginning of the next print zone before printing the item that follows the comma.

Example 1

Assume the following program has been entered:

```
20 LET PROFIT = 4.45 - 2.45
40 LET BREAKEVEN = 10000 / PROFIT
60 PRINT BREAKEVEN, PROFIT
```

If the RUN command is entered, these instructions are executed in sequence. The computer first subtracts 2.45 from 4.45 and stores the result of 2.00 under the variable name PROFIT. Then the computer divides 10000 by the current value of PROFIT (2.00) and stores the result (5000) under the variable name BREAKEVEN.

Finally, the statement on line 60 instructs the computer to print the current values of BREAKEVEN and PROFIT. Since a comma appears after BREAKEVEN, the computer advances to the next print zone before printing the current value of PROFIT.

The result of running this program is shown below.

```
RUN
  5000            2
```

The large space between the printed items is the result of using the comma in the PRINT statement, causing the second item to be printed in the next print zone. Notice also that in BASIC, trailing zeros after the decimal point are not shown when a numeric value is printed.

Example 2

The following simple program is used to further illustrate the effect of the comma in a PRINT statement.

```
LIST
10 LET W1SALES = 1245.70
20 LET W2SALES = 1023.85
30 PRINT "LAST TWO WEEKS' SALES =", W1SALES, W2SALES
```

The first two lines of this program assign values to the variables W1SALES, and W2SALES. Line 30 then causes three items to be printed. As each comma is encountered in the PRINT statement, the computer advances to the next print zone before printing the next item.

The output of this program is:

```
RUN
LAST TWO WEEKS' SALES =            1245.7          1023.85
```

Notice the first item printed is wider than its print zone. When the comma is encountered after this string, the computer advances to the next available print zone, which is the third zone in this case.

PRINTING A BLANK LINE

When the BASIC command PRINT is used by itself, the computer prints a blank line. We can use blank lines to improve the readability of the output.

Example

This sample program computes the breakeven point for a product and presents the results in columns with column headings.

```
10 LET SELLINGPRICE = 4.49
20 LET CSTPERITEM = 3.24
30 LET UNITPROFIT = SELLINGPRICE - CSTPERITEM
40 LET BREAKEVEN = 10000 / UNITPROFIT
50 PRINT "SELLING PRICE", "PROFIT", "BREAKEVEN"
60 PRINT
70 PRINT SELLINGPRICE, UNITPROFIT, BREAKEVEN
```

The first two lines of this program assign values to the variables SEL-LINGPRICE and CSTPERITEM. Line 30 uses these values to compute the profit per unit, and the resulting value of 1.25 is assigned to UNITPROFIT. The next line divides the overhead cost of 10000 by the current value of UNITPROFIT (1.25). The result (8000 units) is stored under the variable name BREAKEVEN.

In the PRINT statement on line 50, each of the strings is separated by commas, so they are printed in the print zones. The single word PRINT on line 60 causes a blank line to be printed. Line 70 then causes the current values of the variables SELLINGPRICE, UNITPROFIT, and BREAKEVEN to be printed. Since these variables are separated by commas, they are also printed in the print zones.

When this program is RUN, the output appears as:

```
RUN
SELLING PRICE    PROFIT           BREAKEVEN

   4.49            1.25              8000
```

TEST YOUR UNDERSTANDING

7. Create variables for storing a name and an address. Write a program which assigns your name and address to these variables, and produces output in the following format:

```
NAME:          JOHN  SMITH

ADDRESS:       404  MAIN  STREET
```

8. Rewrite the program above so that the output is produced in different format, as follows:

```
NAME            ADDRESS

JOHN  SMITH     404  MAIN  STREET
```

Section 4. Formatting Numeric Output

INTRODUCTION

When numeric data is printed, the computer displays up to 8 significant digits. This degree of accuracy is often unnecessary. In fact, when dealing with money, a value of $1.8957236 is impractical. Similarly, when calculating the distribution of 90 bicycles among 25 retail stores, the result of 3.6 bicycles per store is hardly realistic.

To make the output practical and realistic requires that we make some adjustments to the data before it is printed. This may involve the use of a function in BASIC called INT—the *integer function*. There are several techniques for formatting the output of a program which involve the INT function.

(Another method of formatting output involves the use of the PRINT USING statement. Because PRINT USING is not available in all versions of

BASIC, we will not use it in this text. Instead, we will concentrate on the uses of the more commonly available INT function.)

This section has three parts:

- The INT Function
- Rounding Off Whole Numbers
- Rounding Dollar Values

THE INT FUNCTION

The INT function converts a non-integer numeric value into the next lower integer.

The format of the INT function is:

$$INT \,(value)$$

For the value in parentheses, we may use a numeric literal, a numeric variable name, or an arithmetic expression. The INT function can be used in the same statements in which an arithmetic expression can be used. Where it appears, the INT function is evaluated as the integer portion of the value in parentheses.

Example 1

When the following BASIC statement is executed,

```
PRINT INT(3.8)
```

the computer prints:

```
3
```

Prior to being printed, the INT function is evaluated, and the printed value is the integer of 3.8.

Example 2

A specialty coffee shop has received a 50-lb. sack of imported coffee beans. The beans will be ground and packed in 12-ounce bags. The following program computes the number of 12-ounce bags that can be filled from the 50-lb. sack.

```
10 REM TOTAL OUNCES = LBS * 16 OUNCES PER LB.
20 LET OUNCES = 50 * 16
30 LET BAGS = OUNCES / 12
40 PRINT INT(BAGS); " TWELVE OUNCE BAGS"
```

When this program is RUN, the computer starts executing instructions beginning at line 10. Since this is a REMark, the computer ignores line 10 and continues to the next line.

Line 20 causes the value 50 to be multiplied by 16, and the result of 800 is stored under the variable name OUNCES. At line 30, the current value of OUNCES is divided by 12 to determine how many bags can be filled. The result (66.666667) is stored under the variable name BAGS.

Since the owner of the shop wants to know how many *full* bags he will end up with, the fractional part of the result must be dropped. In line 40, the INT function converts the current value of BAGS (66.666667) to an integer (66) before the result is printed. The output of this program is shown below:

```
RUN
 66 TWELVE OUNCE BAGS
```

ROUNDING OFF WHOLE NUMBERS

A value can be rounded to the nearest whole number by adding .5 to the value and taking the integer of the result.

It is often desirable to round a value rather than simply dropping the digits after the decimal. If the decimal fraction is .5 or more, we round the value up to the next whole number. This is accomplished by adding .5 to the value before taking its integer.

$$INT (value + .5)$$

Example 1

The following program computes a real estate company's average weekly sales for a four week period, with the result rounded off.

```
10 LET TTLSALES = 60 + 56 + 22 + 81
20 LET AVERAGE = TTLSALES / 4
30 PRINT "AVERAGE WEEKLY SALES ="; INT (AVERAGE + .5)
```

When this program is executed, line 10 causes the four weekly sales figures to be added, and the sum (219) is stored under the variable name TTLSALES. Line 20 causes the current value of TTLSALES to be divided by 4 and the result (54.75) stored under the variable name AVERAGE.

On line 30, a value of .5 is added to the current value of AVERAGE (54.75), giving 55.25; then the INT function is evaluated as the integer portion of that value. Thus, the average weekly sales is successfully rounded to the next higher whole number before it is printed.

The output of this program is:

```
RUN
AVERAGE WEEKLY SALES = 55
```

Example 2

This short program computes the average speed on a cross-country trip. Again, the result is to be rounded.

```
80 LET MILES = 627
90 LET HOURS = 12
100 LET MPH = MILES / HOURS
110 PRINT "AVERAGE SPEED ="; INT (MPH + .5); " M.P.H."
```

The first two statements in this program assign values to the variables MILES and HOURS. The third statement divides the value of MILES by the value of HOURS. This gives 52.25 as the value of MPH.

The last line causes .5 to be added to the value of MPH before the INT function is applied. Adding .5 to 52.25 gives 52.75, and the integer of 52.75 is 52. Therefore, the result is rounded down correctly before printing.

The RUN command and the output of this program are shown below:

```
RUN
AVERAGE SPEED = 52 M.P.H.
```

ROUNDING DOLLAR VALUES

Rounding to two decimal places is accomplished by multiplying the value by 100 *before* rounding, and then dividing by 100 *after* rounding.

When the output of a program is dollar values, we usually like the results to be rounded to the nearest penny. Thus, $1.8762 would be rounded to

$1.88, and $5.6739 would be rounded to $5.67. To do this, we multiply the value by 100 to shift the decimal two places to the right, then round off. After rounding, we divide by 100 to shift the decimal back to its proper position.

$$\text{INT} \ (\ \text{value} \ * \ 100 \ +.5) \ / \ 100$$

Example

In computing payroll deductions, an employee's gross pay is multiplied by the FICA tax rate of .067. The result must be rounded to the nearest penny. The following program demonstrates how this is done, using gross pay of $375.

```
60 LET TAX = 375 * .067
70 REM ROUND THE TAX TO THE NEAREST PENNY
80 LET TAX = INT (TAX * 100 + .5) / 100
90 PRINT "DEDUCTION = $"; TAX
```

When line 60 is executed, gross pay of 375 is multiplied by the tax rate of .067, and the result of 25.125 is assigned to the variable name TAX. The next line is a REMark statement (which the computer ignores), so execution continues to line 80 where the rounding is performed.

The expression to the right of the assignment operator (=) in line 80 is first evaluated, then the result is assigned to the variable TAX. In evaluating the expression, the operations contained in parentheses are performed first.

```
INT (25.125 * 100 + .5) / 100
INT (    2512.5    + .5) / 100    (Multiplication before addition)
```

Multiplying by 100 has shifted the decimal two places to the right before rounding. Evaluation of the expression continues by performing the remaining operation in the parentheses.

```
INT (2512.5 + .5) / 100
INT (    2513.0  ) / 100
```

The INT function is evaluated next.

```
INT (2513.0) / 100
       2513 / 100
          25.13
```

The final operation of dividing by 100 causes the decimal to be shifted back to its original position. Therefore, the value of the expression is 25.13, and it is assigned as the new value of the variable TAX. Line 90 then displays the result.

```
RUN
DEDUCTION = $ 25.13
```

Notice that the tax of $25.125 has been correctly rounded off to the nearest penny.

TEST YOUR UNDERSTANDING

9. Write a program to compute the number of 14 1/2-inch-long blocks that can be obtained from a 10-foot-long piece of lumber. Display the result with an explanatory message.

10. In an elementary school with 37 teachers, there are 1180 students. Write a program to compute the number of students per teacher, rounding the result to the nearest whole number. The output is to appear as follows:

EACH TEACHER HAS APPROXIMATELY _____ STUDENTS.

11. Assuming a property tax rate of 1.7 percent of assessed value, write a program to compute the property tax due on a building assessed at $57,385, rounding the result to the nearest penny.

Section 5. Getting Data into a Program

INTRODUCTION

The examples we have seen so far have assumed that we know the values to be used in the calculations before we write the program. Such programs are very limited in their usefulness since they only solve one specific problem. For instance, the program computing the average speed on a 627-mile trip does not work for an 800-mile trip. This program would be much more useful if it could calculate the average speed for *any* trip. The question is:

How can we write a program to perform calculations when we don't know the values to be used?

This section introduces the INPUT statement, used in a program to read data from the keyboard while the program is running.

This section has two parts:

- The INPUT Statement
- INPUT with Prompt

THE INPUT STATEMENT

We use the INPUT statement when it is necessary to enter a value into memory while a program is running.

The general format for the INPUT statement is:

INPUT variable-name

The word INPUT followed by a variable name causes the computer to print a question mark, and stop execution until someone at the keyboard enters an appropriate value. After the value is entered, it is stored under the variable name and execution of the program continues.

If a numeric variable name is used, a numeric value must be entered. Entering a non-numeric character causes an error message to be displayed, and the INPUT statement is executed again. Execution does not go beyond the INPUT statement until a numeric value is typed at the keyboard, and the ENTER key is pressed. The numeric value is then stored under the numeric variable name, and execution passes to the next statement in the program.

When entering numeric values, do *not* use a comma in the value. An INPUT statement can be written with more than one variable name (though we won't do it in this text). To enter the values for these variables when this INPUT statement is executed, we separate the values by a comma. If your INPUT statement has only one numeric variable and you enter a value that contains a comma, the computer will view your input as two values and give the message EXTRA IGNORED.

If a string variable name is used, any characters may be entered. When the ENTER key is pressed, the characters typed at the keyboard are stored under the string variable name, and execution resumes with the next statement in the program.

An INPUT statement may be used only in a program. Typing an INPUT statement without a preceding line number will give you an error message.

Example

The following program obtains values from the keyboard for destination, miles, and hours, then computes the average speed to the destination.

```
60   PRINT "WHAT WAS YOUR DESTINATION?"
70   INPUT CITY$
80   PRINT "HOW MANY MILES?"
90   INPUT MILES
100 PRINT "HOW MANY HOURS?"
110 INPUT HOURS
120 LET MPH = MILES / HOURS
130 PRINT MPH; " MILES PER HOUR TO "; CITY$
```

The first line of this program prints a message requesting data. The INPUT statement on the second line causes the computer to print a question mark and then stop execution. At this point, the output appears:

RUN
```
WHAT WAS YOUR DESTINATION?
?  _
```

Execution of the program will not resume until someone at the keyboard types a response and presses the ENTER key. Assume that the destination of HOUSTON is typed. When the ENTER key is pressed, the string of characters HOUSTON is stored under the string variable name CITY$, and execution of the program continues.

Line 80 causes another message to be displayed. The INPUT statement on line 90 causes a question mark to be printed, and the program stops execution again until a value is entered at the keyboard. The output is shown below as it now appears:

RUN
```
WHAT WAS YOUR DESTINATION?
?  HOUSTON
HOW MANY MILES?
?  _
```

Since the variable in this INPUT statement (MILES) is a numeric variable instead of a string variable, the computer will not accept any response unless it is numeric. If the response 1400 MILES is entered, an error message will be displayed and the computer will re-execute the INPUT statement. This error is demonstrated below:

```
RUN
WHAT WAS YOUR DESTINATION?
?  HOUSTON
HOW MANY MILES?
?  1400 MILES
REDO                              (NOTE: On some computers, the
?  _                              error message may be REENTER. )
```

The program will not continue past the INPUT on line 90 until a numeric value is entered. Assume the value 1400 is typed. When the ENTER key is pressed, the computer stores the value 1400 under the variable name MILES, and continues by executing the next line of the program.

After line 100 prints another request for data, the INPUT on line 110 causes another question mark to be printed. Execution stops again until a numeric value is entered. The exchange now appears:

```
RUN
WHAT WAS YOUR DESTINATION?
?  HOUSTON
HOW MANY MILES?
?  1400 MILES
REDO
?  1400
HOW MANY HOURS?
?  _
```

Assume the person at the keyboard enters the value 25. When the ENTER key is pressed, the computer stores the value 25 under the variable name HOURS, and execution of the program continues.

On line 120, the current value of MILES is divided by the current value of HOURS, and the result is assigned to the variable MPH. The final result is printed by line 130.

The complete exchange between the program and the person at the keyboard is as follows:

```
RUN
WHAT WAS YOUR DESTINATION?
?  HOUSTON
```

```
HOW MANY MILES?
? 1400 MILES
REDO
? 1400
HOW MANY HOURS?
? 25
56 MILES PER HOUR TO HOUSTON
```

Because this program uses INPUT statements to obtain its data, it can be used to calculate the average speed on any trip, anywhere. Each time the program is run, new data can be entered and a different result produced.

INPUT WITH PROMPT

When a message is included in the INPUT statement, the computer prints the message before it stops to get a value from the keyboard.

The previous example used PRINT statements to display messages requesting data. The message that asks for data is called a *prompt,* which can be included as part of the INPUT statement itself.

The general format of the INPUT statement with a prompt is:

INPUT "prompt"; variable-name

In the INPUT statement, the prompt is enclosed in quotation marks, and immediately follows the word INPUT. The prompt is separated from the variable name by a semicolon.

When this statement is executed, the prompt is displayed, followed by the question mark. The program then stops execution until an appropriate value is entered.

NOTE: On some computers, the presence of a prompt in the INPUT statement suppresses the display of the question mark. In this case, you must include the question mark as part of the prompt.

Example

At this point, we know enough BASIC to write a partial solution for the breakeven analysis problem. In this example, a company is introducing a line of novelty keychains. The manufacturing operation will have fixed overhead costs of $10,000 per month. The marketing director believes that the keychains will cost about $1.20 each to produce.

This sample program allows the user to enter any potential selling price. The program then calculates the number of keychains that would have to be sold in order for the profits to meet the overhead expenses. This is the breakeven point.

```
10 LET OVERHEAD = 10000
20 LET CSTPERITEM = 1.20
30 INPUT "WHAT SELLING PRICE"; SELLINGPRICE
40 LET UNITPROFIT = SELLINGPRICE - CSTPERITEM
50 LET BREAKEVEN = OVERHEAD / UNITPROFIT
60 PRINT INT (BREAKEVEN); " UNITS TO BREAKEVEN"
```

The first two lines assign values to the variable names OVERHEAD and CSTPERITEM. The INPUT statement on line 30 then causes a prompt to be displayed and execution of the program stops until a numeric value is entered. The output of the program up to this point appears:

RUN
WHAT SELLING PRICE? _

Assume the marketing director selects 1.99 as a possible selling price. When entered, the computer assigns the value 1.99 to the variable SELLINGPRICE and execution resumes at line 40.

The profit is calculated by subtracting the current value of CSTPERITEM from the current value of SELLINGPRICE. In this case, 1.99 - 1.20 is .79, which is assigned to UNITPROFIT.

Line 50 then causes the current value of OVERHEAD to be divided by the current value of UNITPROFIT, and the result of 12658.227 units is assigned to the variable BREAKEVEN. Since fractional units are not meaningful, the INT function is used to convert the result to a whole number before printing.

The output of the program is as follows:

RUN
WHAT SELLING PRICE? **1.99**
 12658 UNITS TO BREAKEVEN

If the marketing director feels he could not sell that many keychains per month, he could try another value for the selling price. The program is run again, this time using 2.49 as the selling price.

RUN
WHAT SELLING PRICE? **2.49**
 7751 UNITS TO BREAKEVEN

This program could be run many times using various selling prices to establish a suitable level of production and sales price.

TEST YOUR UNDERSTANDING

12. What is the purpose of the INPUT statement?

13. What three things occur when an INPUT statement is executed?

14. When an INPUT statement is executed, the program stops execution until the _____ key is pressed.

Assume the following program has been entered:

```
10 REM THIS PROGRAM COMPUTES A CHECKING ACCOUNT BALANCE
20 INPUT "PREVIOUS CHECKING BALANCE"; BALANCE
30 INPUT "TOTAL DEPOSITS"; DEPSITS
40 INPUT "TOTAL CHECKS"; CHECKS
50 LET BALANCE = BALANCE + DEPSITS - CHECKS
60 PRINT "NEW BALANCE IS $"; BALANCE
```

15. How many times will this program stop execution to accept values from the keyboard?

16. When this program is run, the following message appears on the screen, and the program stops:

```
PREVIOUS CHECKING BALANCE?
```

What line is being executed when this message appears? Assume you type 327.50 and press the ENTER key. Where will this value be stored? What appears on the screen next?

Section 6. Performing Repetitive Calculations

INTRODUCTION

Although the program in the last example solved the problem of calculating a breakeven point for any price, it is inconvenient to run the program over and over for various selling prices. We could do a great service for the marketing director if we wrote the program to produce a list of possible selling prices and corresponding breakeven points. This would require that the breakeven calculation be repeated a number of times using various selling prices.

One method for performing repetitive calculations in BASIC involves the use of the FOR and NEXT statements, which are introduced in this section.

This section has two parts:

- The FOR . . . NEXT Loop
- The STEP

THE FOR . . . NEXT LOOP

The FOR . . . NEXT loop is a series of statements beginning with a FOR statement, and ending with a NEXT statement. The statements between them are executed one or more times depending on the values supplied in the FOR statement.

The FOR . . . NEXT loop is constructed using two statements placed on separate lines of the program. The lines between the FOR and NEXT statements contain the instructions to be repeated.

There are two keywords required in the FOR statement; FOR and TO. The general format of the FOR statement is:

FOR counter-variable = lower-limit TO upper-limit

Either a numeric value or a numeric variable name can be used for the lower limit and upper limit. Only a numeric variable name can be used for the counter-variable. When the FOR statement is executed, the value of the lower limit is assigned to the counter-variable. Execution then continues to the statement following the FOR.

The NEXT statement must appear somewhere in the program after the FOR statement. The general format of this statement is:

NEXT counter-variable

The variable name used for the counter-variable in the NEXT statement must match the variable name used in the FOR statement. When the NEXT statement is executed, 1 is added to the value of the counter-variable, and a comparison is made between the counter-variable and the upper limit. What the computer does next depends on the result of this comparison.

If the new value of the counter-variable is not greater than the upper limit specified in the corresponding FOR statement, control returns to the statement following the FOR; then the statements following FOR are executed once more. When the NEXT statement is reached, 1 is added to the counter-variable and the comparison is made again.

Whenever the new value of the counter-variable is greater than the upper limit, the loop is completed, and execution passes to the statement following the NEXT.

A NEXT statement without a corresponding FOR preceding it causes the error NEXT WITHOUT FOR. If FOR appears without a corresponding NEXT, the effect of the FOR is only to assign the value of lower limit to the counter-variable. Repetition of the statements following the FOR does not occur unless a corresponding NEXT is encountered.

Example

This simple program demonstrates the operation of the FOR and NEXT statements. (NOTE: We have indented the statement that appears between the FOR and NEXT to emphasize the instruction in the loop. Indenting is *not* supported on all computers.)

```
10  PRINT "FOR...NEXT DEMONSTRATION"
15  PRINT
20  FOR NUMBER = 3 TO 9
25    PRINT "COUNTER VARIABLE IS NOW EQUAL TO"; NUMBER
30  NEXT NUMBER
35  PRINT
40  PRINT "END OF DEMONSTRATION"
45  PRINT NUMBER
```

The result of running this program is:

```
RUN
FOR...NEXT DEMONSTRATION

COUNTER VARIABLE IS NOW EQUAL TO 3
COUNTER VARIABLE IS NOW EQUAL TO 4
COUNTER VARIABLE IS NOW EQUAL TO 5
COUNTER VARIABLE IS NOW EQUAL TO 6
COUNTER VARIABLE IS NOW EQUAL TO 7
```

```
COUNTER VARIABLE IS NOW EQUAL TO 8
COUNTER VARIABLE IS NOW EQUAL TO 9

END OF DEMONSTRATION
10
```

This program begins by printing a message and then a blank line. When the FOR statement on line 20 is executed, the value of the lower limit (3) is assigned to the counter-variable, NUMBER. The computer then continues to the instruction following the FOR statement, which causes a message and the current value of NUMBER to be displayed.

When the matching NEXT statement is reached at line 30, two things occur. First, the NEXT statement causes a value of 1 to be added to the counter-variable NUMBER. At this point, the value of NUMBER becomes 4. The NEXT statement then makes a comparison between the counter-variable and the upper limit.

If the counter-variable has not exceeded the upper limit, the computer will repeat the instructions following FOR. Since NUMBER is now equal to 4, and 4 is not greater than 9, the computer repeats the PRINT instruction on line 25.

The message is printed again using the new value of the variable NUMBER. At line 30, the NEXT statement again causes 1 to be added to NUMBER. This new value of NUMBER is compared to the upper limit to see if the upper limit has been exceeded. As long as the counter-variable is not greater than the upper limit, the instruction between the FOR and the NEXT statements is repeated.

The computer continues to execute the instruction between FOR and NEXT, and add 1 to the counter-variable NUMBER each time the NEXT is reached. Eventually, the value of NUMBER becomes 10. When the counter-variable exceeds the upper limit, then the FOR . . . NEXT loop has been completed. Execution continues with the first statement following the NEXT.

The first instruction after the NEXT statement is the PRINT statement on line 35, which prints a blank line. Line 40 then prints an ending message, and line 45 prints the final value of the variable NUMBER.

Observe that the instructions before the FOR statement and after the NEXT statement were executed only once. The single instruction between FOR and NEXT, however, was executed repeatedly. In fact, this instruction was executed one time FOR *every value from* 3 TO 9.

Also observe that after the loop is completed, the value of NUMBER remains unaltered. We used line 45 in this program to demonstrate that the value of NUMBER did reach 10, and it was this value that terminated the loop.

THE STEP

The keyword STEP used in a FOR statement defines a value to be used for incrementing the counter-variable.

In the previous example, 1 was added to the counter-variable each time the NEXT statement was reached. It is possible to specify a value other than 1 to be added to the counter-variable. This is accomplished by including the keyword STEP in the FOR statement. The general format for the use of the STEP is:

FOR counter-variable = lower-limit TO upper-limit STEP value

The value following the keyword STEP can be a numeric value, a numeric variable name, or an arithmetic expression.

Example 1

To illustrate the use of STEP in the FOR statement, the following program prints the odd numbers between 1 and 10.

```
10 PRINT "ODD NUMBERS LESS THAN 10"
20 PRINT
30 FOR X = 1 TO 10 STEP 2
40    PRINT X
50 NEXT X
60 PRINT "THAT'S ALL"
70 PRINT "(FINAL VALUE OF X IS"; X; ")"
```

The output of this program is shown below:

```
RUN
ODD NUMBERS LESS THAN 10

 1
 3
 5
 7
 9
THAT'S ALL
(FINAL VALUE OF X IS 11)
```

Begining at line 10, a message is printed, then line 20 prints a blank line. At line 30, the FOR...NEXT loop is entered. When the FOR statement is executed, the value of the lower limit (1) is assigned to the counter-variable X. Execution then passes to the following instruction on line 40, which prints the current value of the variable X.

The NEXT statement is reached at line 50, which causes the STEP value of 2 to be added to the counter-variable X. The variable X is now equal to 3, and 3 is less than the upper limit 10. Therefore, the instructions after the FOR statement are executed again.

Each time the NEXT statement is reached, the STEP value of 2 is added to the counter-variable. When this causes the value of X to become 11, then the loop is complete, and the computer does not repeat the instructions in the loop again. Instead, it continues past the NEXT statement to the next instruction (line 60). An ending message is printed, and then line 70 shows us the final value of the counter-variable.

Example 2

To solve our breakeven analysis problem, we must compute the breakeven point at a variety of selling prices between a minimum and maximum price. One technique for accomplishing this involves a FOR...NEXT loop, using the minimum price as the lower limit and the maximum price as the upper limit. This technique is illustrated in the following program, which obtains a minimum and maximum price and prints a list of possible selling prices.

First, let's consider what STEP value should be used in the loop. A STEP value of 1 could be used, but this would give us only two computations if the limits were 2.00 and 3.00. A STEP value of .01 could be used, but this would give us 101 possible prices if the limits were 1.50 to 2.50.

To produce the same number of selling prices each time the program is run, we can divide the price range into a constant number of intervals. This is accomplished by finding the difference between the minimum and maximum selling price, and then dividing by an arbitrary value—say 10. The result is a value used for the STEP to produce 11 prices between the minimum and maximum.

This is illustrated in the following program:

```
10 INPUT "WHAT IS THE MINIMUM SELLING PRICE"; MINPRICE
20 INPUT "WHAT IS THE MAXIMUM SELLING PRICE"; MAXPRICE
30 LET RANGE = MAXPRICE - MINPRICE
40 LET PRICEINCRMENT = RANGE / 10
50 PRINT
60 PRINT "POSSIBLE SELLING PRICES"
```

```
70 FOR SELLINGPRICE = MINPRICE TO MAXPRICE STEP
PRICEINCRMENT
80    PRINT "$"; INT(SELLINGPRICE * 100 + .5) / 100
90 NEXT SELLINGPRICE
```

When this program is RUN, the first instruction causes a prompt to be displayed, and execution then stops until the required data is entered. Assume the value 1.59 is entered as the minimum selling price. This value is stored as MINPRICE, and execution continues to line 20.

The second INPUT statement causes another prompt to be displayed, and execution again stops until data is entered. Assume the value of 1.91 is entered as the maximum price. Before the ENTER key is pressed, the output appears:

RUN
WHAT IS THE MINIMUM SELLING PRICE? **1.59**
WHAT IS THE MAXIMUM SELLING PRICE? **1.91_**

After the ENTER key is pressed, 1.91 is stored as the value of MAXPRICE. Line 30 then computes the difference between the prices, which is 1.91 − 1.59 = .32. This is stored as RANGE, and line 40 divides that range into 10 intervals. Therefore, PRICEINCRMENT is .32 / 10 or .032. A blank line and a heading are printed by lines 50 and 60.

The FOR . . . NEXT loop is entered at line 70, and the counter-variable SELLINGPRICE is assigned the current value of the variable MINPRICE. Therefore, when line 80 is executed the first time, SELLINGPRICE is equal to 1.59.

Line 80 rounds the selling price to the nearest penny before printing it. Although rounding is not necessary at this point, it becomes important as a STEP value of .032 is added to SELLINGPRICE each time the NEXT statement is reached.

The instruction between FOR and NEXT will be executed repeatedly, with a value of .032 being added to the SELLINGPRICE each time through the loop. When the SELLINGPRICE finally exceeds the upper limit of MAXPRICE, the loop is terminated, and execution passes to the instruction following the NEXT statement. Since there are no instructions following the NEXT statement, the program is completed.

The final output of this program is shown below:

RUN
WHAT IS THE MINIMUM SELLING PRICE? **1.59**

WHAT IS THE MAXIMUM SELLING PRICE? **1.91**

POSSIBLE SELLING PRICES
```
$ 1.59
$ 1.62
$ 1.65
$ 1.69
$ 1.72
$ 1.75
$ 1.78
$ 1.81
$ 1.85
$ 1.88
$ 1.91
```

TEST YOUR UNDERSTANDING

17. A service station sells propane gas at $1.27 per gallon. But the propane pump measures only the number of gallons delivered; it does not compute the amount of sale. Write a program to produce a price list in the following format:

```
1  GAL  =  $  1.27
2  GAL  =  $  2.54
3  GAL  =  $  3.81
   •         •
   •         •
   •         •
10 GAL  =  $ 12.7
```

18. Alter the program above so that prices are computed in .1-gallon increments from .1 to 1.0 gallon. The output should appear as shown below. (Note that the price is rounded to the nearest penny.)

```
.1 GAL  =  $  .13
.2 GAL  =  $  .25
.3 GAL  =  $  .38
   •         •
   •         •
   •         •
1  GAL  =  $ 1.27
```

Section 7. The Breakeven Analysis Program

INTRODUCTION

The problem introduced at the beginning of this chapter was to produce a breakeven analysis. To solve this problem using the computer requires a program that obtains input data, performs repetitive calculations, and prints the results. All BASIC statements and techniques for performing these operations have been presented, and we are now ready to formulate a solution to the problem.

In this section we discuss the use of an algorithm to describe the functions of a program, and several additional techniques for writing an understandable program.

This section has three parts:

- Developing an Algorithm
- Writing a BASIC Program
- The Breakeven Analysis Program

DEVELOPING AN ALGORITHM

We can simplify writing a program by first writing an algorithm, a narrative description of the steps required in the solution of a problem.

We can start our algorithm by writing those steps most apparently needed in the solution. We can then refine these steps and add more detail, until we are satisfied that the solution is clearly described.

To develop the algorithm for solving the breakeven analysis problem, let's start with the two calculations for determining a breakeven point. Once a breakeven point is calculated, the result must be displayed, so we will also include this step.

— Calculate unit profit (selling price − cost per unit)
— Calculate breakeven point (overhead / unit profit)
— Print results

Here, we see that, in order to perform the calculations, we must somehow obtain values for selling price, cost per unit, and overhead. The overhead was given as $10,000; this value could be included in the program as a constant. Since the cost and price data are not known, we can input these values when the program is run. Now we have two more steps to add to the algorithm.

— Assign 10000 to overhead constant
— Input cost and price data
— Calculate unit profit (selling price − cost per unit)
— Calculate breakeven point (overhead − unit profit)
— Print results

Recall that we wished to produce a *list* of potential selling prices and corresponding breakeven points. A FOR . . . NEXT loop can be used to repeat the breakeven calculations for a range of prices if we determine a lower and an upper limit and the steps between. As illustrated in the examples, we can input a minimum and maximum price for the limits. The price range can then be divided into an arbitrary number of intervals to determine a price increment for the step value. Let's pick 10 intervals and include this value as a constant in our program. After adding these steps to our algorithm, we have:

— Assign 10000 to overhead, 10 to number of intervals
— Input cost and minimum and maximum selling prices
— Calculate price range (maximum − minimum)
— Calculate price increment (range / intervals)
— Start loop with selling price = minimum price
— Calculate unit profit (selling price − cost per unit)
— Calculate breakeven point (overhead − unit profit)
— Print results
— Add price increment to selling price and repeat loop until maximum price is reached

In reviewing our algorithm, we feel confident we have listed all the steps required to solve the problem.

WRITING A BASIC PROGRAM

When you have written a good algorithm, each step in the problem solution can be easily translated into one or more BASIC instructions.

The first step in our algorithm is to assign values to the constants. Let's use the variable names OVERHEAD and NTERVLS to represent the overhead costs and the number of intervals for the price range. (Although we would like to use the variable name INTERVALS, unfortunately it contains two

keywords, INT and VAL.) To assign values to these variables, we use two
LET. . . = statements.

```
LET OVERHEAD = 10000
LET NTERVLS = 10
```

The next step in the algorithm is to input values for the unit cost, the
minimum price, and the maximum price. For this, we create three variable
names for storing the values input from the keyboard, and we write three
INPUT statements to obtain these values.

```
INPUT "WHAT IS THE COST PER UNIT"; CSTPERITEM
INPUT "WHAT IS THE MINIMUM SELLING PRICE"; MINPRICE
INPUT "WHAT IS THE MAXIMUM SELLING PRICE"; MAXPRICE
```

Note we have to carefully choose the variable names so that each begins
with two unique characters. Also, we try making the names meaningful
without including keywords. CSTPERUNIT could not be used because it
contains the keyword RUN.

The third and fourth steps in the algorithm are calculations for the price
range and the increment. To perform a calculation, we can write it as an
arithmetic expression and include it in a LET. . . = statement. The variables we will use for storing the result of each calculation are PRICERANGE
and INCRMENT.

```
LET PRICERANGE = MAXPRICE - MINPRICE
LET INCRMENT = PRICERANGE / NTERVLS
```

Now we must establish a loop to compute and print the breakeven points.
To do this, we write a FOR statement and create the variable name SEL-
LINGPRICE to use as a counter variable.

```
FOR SELLINGPRICE = MINPRICE TO MAXPRICE STEP INCRMENT
```

Within the loop, we must include instructions for calculating the unit
profit and the breakeven point at the current selling price, and a PRINT
statement to display the result. We create two more variables for storing the
results of the calculations, and use LET. . . = statements to perform the
calculations and assign the results to the proper variables.

```
LET UNITPROFIT = SELLINGPRICE - CSTPERITEM
LET BREAKEVEN = OVERHEAD / UNITPROFIT
```

For output, let's print the selling price and the breakeven point in zones so they appear in columns. We should also round the value of SELLINGPRICE to two decimal places and convert BREAKEVEN to an integer before printing.

```
PRINT INT(SELLINGPRICE * 100 + .5) / 100, INT(BREAKEVEN)
```

After this statement is executed, we direct the computer to repeat the loop for the next selling price.

```
NEXT SELLINGPRICE
```

As we think about the output appearing in columns, we realize that we have not taken column headings into consideration. Since we wouldn't want the column headings to appear before the input prompts, we should print them after inputting the data. We also wouldn't want headings printed for every breakeven point, so they will have to be printed before the loop is entered. Let's print the headings right after inputting the data, and add the following statements to our program.

```
PRINT
PRINT "SELLING PRICE", "BREAKEVEN"
PRINT
```

After assigning line numbers to each of the instructions that we have written, our program appears:

```
100 LET OVERHEAD = 10000
110 LET NTERVLS = 10
120 INPUT "WHAT IS THE COST PER UNIT"; CSTPERITEM
130 INPUT "WHAT IS THE MINIMUM SELLING PRICE"; MINPRICE
140 INPUT "WHAT IS THE MAXIMUM SELLING PRICE"; MAXPRICE
150 PRINT
160 PRINT "SELLING PRICE", "BREAKEVEN"
170 PRINT
180 LET PRICERANGE = MAXPRICE - MINPRICE
190 LET INCRMENT = PRICERANGE / NTERVLS
200 FOR SELLINGPRICE = MINPRICE TO MAXPRICE STEP INCRMENT
210 LET UNITPROFIT = SELLINGPRICE - CSTPERITEM
220 LET BREAKEVEN = OVERHEAD / UNITPROFIT
230 PRINT INT(SELLINGPRICE * 100 + .5) / 100, INT(BREAKEVEN)
240 NEXT SELLINGPRICE
```

Writing a program to solve the problem correctly, however, is not the only consideration; it should also be easy to read and understand. We can write REM statements both to explain the operation of the program and to make it more readable. Here are three ways in which REMs can be used:

1. Use REM statements at the beginning of the program to explain what the program does.
2. Use REMs to describe what is happening within the program, and to divide the program into logical sections. This makes the program easier to follow. If changes are required, it is easier to locate where the changes must be made.
3. Use empty REM statements to create blank lines in the program where they can improve readability.

If your computer allows extra spaces to be inserted in statements, a program can be made easier to read by indenting certain instructions. Notice how this technique is used in the sample program that follows.

THE BREAKEVEN ANALYSIS PROGRAM

In this program, we have inserted REM statements to document the program and make it easier to read. We have also used indenting to improve the readability, although this may not be possible on all computers. Review the program giving special attention to the use of REM statements, as well as the operation of the LET, PRINT, INPUT, FOR, and NEXT statements.

```
LOAD  "PROGRAM3"
LIST
10   REM  ****************************************************
15   REM                        REMARKS
20   REM  ****************************************************
25   REM   THIS PROGRAM PREPARES A BREAKEVEN ANALYSIS BASED
30   REM   ON AN OVERHEAD COST OF $10,000.  INPUT IS THE
35   REM   COST PER UNIT, MINIMUM SELLING PRICE AND MAXIMUM
40   REM   SELLING PRICE.  THE PRICE RANGE IS DIVIDED INTO
45   REM   TEN INTERVALS AND THE BREAKEVEN POINT IS COMPUTED
50   REM   FOR EACH POTENTIAL SELLING PRICE IN THE RANGE.
55   REM  ****************************************************
60   REM                  MAIN PROGRAM SECTION
65   REM  ****************************************************
70   REM
```

```
75   REM ************** INITIALIZE CONSTANTS ******************
80   REM
100      LET OVERHEAD = 10000
110      LET NTERVLS = 10
115  REM
116  REM ******* GET THE INPUT DATA AND PRINT HEADINGS ********
117  REM
120      INPUT "WHAT IS THE COST PER UNIT"; CSTPERITEM
130      INPUT "WHAT IS THE MINIMUM SELLING PRICE"; MINPRICE
140      INPUT "WHAT IS THE MAXIMUM SELLING PRICE"; MAXPRICE
150      PRINT
160      PRINT "SELLING PRICE", "BREAKEVEN"
170      PRINT
175  REM
176  REM **** CALCULATE PRICE INCREMENT TO BE USED IN LOOP ****
177  REM
180      LET PRICERANGE = MAXPRICE - MINPRICE
190      LET INCRMENT = PRICERANGE / NTERVLS
195  REM
196  REM CALCULATE BREAKEVEN FOR EACH POTENTIAL SELLING PRICE *
197  REM
200      FOR SELLINGPRICE = MINPRICE TO MAXPRICE STEP INCRMENT
210         LET UNITPROFIT = SELLINGPRICE - CSTPERITEM
220         LET BREAKEVEN = OVERHEAD / UNITPROFIT
230         PRINT INT(SELLINGPRICE * 100 + .5) / 100,
                INT(BREAKEVEN)
240      NEXT SELLINGPRICE
```

Here are two sample runs of the breakeven analysis program.

RUN
WHAT IS THE COST PER UNIT? **2.45**
WHAT IS THE MINIMUM SELLING PRICE? **2.99**
WHAT IS THE MAXIMUM SELLING PRICE? **3.99**

```
SELLING PRICE     BREAKEVEN

2.99              18518
3.09              15624
3.19              13513
3.29              11904
3.39              10638
```

3.49	9615
3.59	8771
3.69	8064
3.79	7462
3.89	6944
3.99	6493

RUN
WHAT IS THE COST PER UNIT? **2.45**
WHAT IS THE MINIMUM SELLING PRICE? **3.29**
WHAT IS THE MAXIMUM SELLING PRICE? **3.59**

SELLING PRICE	BREAKEVEN
3.29	11904
3.32	11494
3.35	11111
3.38	10752
3.41	10416
3.44	10101
3.47	9803
3.5	9523
3.53	9259
3.56	9009
3.59	8771

PROGRAMMING EXERCISES

Programming Problem 3A:

The marketing director is so pleased with your breakeven analysis program he'd like to use it for setting prices of other products as well. Since the overhead cost varies with the product, you must alter the program so that overhead cost can be input when the program is run.

Programming Problem 3B:

The marketing director has requested that the breakeven analysis compute a larger number of price possibilities between the minimum and maximum selling price. In fact, he'd like to specify the number of intervals for any analysis. Change the program so the number of intervals is input when the program is run.

ANSWERS TO "TEST YOUR UNDERSTANDING" EXERCISES

1. (a) 22 ; (b) 13.5 ; (c) 17 ; (d) 36
2. (a) (6 * 5 + 2) / 8 ;
   (b) (7 - 5) ^ 2 + 3 * 5
3. (a)   (CST + DELIVERY + MARKUP) / QUANTITY
   (b)   (PARTS * TAX + PARTS + LABOR) * PCTDOWN
4. PRINT (256 + 325 + 119 + 200) / 4
5. PRINT "NEW BALANCE IS $"; 187 + 38 - 27
6. PRINT "VALUE OF GOLD IS $"; 512.7 * 17; " LESS $";
   512.7 * 17 * .03; " COMMISSION"
7. Sample solution:

```
10 LET NAM$ = "JOHN SMITH"
20 LET ADDRESS$ = "404 MAIN STREET"
30 PRINT "NAME:", NAM$
40 PRINT
50 PRINT "ADDRESS:", ADDRESS$
```

8. Sample solution:

```
10 LET NAM$ = "JOHN SMITH"
20 LET ADDRESS$ = "404 MAIN STREET"
30 PRINT "NAME", "ADDRESS"
40 PRINT
50 PRINT NAM$, ADDRESS$
```

9. Suggested solution:

```
10 LET TTLINCHES = 10 * 12
20 LET BLCKS = TTLINCHES / 14.5
30 PRINT INT(BLCKS); " BLOCKS FROM A 10-FT. PIECE"
```

10. Suggested solution:

```
10 LET AVERAGE = 1180 / 37
20 LET AVERAGE = INT(AVERAGE + .5)
30 PRINT "EACH TEACHER HAS APPROXIMATELY"; AVERAGE; " STUDENTS"
```

11. Suggested solution:

```
10 LET TAX = 57385 * .017
20 LET TAX = INT (TAX * 100 + .5) / 100
30 PRINT "PROPERTY TAX DUE IS $"; TAX
```

12. The purpose of the INPUT statement is to read a value from the keyboard and store it in memory.

13. A question mark is printed; execution stops; when the ENTER key is pressed, the value entered is stored in memory.

14. ENTER

15. The program will stop 3 times (at lines 20, 30, and 40).

16. Line 20 is being executed; under the variable name BALANCE ; TOTAL DEPOSITS? appears next.

17. Suggested solution:

```
10 FOR GALLNS = 1 TO 10
20   PRINT GALLNS; " GAL = $"; 1.27 * GALLNS
30 NEXT GALLNS
```

18. Suggested solution:

```
10 FOR GALLNS = .1 TO 1.05 STEP .1
20   LET PRICE = GALLNS * 1.27
30   LET PRICE = INT(PRICE * 100 + .5) / 100
40   PRINT GALLNS; " GAL = $"; PRICE
50 NEXT GALLNS
```

(In trying this exercise, you no doubt discovered that FOR GALLNS = .1 TO 1 STEP .1 gives you prices only up to .9 gallon. Because the computer stores values as binary digits, and it has no exact binary equivalent for .1, it uses a close approximation which is only slightly larger. But its approximation is enough larger to make the counter-variable greater than the upper limit when it should have been equal to it; thus, the loop is terminated after its 9th execution. We overcome this problem by making the upper limit a little larger than 1, so the loop is not terminated until the price for 1 gallon is computed. Keep this problem in mind; you may run into it again on different occasions.)

CHAPTER 4

Fundamental Programming Techniques

CHAPTER OBJECTIVE

To introduce the fundamental concepts of loops, conditions, subroutines, and data files, and explain the use of the BASIC statements associated with these concepts.

PROBLEM

Because of company growth, the Payroll Department is currently working overtime to keep up with payroll processing. Using the computer to perform routine payroll calculations would greatly relieve the burden on this department.

The standard payroll calculation involves the computation of total pay—multiplying the hours worked by the employee's pay rate. If the employee has worked more than 40 hours, however, the total pay is computed by calculating the regular pay and overtime pay, and adding the two together. An FICA deduction is then computed as 6.7 percent of the total pay; this is subtracted from the total to arrive at net pay.

CHAPTER OVERVIEW

The preparation of payrolls is one of the most common business uses of a computer. Where it would take hours for a staff of payroll clerks to process a large payroll, the computer can perform all the required calculations in seconds.

The timely processing of large quantities of data often involves the use of data files. In this chapter, you will learn how to use data files, set up a loop to process all the data in a file, direct the computer to perform different operations (depending on the data currently being used), and use subroutines to make programs more understandable.

At the end of this chapter, these fundamental programming techniques are demonstrated in the solution to the payroll problem.

This chapter has five sections:

- **Using Loops to Repeat Instructions**
- **Using and Testing Conditions**
- **Using Subroutines to Simplify Programs**
- **Using A Data File**
- **The Payroll Program**

Section 1. Using Loops to Repeat Instructions

INTRODUCTION

To process large quantities of data, the instructions that process one item must be repeated for every data item—but writing the same instructions 100 times to process 100 items is not feasible. Instead, we write the instructions only once. At the end of the instructions, we direct the computer to go back to the beginning and execute the same instructions again for the next data item. This is a loop.

This section introduces the GOTO statement, used to send the computer back to the beginning of a list of instructions. Also discussed is a problem that occurs when using loops—the endless loop.

This section has two parts:

- The GOTO Statement
- The Endless Loop

THE GOTO STATEMENT

The GOTO statement interrupts the sequential execution of instructions and directs the computer to a specific line in the program where sequential execution resumes.

When a program is executed, the computer starts at the lowest numbered line and executes each line in sequence from the lowest to the highest. We can interrupt the sequential execution of instructions using a GOTO statement.

The GOTO statement consists of the keyword GOTO followed by a line number. When this statement is executed, the computer "goes to" the specified line number. Once there, it resumes execution of instructions in line number sequence.

If the specified line number in the GOTO statement does not actually exist in the program, an UNDEFINED STATEMENT error occurs (or UNDEFINED LINE NUMBER, depending on your computer).

Example

The following program demonstrates the operation of the GOTO statement:

```
20   PRINT "GOTO DEMONSTRATION"
40   GOTO 80
60   PRINT "THIS STATEMENT WILL NEVER BE EXECUTED"
80   PRINT "BECAUSE THE COMPUTER SKIPS DIRECTLY TO"
100 PRINT "LINE 80, AS A RESULT OF THE GOTO"
```

Running this program produces:

```
RUN
GOTO DEMONSTRATION
BECAUSE THE COMPUTER SKIPS DIRECTLY TO
LINE 80, AS A RESULT OF THE GOTO
```

Execution of this program begins at line 20 with the printing of the title of the demonstration. At line 40, the GOTO is encountered. We would normally expect line 60 to be executed after line 40, but the GOTO statement interrupts the sequential execution of instructions. The computer is directed instead to line 80, where execution resumes. Lines 80 and 100 are then executed in sequence.

The effect of the GOTO statement can be illustrated:

```
    20   PRINT "GOTO DEMONSTRATION"
    40   GOTO 80
    60   PRINT "THIS STATEMENT WILL NEVER BE EXECUTED"
    80   PRINT "BECAUSE THE COMPUTER SKIPS DIRECTLY TO"
   100   PRINT "LINE 80, AS A RESULT OF THE GOTO"
```

The result of the GOTO is that line 60 is skipped over. The sequence in which statements are executed is: 20, 40, 80, 100.

THE ENDLESS LOOP

When the computer repeatedly executes a series of instructions, it is in a loop. If there is no provision for stopping the computer from repeating these instructions, the loop is endless.

The previous example demonstrated the use of the GOTO to send the computer forward to an instruction farther down in the program. The GOTO can also be used to send the computer backward to a previous instruction. This creates a loop, in which instructions are repeated. If there is no provision for terminating this repetition, the loop is endless.

When a program enters an endless loop, it will never stop executing the instructions in the loop. Since endless loops are common programming errors, computers are usually equipped with some type of "break" key on the keyboard. Pressing the break key halts execution of a program—even one stuck in a loop.

Note: The break key may be marked BREAK or RESET, depending on the computer. On some models, a combination of two keys may have to be pressed simultaneously. Check the operations manual for your computer.

Example

This example program demonstrates how an endless loop can be created by using a GOTO statement. In this example and those that follow, instructions that are part of a loop are indented.

```
10 PRINT "ENDLESS LOOP DEMONSTRATION"
20 PRINT
30    PRINT "PRESS BREAK KEY TO STOP PROGRAM"
40 GOTO 30
50 PRINT "THE COMPUTER NEVER GETS TO THIS LINE"
```

A *partial* output of this program is shown below:

```
RUN
ENDLESS LOOP DEMONSTRATION

PRESS BREAK KEY TO STOP PROGRAM
PRESS BREAK KEY TO STOP PROGRAM
PRESS BREAK KEY TO STOP PROGRAM
PRESS BREAK KEY TO STOP PROGRAM
PRESS BREAK KEY TO STOP PROGRAM
PRESS BREAK KEY TO STOP PROGRAM
PRESS BREAK KEY TO STOP PROGRAM
PRESS BREAK KEY TO STOP PROGRAM
PRESS BREAK KEY TO STOP PROGRAM
PRESS BREAK KEY TO STOP PROGRAM
PRESS BREAK KEY TO STOP PR
PRESS BREA
PRE
```

The first three lines of this program print a heading, then a blank line, then a message. The fourth line of the program contains a GOTO which sends the computer back to line 30.

After going to line 30, sequential execution resumes, and the message is printed again. Line 40 is executed next, which again sends the computer back to line 30. The program is now in an endless loop. The computer will continue to execute these two instructions until it is interrupted by the BREAK key.

The effect of the GOTO can be illustrated:

```
10 PRINT "ENDLESS LOOP DEMONSTRATION"
20 PRINT
30    PRINT "PRESS BREAK KEY TO STOP PROGRAM"
40 GOTO 30
50 PRINT "THE COMPUTER NEVER GETS TO THIS LINE"
```

Notice that the print statement on line 50 is never executed. Before the computer can get to line 50, line 40 always sends the computer backward in the program. The statements in this program are executed in this sequence: 10, 20, 30, 40, 30, 40, 30, 40, 30, 40, etc.

Endless loops can create interesting effects, but they are never intentionally included in a business program. An endless loop is a programming error to be avoided.

TEST YOUR UNDERSTANDING

Assume the following program is entered.

```
10 GOTO 40
20 PRINT "ANY SENSE UNLESS"
30 GOTO 60
40 PRINT "THIS WON'T MAKE"
50 GOTO 20
60 PRINT "IT IS CORRECT"
```

1. List the sequence in which the lines of this program would be executed.

2. What would be the output of the program above?

Section 2. Using and Testing Conditions

INTRODUCTION

When a loop is used to repeat the same instructions for large quantities of data, a provision must be made to terminate the loop when all data has been processed. This is called "exiting a loop." If an exit is not provided, the loop becomes an endless loop.

In BASIC the IF statement can be used to test for the end of the data, and direct the computer to exit the loop when all data has been processed. The IF statement is also used to determine what type of processing is appropriate. For instance, in the payroll program, regular pay is calculated for the employee who has worked 40 hours or less. If more than 40 hours have been worked, then overtime pay must be calculated at 1½ times the regular pay rate. In this case, an IF statement is used to test the current value of hours worked, and direct the computer to perform the correct calculation depending on the test result.

This section introduces conditions used to control programs, and the IF statement used to test conditions.

This section has two parts:

- Conditions and Relational Operators
- Testing a Condition with the IF Statement

CONDITIONS AND RELATIONAL OPERATORS

A condition is an expression which compares two values. In writing a condition, we use one of six symbols, called the "relational operators," to express a relationship between the values. The computer evaluates a condition by comparing the values to determine if the relationship is true.

To express a relationship between two values, we use one of these six symbols:

Relationship	Symbol
Equal to	=
Greater than	>
Less than	<
Greater than or equal to	>= or =>
Less than or equal to	<= or =<
Not equal	<> or ><

A condition is an expression which uses one of the relational operators to compare two values. It is not a statement of fact, but a question that the computer must answer. Where a condition appears in a BASIC statement, the computer evaluates it as "true" or "false" depending on the values being compared.

The comparison may be between two numeric values or between two string values. However, mixing string and numeric values together in the same condition gives an error message, such as TYPE MISMATCH.

The rules for evaluating a condition are given in the following examples.

Example 1

The following numeric conditions are evaluated as "true" or "false':

Condition	How to Read	Evaluation
7 < 24	7 is less than 24?	True
47 = 12 + 33	47 is equal to 12 + 33?	False
5 <> 3	5 is not equal to 3?	True
6 + 4 <= 8	6 + 4 is less than or equal to 8?	False
16 > 2 * 8	16 is greater than 2 * 8?	False
8/2 >= 10/5	8/2 is greater than or equal to 10/5?	True

Example 2

When a condition contains a variable name, the current value of the variable is used to evaluate the condition. Whether a condition turns out to be true or false depends on the current values of the variables appearing in the condition.

In this example, three numeric variables have been assigned the indicated values:

```
LET AGE = 24
LET HEIGHT = 66
LET WEIGHT = 115
```

The following conditions are evaluated based on the current values of these variables:

Condition	Evaluated as	Evaluation
AGE > 21	24 > 21	True
6 < HEIGHT/12	6 < 66/12	False

```
125 >< WEIGHT              125 >< 115              True
HEIGHT - 2 = 68           66 - 2 = 68            False
HEIGHT <= AGE + WEIGHT    66 <=24 + 115          True
WEIGHT >= 120             115 >= 120             False
```

Example 3

Conditions may also be used to compare string values. The rules for determining whether one string is "less than" or "greater than" another involve character sequence and string length, and can vary from computer to computer. In this text, we will compare strings using only the "equal to" (=) or "not equal to" (<>) operators.

In order for two strings to be equal, each string must have the same number of characters, and each must contain identical characters in identical order.

The following string conditions are evaluated.

Condition	Evaluation	Reason
"PRINT" = "PRIMT"	False	(4th characters not =)
"CATALOG" = "CATALOG"	True	(Identical)
"TIME" <> "TIME"	False	(They *are* identical)
"Y" = "YES"	False	(Unequal number of characters)
"ACE" <> "KING"	True	(Not identical)
" " = " "	False	(Unequal number of characters)
"" = ""	True	(Both contain *no* characters)

Notice in the sixth condition, one string contains two space characters, and the other contains three space characters; thus, the strings are not equal in length. In the last condition, two quotation marks are used with no characters in between them. This represents an *empty* or *null* string. A null string contains no characters.

Example 4

A string variable can be used in a string comparison. When the condition is evaluated, the current value of the string variable is used.

In this example, the string variables below have been assigned the indicated values:

```
LET CITY$ = "NEW YORK"
LET TWN$ = "NEW HAVEN"
```

The current value of each variable is used in evaluating the following conditions:

Condition	Evaluated As	Evaluation
CITY$ = "BRIDGEPORT"	"NEW YORK" = "BRIDGEPORT"	False
TWN$ = CITY$	"NEW HAVEN" = "NEW YORK"	False
"NEWYORK " <> CITY$	"NEWYORK " <> "NEW YORK"	True
TWN$ <> "NEW HEAVEN"	"NEW HAVEN" <> "NEW HEAVEN"	True
CITY$ = "NEW YORK"	"NEW YORK" = "NEW YORK"	True

The equal condition is true only if both strings contain the same number of characters, and identical characters in identical order.

TESTING A CONDITION WITH THE IF STATEMENT

The IF statement contains a condition and an instruction. If the condition is true, the instruction is executed. If the condition is false, the instruction is ignored.

The general format of the IF statement is:

IF condition THEN statement

When the IF statement is executed, the condition is evaluated. If the condition is *true*, the statement following THEN is executed. If the condition is false, the statement following THEN is *not* executed. When the condition is false, the computer ignores the remainder of the IF statement and execution passes to the next line of the program.

Example 1

This example demonstrates how an IF statement can be used to exit an otherwise endless loop.

Assume you are considering investing $100 in a venture promising to double your investment every year for 10 years. You would like to know what the value of that investment would be at the end of the 10-year period. The following program contains a loop which doubles the investment each time it is executed, and an IF statement which terminates the loop after its 10th execution.

```
10 LET YEAR = 0
20 LET INVESTMENT = 100
```

```
30    PRINT "AFTER YEAR"; YEAR; ", INVESTMENT = $";
        INVESTMENT
40    IF YEAR >= 10 THEN GOTO 80
50    LET INVESTMENT = INVESTMENT * 2
60    LET YEAR = YEAR + 1
70    GOTO 30
80 PRINT
90 PRINT "WOW!"
```

The result of running this program is:

```
RUN
AFTER YEAR  0,  INVESTMENT = $  100
AFTER YEAR  1,  INVESTMENT = $  200
AFTER YEAR  2,  INVESTMENT = $  400
AFTER YEAR  3,  INVESTMENT = $  800
AFTER YEAR  4,  INVESTMENT = $  1600
AFTER YEAR  5,  INVESTMENT = $  3200
AFTER YEAR  6,  INVESTMENT = $  6400
AFTER YEAR  7,  INVESTMENT = $  12800
AFTER YEAR  8,  INVESTMENT = $  25600
AFTER YEAR  9,  INVESTMENT = $  51200
AFTER YEAR  10,  INVESTMENT = $  102400

WOW!
```

Lines 10 and 20 of the program assign starting values to YEAR and INVEST-MENT, then line 30 prints the current value of each variable.

At line 40, the condition YEAR >= 10 is evaluated. Since YEAR is equal to 0 now, the condition is false; the computer ignores the remainder of the IF statement and execution passes to line 50.

On line 50, the value of INVESTMENT is multiplied by 2 and the result is assigned as the new value of INVESTMENT. Next, a value of 1 is added to YEAR and this result is stored as the new value of YEAR. The GOTO on line 70 sends the computer back to line 30 to print the new YEAR and INVESTMENT.

Were it not for the IF statement in this loop, the loop would be endless. Every time the computer comes to line 70, it branches back to line 30. The loop is not endless because the IF statement provides an exit.

Since 1 is added to YEAR each time through the loop, eventually the value of YEAR becomes 10. When it does, the condition in the IF statement (YEAR >= 10) is evaluated as true, and the instruction following THEN is executed. This GOTO directs the computer out of the loop to line 80.

Example 2

The following program illustrates the use of IF statements to test data. The output of this program depends on the value of the data entered.

```
50 INPUT "HOW MANY HOURS THIS WEEK"; HOURS
60 IF HOURS > 40 THEN PRINT "OVERTIME OF"; HOURS - 40;
" HOURS THIS WEEK"
70 IF HOURS <= 40 THEN PRINT "NO OVERTIME THIS WEEK"
80 PRINT
90 PRINT "END OF PROGRAM"
```

When this program is run, the INPUT on line 50 displays the prompt and stops execution of the program until a numeric value is entered. Assume that the value 32 is entered. Before the ENTER key is pressed, the screen appears as follows:

```
RUN
HOW MANY HOURS THIS WEEK? 32_
```

After the ENTER key is pressed, 32 is assigned to the variable HOURS and execution continues. At line 60, the condition HOURS > 40 is evaluated. Since the current value of HOURS is 32, the condition is false. The remainder of the IF statement on line 60 is ignored and execution passes to the next line in the program.

The IF test on line 70 now evaluates the condition HOURS <= 40. Since the current value of HOURS is less than 40, this condition is true. The statement following THEN on line 70 is therefore executed, which causes the message NO OVERTIME THIS WEEK to be printed. Execution then continues to the next line in the program.

Lines 80 and 90 print a blank line, and an end-of-program message. The complete output on this run is:

```
RUN
HOW MANY HOURS THIS WEEK? 32
NO OVERTIME THIS WEEK

END OF PROGRAM
```

If the program is run again with the value 48 being entered for HOURS, the output is different. In this case, the condition in line 60 is evaluated as true (48 > 40), so the statement following THEN is executed. This causes a message and the amount of overtime (HOURS – 40) to be printed.

Execution next passes to line 70, where the condition HOURS < = 40 is evaluated as false. Therefore, the remainder of the IF statement on line 70 is ignored, and the computer continues to lines 80 and 90.

On this run, the output appears:

```
RUN
HOW MANY HOURS THIS WEEK?  48
OVERTIME OF 8 HOURS THIS WEEK

END OF PROGRAM
```

TEST YOUR UNDERSTANDING

3. Evaluate the following conditions as true or false:

a. 185 <> 185   d. 25 = 25   g. "RATES" = "RATES "
b. 83 > 75   e. 72 >= 45   h. "SMITH" <> "SMITH"
c. 16 <= 21   f. 16 < 16   i. "20" = "020"

4. What output would be produced by the following program?

```
10   LET EMPLOYEE$ = "MORTON"
20   LET PAY = 5.75
30   LET DEDUCTS = 2
40   IF PAY >= 5.75 THEN PRINT "R"
50   IF DEDUCTS <= 3.1 THEN PRINT "I"
60   IF "EMPLOYEE" = EMPLOYEE$ THEN PRINT "N"
70   IF DEDUCTS > 1 THEN PRINT "G"
80   IF PAY < 4.5 THEN PRINT "T"
90   IF EMPLOYEE$ <> "MARTIN" THEN PRINT "H"
100  IF 3 = DEDUCTS THEN PRINT "A"
110  IF 5.76 <> PAY THEN PRINT "T"
```

5. A company pays its salesmen a 12 percent commission on sales less than $1000. If the sale is $1000 or more, the commission is 16 percent. Write a program which prompts for and inputs the amount of the sale, computes the commission earned, and prints the result. Use the following algorithm:

— Input the amount of sale.
— If the sale is greater than or equal to 1000, then let the commission earned equal 16 percent of the sale.

— If the sale is less than 1000, then let the commission earned equal 12 percent of the sale.

— Print the commission earned.

Section 3. Using Subroutines to Simplify Programs

INTRODUCTION

When we write a program containing a large number of instructions, we may find the same set of instructions used at different places in the program. When this occurs, those instructions can be written as a subroutine.

A subroutine is a set of statements to which we can transfer control temporarily. When we need the instructions it contains, we direct the computer to the subroutine with the provision that it return when execution of the subroutine is complete. Thus, a set of instructions that might otherwise appear more than once in the program can be written in only one place, but called upon from several points in the program—with the computer returning each time to the point of origin.

We can make a subroutine out of any group of instructions, even if it appears in the program only once. We do this to help make the program easier to write and simpler to understand.

This section introduces the GOSUB statement which directs the computer to the subroutine, and the RETURN statement which sends the computer back to its point of origin. The use of the END statement to protect subroutines, and the use of subroutines to simplify programs, are also illustrated.

This section has three parts:

- The GOSUB and RETURN Statements
- The END Statement to Protect Subroutines
- Using Subroutines to Simplify Programs

THE GOSUB AND RETURN STATEMENTS

The GOSUB statement sends the computer to a specific line in the program with the provision that, when a RETURN statement is encountered, the computer is to return to the statement following the GOSUB.

The keyword GOSUB is very much like GOTO. It is followed by a line number, and causes the computer to interrupt the sequential execution of instructions. When the GOSUB is executed, the computer branches to the indicated line, and resumes executing instructions in sequence.

The difference between GOSUB and GOTO is that, before branching to the new line, the computer saves in its memory the address of the statement that *follows* the GOSUB. When the computer later encounters the keyword RETURN, sequential execution is again interrupted, and the computer returns to the address that was saved. Thus, the computer is able to return to the instruction that follows the GOSUB, and resume execution where it originally left off.

Whenever a GOSUB sends the computer to a subroutine, the last statement in the subroutine must be a RETURN statement. If there is no RETURN, the GOSUB does nothing more than a GOTO.

Example

This example illustrates how to recognize when a subroutine is appropriate, develop a subroutine, and use GOSUB and RETURN statements. We have intentionally written the sample program with a flaw, however, to also illustrate an error you may encounter in using a subroutine.

The following program computes the average daily sales for the past week, month, and year. It is written without using subroutines. Extra spacing has been added to some of the instructions to make the program more readable.

```
10   INPUT "TOTAL SALES FOR PAST 7 DAYS"; SALES
20   LET DAYS = 7
30     LET AVERAGE = SALES / DAYS
40     PRINT
50     PRINT "AVERAGE FOR"; DAYS; " DAYS IS $"; AVERAGE
60     PRINT
70   INPUT "TOTAL SALES FOR PAST 30 DAYS"; SALES
80   LET DAYS = 30
90     LET AVERAGE = SALES / DAYS
100    PRINT
110    PRINT "AVERAGE FOR"; DAYS; " DAYS IS $"; AVERAGE
120    PRINT
130  INPUT "TOTAL SALES FOR PAST YEAR"; SALES
140  LET DAYS = 365
150    LET AVERAGE = SALES / DAYS
160    PRINT
170    PRINT "AVERAGE FOR"; DAYS; " DAYS IS $"; AVERAGE
180    PRINT
190  PRINT "END OF PROGRAM"
```

Notice the identical set of instructions appearing in lines 30 through 60, 90 through 120, and 150 through 180. We can turn this set of instructions into a single subroutine by writing it only once, placing it near the end of the program, and adding a RETURN statement as the last line. Where the instructions were originally located, we write a single GOSUB statement directing the computer to the new line number of the first subroutine instruction.

The new version of this program, now using a subroutine, is:

```
10   INPUT "TOTAL SALES FOR PAST 7 DAYS"; SALES
20   LET DAYS = 7
30      GOSUB 120
40   INPUT "TOTAL SALES FOR PAST 30 DAYS"; SALES
50   LET DAYS = 30
60      GOSUB 120
70   INPUT "TOTAL SALES FOR PAST YEAR"; SALES
80   LET DAYS = 365
90      GOSUB 120
100 PRINT "END OF PROGRAM"
110 REM ******** SUBROUTINE TO CALCULATE AVERAGE *******
120    LET AVERAGE = SALES / DAYS
130    PRINT
140    PRINT "AVERAGE FOR"; DAYS; " DAYS IS $"; AVERAGE
150    PRINT
160 RETURN
```

When the program is run, execution begins at the first line. The INPUT at line 10 displays a prompt, and execution stops until a numeric value is entered. At this point, the output appears as follows:

```
RUN
TOTAL SALES FOR PAST 7 DAYS? _
```

Assume the value 3500 is entered, and assigned to the variable SALES; execution resumes at line 20 where the value 7 is assigned to the variable DAYS. At line 30, the GOSUB transfers control to the subroutine, first saving a return address of "line 40".

In the subroutine, the average is calculated and the result printed. The last line of the subroutine is the RETURN, which sends the computer back to its return address of line 40. The INPUT statement on this line displays the next prompt. The output now appears:

RUN

TOTAL SALES FOR PAST 7 DAYS? **3500**

AVERAGE FOR 7 DAYS IS $ 500

TOTAL SALES FOR PAST 30 DAYS? _

Assume we now enter the value 18000. This value is assigned as the new value of SALES, then line 50 assigns the value 30 to DAYS. The next GOSUB on line 60 sends the computer again to the subroutine at line 120, but now the return address is "line 70".

The instructions in the subroutine calculate the average using the new values of SALES and DAYS, then the result is printed. The RETURN this time sends the computer back to line 70, where the third INPUT is executed. The output now appears:

RUN

TOTAL SALES FOR PAST 7 DAYS? **3500**

AVERAGE FOR 7 DAYS IS $ 500

TOTAL SALES FOR PAST 30 DAYS? **18000**

AVERAGE FOR 30 DAYS IS $ 600

TOTAL SALES FOR PAST YEAR? _

If we enter the value 164250, it is stored as the new value of SALES. Then the LET. . . = statement assigns 365 as the new value of DAYS. The GOSUB on line 90 sends the computer to the subroutine for the third time, this time saving "line 100" as the return address.

The subroutine calculates another average using the current values of 164250 for SALES and 365 for DAYS. The result is printed, the computer RETURNs to line 100, and the remainder of the program is executed. This causes the output as follows:

RUN

TOTAL SALES FOR PAST 7 DAYS? **3500**

AVERAGE FOR 7 DAYS IS $ 500

```
TOTAL  FOR  PAST  30  DAYS?  18000

AVERAGE  FOR  30  DAYS  IS  $  600

TOTAL  SALES  FOR  PAST  YEAR?  164250

AVERAGE  FOR  365  DAYS  IS  $  450

END  OF  PROGRAM

AVERAGE  FOR  365  DAYS  IS  $  450

RETURN  WITHOUT  GOSUB  ERROR  IN  LINE  160
```

What has happened? The program is supposed to end after printing the message END OF PROGRAM—but it doesn't. After executing line 100, the computer continues to execute instructions in sequence. Line 110 is a REM statement, so the computer ignores it. Line 120 is next, which computes the average again, using the current values of SALES (164250) and DAYS (365). Line 130 through 150 print a blank line, the result, and another blank line.

Now, when the RETURN is encountered at line 160, the computer discovers that it has *no return address*. The subroutine has been entered because of sequential execution, not because of a GOSUB— so no return address was saved. Without a current return address, the error RETURN WITHOUT GOSUB occurs.

THE END STATEMENT TO PROTECT SUBROUTINES

The END statement terminates execution of a program. We can prevent a subroutine from being entered as a result of sequential execution by placing it after an END statement.

As we just illustrated, if the computer enters the subroutine without being sent there by a GOSUB, an error occurs when RETURN is reached. Since the computer starts at the first line of the program and works its way to the last line of the program, we must stop the computer before it runs into the subroutine.

One way we can do this is to use the END statement. The keyword END terminates execution of the program. By placing the END statement after the main body of instructions, and the subroutine after the END statement, we prevent the computer from entering the subroutine sequentially.

Note: On most microcomputers, one or more END statements can be placed at any point in the program. The program is not terminated until the END statement is actually executed. On some larger systems, however, the computer scans the program prior to execution, and ignores all instructions appearing after the first END statement. In this situation you must place the END statement as the last line of the program. Where we use an END statement in the middle of a program, substitute a GOTO sending the computer to the END.

Example

The following illustration shows how a program can be organized when subroutines are used, and where the END statement is placed.

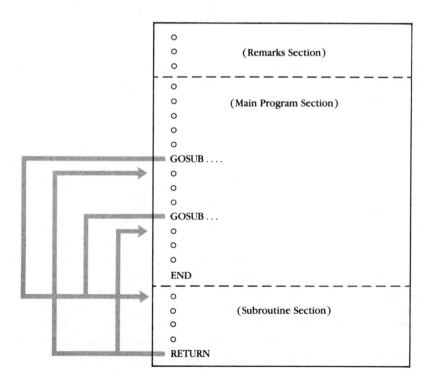

Notice in the illustration that the subroutine can be entered only by placing a GOSUB in the main program section. Whenever the instructions in the subroutine are needed, a GOSUB sends the computer to the subroutine. When the RETURN statement is encountered at the end of the subroutine, the computer returns to its point of origin in the program.

After working its way down the list of instructions in the main program section, the computer encounters the END statement. This statement tells the computer that it has completed everything we wanted it to do, and execution of the program is terminated.

USING SUBROUTINES TO SIMPLIFY PROGRAMS

We can sometimes make a program easier to understand by moving a set of instructions from the main program to the subroutine section—even if those instructions appear in the program only once.

Most business programs perform many functions. As the number of instructions in the program increases, so does the complexity. It may be difficult to follow what a program is doing with hundreds of instructions in the main program section.

Sometimes, the size and complexity of a program can be reduced by moving certain sets of instructions out of the main program section to the subroutine section. Even though the instructions may be needed only once, we can use a subroutine to make the main program section shorter and more understandable.

We move the set of instructions, replacing it by a GOSUB statement. It is also helpful to add a REMark statement to explain what function is being performed by the subroutine. Thus, the main program section gives an outline of the entire program from beginning to END, and subroutines provide detailed instructions for the steps in the main program.

If we keep this approach in mind when organizing a problem's solution, we can write an algorithm in a few simple steps. Those steps needing explanation in greater detail can be written later as another algorithm for a subroutine. Going even farther, when the algorithm describing the steps in the subroutine is completed, any step requiring more detail can be written in another algorithm. This would result in one subroutine calling another subroutine. (The depth to which subroutines can be thus "nested" depends on how many return addresses your computer can save at one time.)

This process of first writing a program in a few simple steps, then describing some of the steps in greater detail later, is called "top down program design". It is widely accepted for making programs simpler and more understandable.

Example

We have been asked to develop a BASIC program for an investor wanting to know how long an investment will take to double at a given interest rate. By his definition, this occurs when the total net earnings on his investment equal or exceed the amount originally invested.

To solve the problem, we can calculate the net earnings year by year, comparing the total to the original investment after each calculation. If we keep count of how many times the calculation is performed, we can stop calculating when the net exceeds the original investment and print the number of years.

To simplify the development of a solution, we consider the calculation of total net earnings as a single step in our algorithm. Using the "top down" approach, we outline the program, then work out the details of the calculations later. We know the program will have to accept data, calculate net earnings, and compare these earnings to the original investment; so we write these steps in our first attempt at an algorithm.

— Input original investment and interest rate
— Calculate net earnings
— Compare net earnings to original investment

Now, let's set up a loop to calculate the total net earnings and compare the result to the original investment. If the comparison is true, then we exit the loop and print the result. If not true, then we add 1 to our counter (for the number of years) and repeat the loop. Since we will be using variables to store both total net earnings and number of years, we must be sure these variables start out with the correct values. We must initialize net earnings to zero, and set the year counter for the first year. The algorithm now appears as follows:

— Input original investment and interest rate
— Initialize earnings to zero, year to 1
— Start loop
— Calculate net earnings to date
— If net earnings >= original investment
   then exit loop and print year
— Otherwise, increase year by 1 and repeat loop

It appears that this algorithm will solve the investor's problem, so we next translate it into BASIC.

```
10   INPUT "ORIGINAL INVESTMENT";  INVESTMENT
20   INPUT "PERCENT INTEREST";  PERCENT
30   LET EARNINGS = 0
40   LET YEAR = 1
50     GOSUB 120 : REM CALCULATE NET EARNINGS
60     IF NET >= INVESTMENT THEN GOTO 90
70     LET YEAR = YEAR + 1
80     GOTO 50 : REM CALCULATE NET EARNINGS FOR NEXT YEAR
90   PRINT "NET EARNINGS = INVESTMENT IN YEAR";  YEAR
100 END
```

This represents the complete main program section for the program—even though we still must create the subroutine called for in line 50. By postponing this task, we have designed the main program section with relative ease. We can now focus our attention on the calculations required for the subroutine.

The investor describes the procedure for computing the net earnings on an investment.

— Calculate the interest earned for the year
— Add interest earned for the year to total earnings
— Net earnings (after tax) is equal to 75% of total earnings (25% tax bracket)

Using this algorithm, we can write the subroutine to calculate net earnings.

```
110 REM *** SUBROUTINE TO CALCULATE NET EARNINGS ***
120    LET YRINCOME = (INVESTMENT + EARNINGS) * (PERCENT / 100)
130    LET EARNINGS = EARNINGS + YRINCOME
140    LET NET = EARNINGS * .75
150 RETURN
```

The complete program and a sample of the output is shown below. Notice that the main program section is easier to read and follow with instructions for calculating net earnings located in the subroutine section. The advantage of this technique is even more significant when programs are more complex, and the subroutines involve an even larger number of instructions.

```
10   INPUT "ORIGINAL INVESTMENT";  INVESTMENT
20   INPUT "PERCENT INTEREST";  PERCENT
30   LET EARNINGS = 0
40   LET YEAR = 1
50     GOSUB 120 : REM CALCULATE NET EARNINGS
60     IF NET >= INVESTMENT THEN GOTO 90
70     LET YEAR = YEAR + 1
80     GOTO 50 : REM CALCULATE NET EARNINGS FOR NEXT YEAR
90   PRINT "NET EARNINGS = INVESTMENT IN YEAR";  YEAR
100 END
110 REM *** SUBROUTINE TO CALCULATE NET EARNINGS ***
120    LET YRINCOME = (INVESTMENT + EARNINGS) * (PERCENT / 100)
130    LET EARNINGS = EARNINGS + YRINCOME
140    LET NET = EARNINGS * .75
150 RETURN
```

```
RUN
ORIGINAL INVESTMENT? 2000
PERCENT INTEREST? 12
NET EARNINGS = INVESTMENT IN YEAR 8
```

TEST YOUR UNDERSTANDING

6.   How are GOSUB and GOTO statements similar? How are they different?

7.   What does the computer do when it executes a RETURN statement?

8.   What error can occur when a RETURN statement is executed? What causes this?

9.   What happens when an END statement is executed?

10.   What precaution must you take when using a subroutine in a program?

11.   In what situations would you use a subroutine?

12.   Refer to the third exercise in Section 2 of this chapter. Write a program which solves the problem, and which uses a subroutine containing both IF statements described in the algorithm.

Section 4. Using a Data File

INTRODUCTION

When a large quantity of data is to be processed by a program, it's often prepared in advance and stored in a computer file. A *file* is a group of related data stored in a computer-readable form. On microcomputers, magnetic diskettes are commonly used for storing files. The file is assigned a name when created, so that the data it contains can be retrieved when needed.

The advantage of data files is that data entered into the computer just once is then available for use by many programs. For instance, a payroll data file could be used by one program to print a list of earnings and deductions, and by another program to prepare government tax reports. A third could use this file to prepare employee insurance reports. Without this data file, the same information would have to be entered into the computer three times.

In using a data file, we must understand how the file is organized. When a file is created, a program accepts data entered from the keyboard, and transfers the data to a file on diskette. Programs that later use this data file must retrieve the data in the same sequence it was entered. Therefore, the programmer must know the organization of the data file to write a program retrieving the data in proper sequence.

This section illustrates the organization of files, how data is transferred to a file on diskette, and how data is retrieved from a file.

This section has three parts:

- The Organization of Data Files
- Putting Data into a File
- Getting Data from a File

Note: Programs using data files represent an important and common business application of the computer. The concepts presented in this section apply to computers in general, but the file statements in the examples are specific to the IBM PC. If you use a different computer, read this section, then consult your BASIC reference manual for the exact format of file-related statements for your computer. If you use an APPLE, refer to Appendix A for a discussion of file handling on this computer.

THE ORGANIZATION OF DATA FILES

A file contains one or more records, each consisting of one or more data items called fields.

File data is divided into logical groups called *records*, each record containing one or more items of related data. Each data item is called a *field*, which is a group of one or more characters treated as one unit.

In BASIC, fields are of two types, *string* and *numeric*. A numeric field contains one or more digits representing a numeric value. A string field contains a sequence of characters representing one item of data.

The smallest possible file (if not absolutely empty) would contain one record containing a single field with only one character. On the other end of the scale, a file could contain millions of records, each containing hundreds of fields of varying sizes. Most files fall somewhere between these two extremes.

Example

A payroll file has been created consisting of one record for each employee in the company. In this and following examples, we assume 10 employees and 10 employee records. The data used to prepare the payroll file were:

Employee Name	Hours Worked	Pay Rate
G. HOLMES	38	5.80
B. PARSONS	40	7.20
C. BARTLETT	25	6.50
H. PAINTER	50	8.80
S. JONES	20	4.10
A. SMITH	48	6.50
M. TURNER	40	9.20
J. ALLEN	17	4.10
R. PASS	44	5.90
K. O'BRIEN	31	6.60

The three fields for each employee record are employee name, hours worked, and pay rate. Employee name is a string field. Hours worked and pay rate are numeric fields.

We can picture data in a file as a sequence of fields. Each field may be followed by an end-of-field character—depending on the computer—and each group of related fields—a record—is followed by an end-of-record character. The last record in the file is followed by an end-of-file character.

The special characters which separate fields, records, and files, and the manner in which they are used, varies among computers. The characters themselves are not printable, but we can illustrate the contents of a file as follows:

G. HOLMES,38,5.8/B. PARSO⌐ ⌐SS,44,5.9/K. O'BRIEN,31,6.6\

This is how the file appears to the computer—as a series of characters. As humans, however, we visualize each record as a line of data:

G. HOLMES, 38, 5.80
B. PARSONS, 40, 7.20
C. BARTLETT, 25, 6.50
H. PAINTER, 50, 8.80
S. JONES, 20, 4.10
A. SMITH, 48, 6.50
M. TURNER, 40, 9.20
J. ALLEN, 17, 4.10
R. PASS, 44, 5.90
K. O'BRIEN, 31, 6.60

Because some computers use end-of-field characters and some don't, we will create a file that can be used on different types of computers by organizing it slightly differently. Instead of having one employee record containing three fields, ours will contain a sequence of three records for each employee, each record containing only one field. We visualize this as:

G. HOLMES
38
5.80
B. PARSONS
40
7.20
C. BARTLETT

17
4.10
R. PASS
44
5.90

K. O'BRIEN
31
6.60

When using this file to prepare the payroll, we must retrieve three single-field records in sequence for each employee. We are going to consider this three-record sequence a *logical* record.

PUTTING DATA IN A FILE

Putting data in a file involves three steps: opening the file, writing the data to the file, and closing the file.

To put data in a file, the file must first be opened for output—to establish the file and prepare the computer to transfer data to it. Each computer has some form of OPEN statement to accomplish this.

Putting data in the file is very similar to printing data on the screen. Depending on the computer, a keyword such as PRINT, PRINT # or WRITE is followed by a literal value or a variable name. When the command is executed, the literal value (or the value stored under the variable name) is transferred to the file.

In most cases, the data being transferred to a file is stored temporarily in a section of the computer's memory called an *output buffer*. When enough data has accumulated for an efficient transfer, the computer automatically copies the data from the buffer to the diskette file. Before the program ends, a CLOSE statement must be executed to make the final transfer of data from the buffer and write an end-of-file character following the last record.

Example

The program in this example creates the payroll file, and demonstrates the use of the OPEN OUTPUT, PRINT #, and CLOSE statements—the BASIC statements for creating a data file on the IBM PC.

```
10   PRINT "ENTER PAYROLL DATA"
20   PRINT "WHEN DONE, USE EMPLOYEE NAME = 'END OF DATA' "
30   OPEN "PAYDATA" FOR OUTPUT AS #1
40     INPUT "EMPLOYEE NAME"; EMPLOYEE$
50     IF EMPLOYEE$ = "END OF DATA" THEN GOTO 130
60     PRINT #1, EMPLOYEE$
70     INPUT "HOURS WORKED THIS WEEK"; HOURS
```

```
80      PRINT #1, HOURS
90      INPUT "HOURLY PAY RATE"; PAY
100     PRINT #1, PAY
110     GOTO 40
120 REM ******* END OF INPUT *******
130     PRINT #1, "END OF DATA"
140     PRINT #1, 00.0
150     PRINT #1, 0.00
160     CLOSE #1
170 PRINT "END OF PROGRAM"
180 END
```

The OPEN OUTPUT statement establishes a file and prepares it to receive data. When the file is opened, we assign it a name to distinguish it from other files on the diskette. A number from 1 to 3 is also assigned to the file, because we can have more than one file open at a time.

The PRINT # statement is used to "print" data into the file. The keywords PRINT # are followed by the number of the file being written to, a comma, and the data to be stored in the file. To close the file, we use a CLOSE # statement, indicating the number of the file that is to be closed.

Although file commands may be different for your computer, you can use the technique illustrated in this program. The first two lines display instructions to the person at the keyboard. Since we are using a loop to collect the data for each employee, an exit from the loop must be provided. The exit is provided at line 50 and will be taken when END OF DATA is entered for the employee name.

Line 30 opens the file and assigns it the name "PAYDATA" and the file number #1. A prompt for the employee name is then displayed by the INPUT statement on line 40, and execution stops until data is entered from the keyboard.

When a name is entered, the IF statement checks the condition EMPLOYEE$ = "END OF DATA". If the condition is true, the exit from the loop is taken. If the employee name is not END OF DATA, the remainder of the IF statement is ignored, and execution passes to line 60. This PRINT # statement transfers to the data file the employee name just entered.

Lines 70 through 100 prompt for hours and pay rate, and transfer the data that is entered to the file. Each data item being written is a single-field record, and the program writes three records in sequence to form a logical record. The GOTO statement on line 110 sends the computer back to line 40 to get the data for the next logical record.

The loop from line 40 to line 110 continues to input data for each employee and transfer the data to the file. When the employee name of END OF DATA is entered, the IF statement on line 50 causes the computer to exit the loop and branch to line 130.

Before the file is closed, a special three-record sequence is written to the file. This logical record is called a *trailer* record, and we will discuss its significance in the next example. The three data items for the trailer record are written to the file by the PRINT # statements on lines 130 to 150. (Note that in these PRINT # statements, the values are literal.) Line 160 closes the file, then an ending message is printed and execution stops with the END statement on line 180.

When we run this program, a file is created which contains all the data entered at the keyboard plus the trailer record. This file is stored on the diskette under the name "PAYDATA", and it can be retrieved by other programs for use as input.

A portion of the RUN for this program is shown:

```
RUN
ENTER PAYROLL DATA
WHEN DONE, USE EMPLOYEE NAME = 'END OF DATA'
EMPLOYEE NAME? G. HOLMES
HOURS WORKED THIS WEEK? 38
HOURLY PAY RATE? 5.80
EMPLOYEE NAME? B. PARSONS
HOURS WORKED THIS WEEK? 40
HOURLY PAY RATE? 7.20
EMPLOYEE NA
HOU
        O'BRIEN
       D THIS WEEK? 31
  RLY PAY RATE? 6.60
EMPLOYEE NAME? END OF DATA
END OF PROGRAM
```

GETTING DATA FROM A FILE

Retrieving data from a file involves three steps: opening the file, inputting data from the file, and closing the file.

To retrieve the data stored in a file, that file must first be opened for input. The computer locates the file on the diskette, and prepares to receive its data. If the file cannot be found on the diskette, an error occurs, such as FILE NOT FOUND. When the file is opened, a "pointer" indicates the first item of data in the file. As each data item is read from the file, the pointer advances to indicate the next item.

Inputting data from the file is similar to inputting data from the keyboard. A keyword such as INPUT, or INPUT # is followed by a variable name under which the input data is to be stored. When the instruction is executed, the value being indicated by the pointer is read from the file and stored under the variable name. Although inputting data from a file may be similar to inputting from the keyboard, a prompt is not allowed. Since the input data is coming from a file, no prompting is necessary.

After inputting all data, we execute a CLOSE statement to terminate the input of data from the file.

Example

The program in this example lists the contents of the payroll file named "PAYDATA". It demonstrates the use of the OPEN INPUT, INPUT #, and CLOSE statements, used on the IBM PC for inputting data from a file. This program also illustrates a variation on the technique of setting up and exiting a loop.

```
10   PRINT "CONTENTS OF PAYDATA FILE"
20   PRINT
30   PRINT "NAME", "HOURS WORKED", "PAY RATE"
40   PRINT
50   OPEN "PAYDATA" FOR INPUT AS #1
60   REM ********** INPUT LOOP **************
70     INPUT #1, EMPLOYEE$, HOURS, WAGE
80     PRINT EMPLOYEE$, HOURS, WAGE
90     IF EMPLOYEE$ <> "END OF DATA" THEN GOTO 70
100  REM ******** TERMINATE PROCESSING **********
110    CLOSE #1
120    PRINT
130    PRINT "END OF PAYDATA FILE"
140    END
```

The output of this program is a listing of the contents of the payroll file:

```
RUN
CONTENTS OF PAYDATA FILE

NAME              HOURS WORKED    PAY RATE

G.  HOLMES          38              5.8
B.  PARSONS         40              7.2
```

```
C.  BARTLETT        25              6.5
H.  PAINTER         50              8.8
S.  JONES           20              4.1
A.  SMITH           48              6.5
M.  TURNER          40              9.2
J.  ALLEN           17              4.1
R.  PASS            44              5.9
K.  O'BRIEN         31              6.6
END OF DATA          0              0
```

END OF PAYDATA FILE

The OPEN INPUT statement causes the computer to locate the file on the diskette, and prepare to receive its data. Since we can have more than one file open at a time, we assign the file a number from 1 to 3 when it is opened.

We use the INPUT # statement to input data from the file. The number following INPUT # must correspond to the file number assigned when it was opened. A prompt is not allowed in the INPUT # statement, since it accepts data from the diskette file rather than the keyboard.

If the INPUT # statement is executed after all data has been read from the file, an error occurs, such as OUT OF DATA (or INPUT PAST END). To prevent this, a trailer record has been placed as the last logical record in the file. Our program checks for this record, and stops inputting data from the file when the trailer is encountered. The CLOSE # statement is used to terminate input from the file.

Again, the file commands may be different for your computer, but the same technique can be used. In this program, lines 10 through 40 print a title and column headings, with blank lines used to improve readability.

The OPEN INPUT statement on line 50 causes the computer to locate the PAYDATA file on the diskette, and assign the number #1 to the file. The file must actually exist on the diskette being searched by the computer, or the error FILE NOT FOUND occurs.

Line 60 is a REMark statement which the computer ignores, and execution passes to the INPUT # statement on line 70, to read three data items from the file. The first item is stored under the string variable name EMPLOYEE$, the second item under the numeric variable name HOURS, and the third under WAGE.

Line 80 then prints the data items just read from the file. The items in this PRINT statement are separated by commas, so they are positioned in the print zones under the appropriate headings.

The IF statement on line 90 checks to see if this is the last logical record in the file. The last logical record is the trailer record, with an employee name of END OF DATA. Notice that this IF statement is not used to *exit* the loop; it is used to *create* the loop.

As long as the employee name is not equal to END OF DATA, the "not equal to" condition in this IF statement is true, and the GOTO 70 is executed. This sends the computer back to line 70 to input and print the next employee record. The loop continues to input and print records until the trailer record is reached.

After the trailer record is input and printed, the IF statement checks the condition EMPLOYEE$ <> "END OF DATA". This time EMPLOYEE$ *is* equal to END OF DATA, so the "not equal" condition is false. Therefore, the statement following THEN is ignored, and the computer proceeds to the next line in the program.

After exiting the loop, the computer executes lines 100 through 140 in sequence. The REMark on line 100 is ignored, and line 110 causes the file to be closed. A blank line and an ending message are printed, and then the END statement halts the program.

Notice that when we created the payroll file, we used the variable name PAY for the pay rate. Now, in this program we are using the variable name WAGE for the same data item. This illustrates that the file contains only data. The variable names are created in the programs, and different programs might use different variable names to reserve storage areas for the data input from a file.

TEST YOUR UNDERSTANDING

13. A file contains one or more _____ , each containing one or more _____ .

14. A field is _____ which is treated as one item of data.

15. In BASIC, there are two types of fields, _____ and _____ .

16. To input data from a file or to write data to a file, the file must first be _____ .

17. What error occurs if we attempt to input data from a file after all the data has been read? What is one technique we can use to prevent this from occurring?

Section 5. The Payroll Program

INTRODUCTION

The problem introduced at the beginning of this chapter was the calculation of gross pay, deductions, and net pay for all the employees of a company. The benefit of using a computer here is that it can perform these calculations for a large number of employees much faster and more accurately than humans.

The payroll program illustrates the statements and the techniques involved in using a data file, creating a loop, providing an exit for a loop, using IF tests, and using subroutines. In this section, we discuss the organization of a program, and present one solution to the payroll problem.

This section has two parts:

- Organizing a Program
- The Payroll Program

ORGANIZING A PROGRAM

Solutions for most problems can be organized in a variety of ways. The most important considerations in organizing a program are that it solve the problem correctly, and be easy to read and understand.

We can organize a BASIC program into three sections— remarks, the main program section, and the subroutine section. Each section can be divided into two or more parts as necessary. Using REMark statements, we can separate and identify each section, and each functional part within a section.

Here is an outline of the payroll program, illustrating the sections and their parts:

I. Remarks
   a. Purpose of program
   b. List of variables

II. Main program section
   a. Prepare to input data
   b. Input and print loop
   c. Terminate input and end

III.Subroutine section
   a. Calculate and print results subroutine
     i.   Calculate regular pay subroutine
     ii. Calculate overtime pay subroutine.

While reading the following, refer to the program listing at the end of this chapter, and identify which lines in the program are performing each of the outline functions.

The first section of the program contains only REM statements. For those who may have to later modify the program, we describe its purpose, and we list the variable names and what each represents. These two introductory elements can be included in any BASIC program.

We have divided the main program section into three parts. The first part assigns starting values to the constants, opens the file, and prints the title and column headings.

The second part of the main program section is the loop that processes each employee record from the file. In this loop, an INPUT # statement reads one logical record, and an IF statement checks to see if the trailer record has been input. If not, a GOSUB sends the computer to a subroutine— to calculate the pay and print the results for the employee whose data has just been read. The loop is then created by a GOTO statement which sends the computer back to input the next employee record.

When the trailer record is input, the condition EMPLOYEE$ = "END OF DATA" is true, and the GOTO 520 is executed. This directs the computer out of the loop to the "terminate processing" part of the program. An ending message is printed, the file is closed, and the program ends.

The third section of the program contains three subroutines. The first is the only one entered from the main program section. The other two are entered from the first. Notice how this is represented in the outline above.

The first subroutine calculates the pay and prints the results for one employee. Two IF statements are used to test for overtime. If the hours worked are over 40, the first IF statement sends the computer to another subroutine to calculate regular and overtime pay. If the hours worked are less than or equal to 40, the second IF statement sends the computer to a different subroutine to calculate regular pay and set overtime pay equal to zero.

After returning from the appropriate subroutine, the regular pay and over-time pay are added for total pay. The FICA deduction is calculated, then rounded to the nearest penny. The next statement computes the net pay by subtracting the deduction from the total pay. After the results are printed in the proper print zones, a RETURN statement sends the computer back to the main program section for the next employee record.

THE PAYROLL PROGRAM

Correlate the listing that follows with the outline given above for this program. Notice that the main program section describes the function of the entire program with the subroutines providing the detailed instructions for the calculations. (This program is written for the IBM PC. See Appendix A for a listing of the payroll program written for the APPLE.)

```
LOAD  "PROGRAM4"
LIST
10   REM  *********************************************************
20   REM                        REMARKS
30   REM  *********************************************************
40   REM THIS PROGRAM PREPARES A PAYROLL REPORT USING THE DATA
50   REM FILE "PAYDATA". IT OPENS THE FILE, READS THREE RECORDS,
60   REM AND CALCULATES TOTAL PAY, DEDUCTIONS AND NET PAY FOR
70   REM EACH EMPLOYEE. THE LAST EMPLOYEE NAME RECORD IN THE
80   REM FILE CONTAINS THE STRING "END OF DATA". WHEN THIS
90   REM RECORD IS DETECTED, THE FILE IS CLOSED AND AN END OF
100  REM REPORT MESSAGE IS PRINTED.
110  REM  *********************************************************
120  REM               LIST OF VARIABLES
130  REM INPUT
140  REM VARIABLES:  EMPLOYEE$ = EMPLOYEE NAME
150  REM               HOURS = HOURS WORKED THIS WEEK
160  REM               WAGE = HOURLY PAY RATE
170  REM PROGRAM
180  REM VARIABLES:  REGULARPAY = PAY FOR HOURS UP TO 40 PER WEEK
190  REM               OVERTIMEPAY = PAY FOR HOURS OVER 40 PER WEEK
200  REM               EXTRAHOURS = HOURS WORKED OVER 40
210  REM PROGRAM
220  REM CONSTANTS:  WRKWEEK = 40 HOURS PER WEEK
230  REM               FICA = .067 (6.7% OF TOTAL PAY)
240  REM OUTPUT
250  REM VARIABLES:  EMPLOYEE$ = EMPLOYEE NAME
260  REM               TTLPAY = TOTAL PAY (REGULAR + OVERTIME)
270  REM               DEDUCT = FICA DEDUCTION
280  REM               NETPAY = NET PAY AFTER DEDUCTION
290  REM  *********************************************************
300  REM               MAIN PROGRAM SECTION
310  REM  *********************************************************
```

```
320 REM
330 REM **** INITIALIZE CONSTANTS, OPEN FILE, PRINT HEADINGS ***
340 REM
350     LET WRKWEEK = 40
360     LET FICA = .067
370     OPEN "PAYDATA" FOR INPUT AS #1
380     PRINT "PAYROLL REPORT"
390     PRINT
400     PRINT "EMPLOYEE", "TOTAL PAY", "DEDUCTION", "NET PAY"
410     PRINT
420 REM
430 REM ************** INPUT AND PRINT LOOP ******************
440 REM
450     INPUT #1, EMPLOYEE$, HOURS, WAGE
460     IF EMPLOYEE$ = "END OF DATA"
             THEN GOTO 520: REM TERMINATE INPUT AND END
470     GOSUB 630: REM CALCULATE PAY AND PRINT RESULTS
480     GOTO 450: REM GET DATA FOR NEXT EMPLOYEE
490 REM
500 REM ************ TERMINATE INPUT AND END *****************
510 REM
520     PRINT
530     PRINT "END OF REPORT"
540     CLOSE #1
550     END
560 REM
570 REM ************************************************************
580 REM                    SUBROUTINE SECTION
590 REM ************************************************************
600 REM
610 REM **** SUBROUTINE TO CALCULATE PAY AND PRINT RESULTS *****
620 REM
630     IF HOURS > WRKWEEK THEN GOSUB 800: REM OVERTIME PAY
640     IF HOURS <= WRKWEEK THEN GOSUB 740: REM NO OVERTIME PAY
650     LET TTLPAY = REGULARPAY + OVERTIME PAY
660     LET DEDUCT = TTLPAY * FICA
670     LET DEDUCT = INT(DEDUCT * 100 + .5) / 100
680     LET NETPAY = TTLPAY - DEDUCT
690     PRINT EMPLOYEE$, TTLPAY, DEDUCT, NETPAY
700     RETURN
710 REM
```

```
720 REM *********** SUBROUTINE FOR NO OVERTIME PAY *************
730 REM
740      LET REGULARPAY = HOURS * WAGE
750      LET OVERTIMEPAY = 0
760      RETURN
770 REM
780 REM ************ SUBROUTINE FOR OVERTIME PAY **************
790 REM
800      LET REGULARPAY = WAGE * WRKWEEK
810      LET EXTRAHOURS = HOURS - WRKWEEK
820      LET OVERTIMEPAY = EXTRAHOURS * WAGE * 1.5
830      RETURN
```

Here is the output of this program (assuming that PAYDATA contains the data illustrated in the examples from Section 4):

```
RUN
PAYROLL REPORT
```

EMPLOYEE	TOTAL PAY	DEDUCTION	NET PAY
G. HOLMES	220.4	14.77	205.63
B. PARSONS	288	19.3	268.7
C. BARTLETT	162.5	10.89	151.61
H. PAINTER	484	32.43	451.57
S. JONES	82	5.49	76.51
A. SMITH	338	22.65	315.35
M. TURNER	368	24.66	343.34
J. ALLEN	69.7	4.67	65.03
R. PASS	271.4	18.18	53.22
K. O'BRIEN	204.6	13.71	190.89

PROGRAMMING EXERCISES

Programming Problem 4A:

The city has adopted an income tax requiring employers to withhold 2 percent of the gross pay of all employees. This must be calculated and included in the computation of deductions. Make the appropriate change to the program to add 2 percent of gross pay to the calculation of deductions. Insert a new constant in the program for CITYTAX, and use this for making the new calculation.

Programming Problem 4B:

The president of the company has declared that each employee should receive a bonus of $50.00. Since this bonus is taxable, it must be added to the employee's total pay. Insert a new constant in the program for BNSPAY, and change the computation of total pay to add the bonus. Also insert a new PRINT statement to cause this message to print immediately under the report heading: GROSS PAY INCLUDES $50.00 BONUS.

ANSWERS TO "TEST YOUR UNDERSTANDING" EXERCISES

1. Sequence of execution is 10, 40, 50, 20, 30, 60.

2. Output appears as: THIS WON'T MAKE
　　　　　　　　　　　ANY SENSE UNLESS
　　　　　　　　　　　IT IS CORRECT

3. (a) False; (b) True; (c) True; (d) True; (e) True; (f) False; (g) False; (h) False; (i) False.

4. Output appears as : R
　　　　　　　　　　　I
　　　　　　　　　　　G
　　　　　　　　　　　H
　　　　　　　　　　　T

5. Suggested solution:

```
10  INPUT "WHAT IS THE AMOUNT OF SALE"; SALE
20  IF SALE >= 1000 THEN LET COMMISSN = SALE * .16
30  IF SALE < 1000 THEN LET COMMISSN = SALE * .12
40  PRINT "COMMISSION EARNED IS $"; COMMISSN
```

6. Both the GOSUB and GOTO transfer control to another line in the program. Before branching to the new line, the GOSUB saves the address of the statement following it; the GOTO does not.

7. It interrupts sequential execution and returns to the address previously saved in memory.

8. The RETURN WITHOUT GOSUB error can occur if the RETURN is executed without a current return address.

9. Execution of the program is terminated.

10. You must not allow the subroutine to be entered through sequential execution of statements.

11. A subroutine can be used when an identical set of statements is needed at different points in the program, or when moving a set of instructions out of the main program section will simplify that section.

12. Suggested solution:

```
10  INPUT "WHAT IS THE AMOUNT OF SALE"; SALE
20  GOSUB 60 : REM CALCULATE COMMISSION
30  PRINT "COMMISSION EARNED IS $"; COMMISSN
40  END
50  REM *** SUBROUTINE TO CALCULATE COMMISSION ***
60  IF SALE >= 1000 THEN LET COMMISSN = SALE * .16
70  IF SALE < 1000 THEN LET COMMISSN = SALE * .12
80  RETURN
```

13. Records; fields.

14. Group of characters.

15. String; numeric.

16. Opened.

17. OUT OF DATA (or INPUT PAST END) error; place a trailer record in the file, and test for it when inputting data. When the trailer record is detected, terminate input from the file.

CHAPTER 5

Decision Making

CHAPTER OBJECTIVE

To demonstrate the techniques for analyzing a decision-making process, and the BASIC statements and techniques used to solve decision problems.

PROBLEM

When considering a loan application, the Loan Department uses the annual income and net worth of the applicant to compute the maximum authorized loan—a percentage of the income plus a percentage of the net worth. These percentages vary, however, depending on the particular combination of the applicant's income and net worth. Before the maximum loan amount can be computed, the Loan Department must decide which of four loan classifications applies to this customer.

Because of a backlog in the Loan Department, you have been asked to write a program using the applicant's income and net worth to determine which loan classification is appropriate, and to then compute the maximum amount that may be loaned to the applicant. The loan classification is determined from the following table:

Income less than $15,000	Income $15,000 to $34,999	Income $35,000 to $99,999	Income $100,000 or more
(CLASS = 4)	Net less than $20,000 (CLASS = 4)	Net less than $20,000 (CLASS = 4)	Net less than $20,000 (CLASS = 4)
	Net between $20,000 and 149,999 (CLASS = 3)	Net between $20,000 and 49,999 (CLASS = 3)	Net between $20,000 and 49,999 (CLASS = 2)
	Net $150,000 or more (CLASS = 2)	Net between $50,000 and 149,999 (CLASS = 2)	Net $50,000 or more (CLASS = 1)
		Net $150,000 or more (CLASS = 1)	

The percentages used in computing the maximum amount for each loan class are:

Class	Percentage of Income	Percentage of Net Worth
1	20	25
2	20	20
3	15	20
4	10	15

CHAPTER OVERVIEW

A decision involves selecting one course of action from among two or more possibilities. Decisions, however, are not made by computers. Decisions are *made* by humans, and programs are written to implement those decisions.

Decision programs are valuable because they reduce the chance of human error in a complex decision process, and because the computer operates at incredible speed. Once given the rules for selecting a course of action, the computer can evaluate thousands of conditions and arrive at a result in seconds.

The computer's ability to implement decisions is limited only by the programmer's ability to express rules for selecting a course of action. In this chapter, you will learn several techniques for analyzing a decision process, the BASIC statements used to implement decisions, and some decision structures used in BASIC programs.

This chapter has five sections:

- **Analyzing A Decision Program**
- **Deciding Between Two Alternatives**
- **Choosing One of Many Alternatives**
- **Complex Decisions**
- **The Loan Program**

Section 1. Analyzing a Decision Program

INTRODUCTION

When a program is RUN, the computer executes each program instruction in sequence from the lowest-numbered to the highest. We have already discussed the GOTO and GOSUB statements used to alter this sequence of execution. Such altering is called "branching." When a GOTO or a GOSUB is encountered, the computer "branches" to the specified line number.

We have also discussed the IF statement, which evaluates a condition and executes a given instruction when the condition is true. The instruction we include in the IF statement may be a GOTO or a GOSUB which transfers control to another line in the program. A decision program often includes several such IF statements—which may make the program difficult to follow because of all the branching that can occur.

This section introduces the techniques we can use to simplify the analysis and writing of decision programs.

This section has two parts:

- Blocks of Instructions
- Flow Lines

BLOCKS OF INSTRUCTIONS

Directing the computer to perform a certain function often requires more than one instruction. A set of instructions which performs a specific function can be viewed as a "block" of instructions, called a routine.

We can simplify a program analysis by picturing it in terms of the functions performed by routines, and drawing a diagram illustrating the routines as blocks. This reduces the amount of detail we must consider and allows us overview of the program.

This diagramming technique can be used as a developmental tool to aid in writing a program, or as an analytical tool to aid in understanding a program's operation.

Example

The following simple program computes the total amount of a purchase order.

```
10 INPUT "PRICE OF ITEM ORDERED"; PRICE
20 INPUT "QUANTITY ORDERED"; QUANTITY
30 LET SUBTTL = PRICE * QUANTITY
40 LET TAX = SUBTTL * .06
50 LET TTL = SUBTTL + TAX
60 PRINT
70 PRINT "TOTAL WITH TAX IS $"; TTL
```

The instructions in this program can be grouped according to the functions being performed, and the program can then be written:

```
5   REM ******** OBTAIN DATA **********
10     INPUT "PRICE OF ITEM ORDERED"; PRICE
20     INPUT "QUANTITY ORDERED"; QUANTITY
25  REM
28  REM **** CALCULATE ORDER TOTAL ****
30     LET SUBTTL = PRICE * QUANTITY
40     LET TAX = SUBTTL * .06
50     LET TTL = SUBTTL + TAX
55  REM
58  REM ******* DISPLAY RESULT ********
```

```
60      PRINT
70      PRINT "TOTAL WITH TAX IS $";  TTL
```

This program could also be illustrated by a diagram showing the main routines of the program as blocks of instructions.

10	Obtain Data
30	Calculate Order Total
60	Display Result

When using a block diagram to illustrate the routines in a program already written, we can include in each block the line number of the first instruction in that routine. This helps us associate the diagram with the listing.

FLOW LINES

When a GOTO or GOSUB statement is encountered in a program, the computer branches to the specified line number. In a block diagram, this branching can be illustrated by a flow line.

We can use a flow line to illustrate the transfer of control from a GOTO or GOSUB statement to a specified instruction or block of instructions, and also to indicate the RETURN of control at the end of the subroutine. By using flow lines in a block diagram, we can picture the flow of control between the routines. This technique simplifies the analysis or development of a program containing branching instructions.

Example

The following program is similar to the order total program in the previous example. In this case, however, a 10% discount is calculated if the amount of the order (before tax) is $100.00 or more.

```
10  REM ***** DETERMINE SUBTOTAL ******
20     INPUT "PRICE OF ITEM ORDERED"; PRICE
30     INPUT "QUANTITY ORDERED";  QUANTITY
40     PRINT
```

```
50      LET SUBTTL = PRICE * QUANTITY
60       IF SUBTTL < 100 THEN GOTO 130
70    REM
80    REM ***** CALCULATE DISCOUNT ******
90      LET DISCOUNT = SUBTTL * .10
100      LET SUBTTL = SUBTTL - DISCOUNT
110      PRINT "DISCOUNT AMOUNT = $"; DISCOUNT
120   REM
130   REM **** CALCULATE ORDER TOTAL ****
140      LET TAX = SUBTTL * .06
150      LET TTL = SUBTTL + TAX
160   REM
170   REM ******* DISPLAY RESULT ********
180      PRINT "TOTAL WITH TAX IS $"; TTL
190      END
```

We can analyze this program using the following diagram:

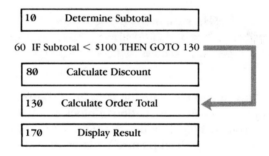

In this program, a decision must be made whether to calculate a discount for the order. If the order is less than $100, no discount is calculated. This decision is represented by the condition (SUBTTL < 100) on line 60.

When the condition is true, the IF statement directs the computer to line 130. Thus, the computer skips the routine for calculating the discount, and goes directly to calculate the order total without a discount. This transfer of control is illustrated by the flow line in the diagram.

When the condition (SUBTTL < 100) is false, the remainder of the IF statement is ignored, and execution passes to the next instruction in sequence. Here, the computer enters the routine for calculating the discount. Next, the computer continues in sequence to figure the order total and display the result.

It is important to recognize two paths that can be taken through this program. Each time the program is RUN, only one of the two paths is taken. The path taken is determined by the IF statement on line 60.

To illustrate the output of the program in each case, let's run the program twice, once with values that make the condition true, and once with values that make it false.

```
RUN
PRICE OF ITEM ORDERED? 35.00
QUANTITY ORDERED? 2

TOTAL WITH TAX IS $ 74.2
```

In this case, SUBTTL equals 35.00 * 2, or 70.00. Since this is less than 100, the IF statement directs the computer along the alternate path directly to line 130. The block of instructions for calculating the discount is skipped.

When the subtotal is $100 or more, a discount is calculated and the discount amount displayed. This is demonstrated in a second RUN of this program.

```
RUN
PRICE OF ITEM ORDERED? 20.00
QUANTITY ORDERED? 6

DISCOUNT AMOUNT = $ 12
TOTAL WITH TAX IS $ 114.48
```

On this run, the SUBTTL is 20.00 * 6, or 120.00. Since the condition in the IF statement is now false, the alternate path directly to line 130 is *not* taken. The computer continues in sequence to the instruction following the IF statement, where the discount is calculated.

Notice how the flow line in the block diagram is used to indicate the alternate path through the program. Whether this path is taken depends on the result of the condition test.

TEST YOUR UNDERSTANDING

1. What is a routine?

2. Identify the routines in the following program by drawing a block around the statements in each one.

```
10 INPUT "HOW MUCH WILL YOU DEPOSIT"; DEPSIT
20 INPUT "WHAT ANNUAL INTEREST RATE (IN PERCENT)"; PCT
30 INPUT "FOR HOW MANY YEARS"; TERM
40 FOR YEAR = 1 TO TERM
50   NTEREST = DEPSIT * PCT / 100
60   DEPSIT = DEPSIT + NTEREST
70 NEXT YEAR
80 PRINT
90 PRINT "YOUR DEPOSIT WILL BE WORTH"; DEPSIT
```

3. For the following program, draw a block diagram showing the routines and flow of control.

```
10 INPUT "WHAT ARE YOUR TOTAL SALES THIS WEEK"; SALES
20 PRINT
30 LET COMMISSN = SALES * .05
40 PRINT "YOUR COMMISSION IS $"; COMMISSN
50 IF SALES < 1000 THEN GOTO 90
60 LET BNUS = (SALES - 1000) * .01
70 PRINT "AND YOU'VE EARNED A BONUS OF $"; BNUS
80 PRINT "FOR A TOTAL OF $"; COMMISSN + BNUS
90 END
```

Section 2. Deciding Between Two Alternatives

INTRODUCTION

In the last example, we saw a technique for deciding whether a certain process should be performed. If it should not, the computer skips over the routine performing the process. This is a simple yes-or-no decision.

Sometimes a problem requires an either/or decision. Either perform one process, or the other, but not both. In this section, you will learn two techniques for making an either/or decision and directing the computer to take only one of two possible courses of action.

This section has two parts:

- The GOTO Approach
- The GOSUB Approach

THE GOTO APPROACH

In writing a program to perform only one of two possible processes, we must include a routine for each alternative. By using GOTOs in the proper places, we can direct the computer to skip over the inappropriate routine.

The problem with writing a program to execute only one of two routines is that they must both be included in the program, one after the other. If we direct the computer to perform the first routine, we must also tell it to skip the second. If we want it to execute only the second routine, we must direct it to skip the first. This can be accomplished by the appropriate use of the GOTO statement, illustrated in the following example.

Example

A hotel has two rooms available for banquets. The Silver Room has a capacity of 20 people, and charges $3.00 per person for table setup, plus $25 for room rental. If more than 20 people attend, the Gold Room must be used. The charge here is $2.50 per person for table setup, and $55 for room rental. A program is required to determine which room is to be used, based on the number of people attending, and to compute the total charges.

A program to solve this problem is:

```
10   REM *** DETERMINE NUMBER OF PEOPLE ATTENDING ***
20      INPUT "HOW MANY PEOPLE WILL ATTEND"; PARTY
30      PRINT
40      IF PARTY > 20 THEN GOTO 200
50   REM
100  REM ********** SILVER ROOM CHARGES ***********
110     LET TABLECHG = PARTY * 3.00
120     LET ROOMCHG = 25
130     PRINT "RESERVE THE SILVER ROOM FOR"; PARTY; " PEOPLE."
140     GOTO 300
150  REM
200  REM *********** GOLD ROOM CHARGES ************
210     LET TABLECHG = PARTY * 2.50
220     LET ROOMCHG = 55
230     PRINT "RESERVE THE GOLD ROOM FOR"; PARTY; " PEOPLE."
240     REM
300  REM ********* COMPUTE TOTAL AND PRINT **********
```

```
310 LET TTLCHG = ROOMCHG + TABLECHG
320 PRINT "THE TOTAL CHARGE IS $"; TTLCHG
330 END
```

The flow of control in this program is illustrated as follows:

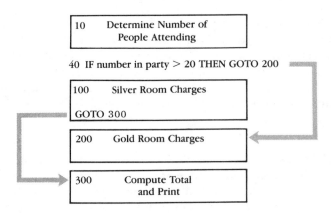

Notice the use of line numbers to identify the routines. In this program, we begin each routine with a line number that is a multiple of 100. This leaves many more available line numbers between the routines than numbering by tens straight through. This makes it easier to add instructions to a routine, if necessary, without having to change line numbers used in the GOTO statements.

Each time this program is executed, one of two possible paths is taken. If the number of people in the party is 20 or less, the condition in the IF statement (PARTY > 20) is false. The computer ignores the remainder of the IF statement and goes to the next line in the program, thereby entering the routine for the Silver Room charges. At the end of this routine, a GOTO on line 140 sends the computer around the routine for the Gold Room charges, directly to the routine to compute and print the total. This is illustrated in the following run.

RUN
```
HOW MANY PEOPLE WILL ATTEND? 18

RESERVE THE SILVER ROOM FOR 18 PEOPLE.
THE TOTAL CHARGE IS $ 79
```

On the other hand, if the number in the banquet party is over 20, an alternate path through the program is taken. In this case, the condition (PARTY > 20) is true. The IF statement directs the computer to skip over the routine for the Silver Room, and proceed directly to line 200 where the Gold Room charges are computed. After this routine is executed, the computer continues in sequence to the next instruction, entering the routine to compute and print the total. The output in this case appears:

```
RUN
HOW MANY PEOPLE WILL ATTEND? 30

RESERVE THE GOLD ROOM FOR 30 PEOPLE.
THE TOTAL CHARGE IS $ 130
```

It's important to note in this decision structure the order of the routines for the true and false conditions following the IF test, and the use of the GOTOs to bypass the inappropriate routine.

THE GOSUB APPROACH

A second method for organizing a program to perform only one of two processes is to write the alternate processes as subroutines. The command which transfers control in this case is GOSUB.

When GOSUB is used, we must write two IF statements to determine which subroutine is needed. The first tests a condition and sends the computer to the appropriate subroutine if the condition is true. The second IF statement tests for the opposite condition, then sends the computer to the second subroutine if that condition is true.

The second IF statement is required because the computer RETURNs to this statement after executing the first subroutine. If the first subroutine has been executed because the first condition is true, the second IF statement, testing the opposite condition, prevents the second subroutine from being executed.

Example

The program from the previous example can be rewritten using the GOSUB approach. The diagram below shows the flow of control to and from the subroutines.

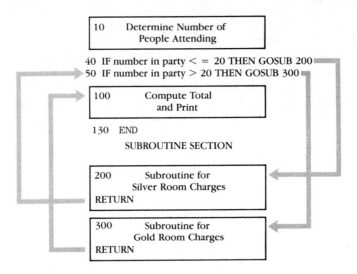

Notice in this and the previous diagram that some flow lines are drawn on the right side of the diagram, and some on the left. The transfer of control resulting from a condition test, as in the IF statement, is shown on the right. These flow lines indicate transfers that may or may not occur, depending on the conditions being tested. Transfers of control not depending on a condition test are drawn on the left. Note also that a flow line is used to indicate the return of control to the statement following a calling GOSUB.

The code for this program is:

```
10  REM *** DETERMINE NUMBER OF PEOPLE ATTENDING ***
20     INPUT "HOW MANY PEOPLE WILL ATTEND"; PARTY
30     PRINT
40     IF PARTY <= 20 THEN GOSUB 200
50     IF PARTY > 20 THEN GOSUB 300
60  REM
100 REM ********* COMPUTE TOTAL AND PRINT **********
110    LET TTLCHG = ROOMCHG + TABLECHG
120    PRINT "THE TOTAL CHARGE IS $"; TTLCHG
130    END
140 REM
180 REM *********** SUBROUTINE SECTION *************
```

```
190 REM
200 REM ********** SILVER ROOM CHARGES ************
210    LET TABLECHG = PARTY * 3.00
220    LET ROOMCHG = 25
230    PRINT "RESERVE THE SILVER ROOM FOR"; PARTY; " PEOPLE."
240    RETURN
250 REM
300 REM *********** GOLD ROOM CHARGES ************
310    LET TABLECHG = PARTY * 2.50
320    LET ROOMCHG = 55
330    PRINT "RESERVE THE GOLD ROOM FOR"; PARTY; " PEOPLE."
340    RETURN
```

Note: If your computer does not permit an END statement in the middle of a program, change line 130 to GOTO 350, and add line 350, END.

This program performs exactly the same function as the previous program. As you see from these examples, there is more than one way to write a problem-solving program. Which way do we choose? We choose the method that provides the correct solution and is easy to read, understand, and modify, if necessary.

Subroutines are used to organize programs and simplify the main program section. When designing a program that involves decisions, use subroutines whenever they can simplify the solution of the problem.

TEST YOUR UNDERSTANDING

4. A car rental agency charges $15 per day plus 10 cents per mile for a car rented seven days or less. If rented more than seven days, the charge is 8 cents per mile, $14 per day for the first seven days, and $12 per day for each day after the seventh.

Using either the GOTO or GOSUB approach, write a program to input the number of days rented and the mileage, and compute the rental charge. Organize your solution by first drawing a block diagram showing the major routines (and subroutines, if you plan to use them). Next, add the IF statement(s) to the diagram, indicating the necessary transfer of control. Write the BASIC instructions needed for each routine and assemble the routines into a BASIC program.

Section 3. Choosing One of Many Alternatives

INTRODUCTION

Many problems we face require more than just a simple either/or decision; there may be many alternatives. Writing a program to choose one alternative from among three or more possibilities often involves a sequence of IF statements.

In this section, you will be introduced to two techniques using a sequence of IF statements, two new BASIC keywords, and the concept of error trapping.

This section has five parts:

- A Sequence of IF Statements
- Error Trapping
- Using OR
- Using AND
- Finding a Value in a Range

A SEQUENCE OF IF STATEMENTS

A problem involving more than two possible conditions, only one of which can be true, requires a sequence of IF statements to determine the true condition.

Following the sequence of IFs is a sequence of routines, one for each possible condition. Each IF statement tests one condition, then directs the computer to the matching routine if the condition is true. Each routine, except the last in the sequence, ends with a GOTO statement causing the computer to skip over the subsequent routines. This structure is illustrated in the following example.

Example

A manufacturing company is about to convert to the metric system of measurement. The company has many technical drawings which contain measurements in inches, square inches, and cubic inches. These measurements must be converted to centimeters, square centimeters, and cubic centimeters. This is not difficult, but a computer program would make the conversion much faster.

The following program asks for the measurement in inches, square inches or cubic inches. To reduce the amount of typing required to use the program, we use single-letter codes to indicate each type of measurement. We determine which code was entered, and direct the computer to the appropriate conversion routine by using a sequence of IF statements to test for each one of the codes. At the end of the program, we create a loop to repeat the program for further measurement conversions.

```
10   REM **************** OBTAIN DATA ********************
20      INPUT "WHAT IS THE MEASUREMENT IN INCHES"; INCHES
30      PRINT "INCHES? SQUARE INCHES? CUBIC INCHES?"
40      INPUT "ENTER I, S, OR C"; CODE$
50      PRINT
60   REM
100  REM ************ DETERMINE WHICH CODE **************
110     IF CODE$ = "I" THEN GOTO 200
120     IF CODE$ = "S" THEN GOTO 300
130     IF CODE$ = "C" THEN GOTO 400
140  REM
200  REM ************ INCHES TO CENTIMETERS **************
210     LET CENT = INCHES * 2.54
220     PRINT INCHES; " INCHES ="; CENT; " CENTIMETERS"
230     GOTO 500
240  REM
300  REM ****** SQUARE INCHES TO SQUARE CENTIMETERS *******
310     LET CENT = INCHES * (2.54 ^ 2)
320     PRINT INCHES; " SQ. INCHES ="; CENT; " SQ. CENTIMETERS"
330     GOTO 500
340  REM
400  REM ****** CUBIC INCHES TO CUBIC CENTIMETERS ********
410     LET CENT = INCHES * (2.54 ^ 3)
420     PRINT INCHES; " CUBIC INCHES = "; CENT; " CC's"
430  REM
500  REM ********** DO IT AGAIN IF THERE'S MORE ***********
510     PRINT
520     INPUT "DO YOU HAVE MORE (Y OR N)"; ANSWER$
530     IF ANSWER$ = "Y" THEN GOTO 10
540  REM
```

```
600  REM ********** OTHERWISE, END THE PROGRAM **********
610     PRINT "END OF CONVERSION PROGRAM"
620     END
```

The flow of control in this program is illustrated here:

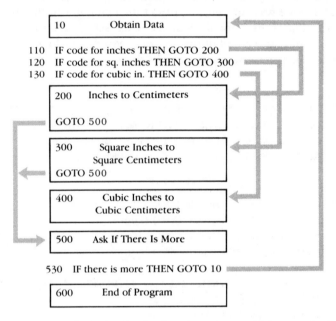

This program is relatively simple, but it serves to illustrate the function of a sequence of IF statements and the use of the GOTO in the matching routines. A sample RUN of this program might look like this:

```
RUN
WHAT IS THE MEASUREMENT IN INCHES? 250
INCHES? SQUARE INCHES? CUBIC INCHES?
ENTER I, S, OR C? C

 250 CUBIC INCHES = 4096.77 CC's

DO YOU HAVE MORE (Y OR N)? Y
WHAT IS THE MEASUREMENT IN INCHES? 1.25
INCHES? SQUARE INCHES? CUBIC INCHES?
ENTER I, S, OR C? I

 1.25 INCHES = 3.165 CENTIMETERS
```

```
DO YOU HAVE MORE (Y OR N)? Y
WHAT IS THE MEASUREMENT IN INCHES? 45
INCHES? SQUARE INCHES? CUBIC INCHES?
ENTER I, S, OR C? S

 45 SQ. INCHES = 290.322 SQ. CENTIMETERS

DO YOU HAVE MORE (Y OR N)? Y
WHAT IS THE MEASUREMENT IN INCHES? 12
INCHES? SQUARE INCHES? CUBIC INCHES?
ENTER I, S, OR C? I

 12 INCHES = 30.48 CENTIMETERS

DO YOU HAVE MORE (Y OR N)? N
END OF CONVERSION PROGRAM
```

Note the sequence of IF statements to test for each of the possible codes, the sequence of routines corresponding to each possible code, and use of the GOTO statements to skip over the inappropriate routines.

Notice also the use of the INPUT and IF statements at the end of the program; these start the program again if there are more measurements to convert.

ERROR TRAPPING

If there is a chance that an error may occur in a program, we should include instructions to test for that error and allow corrective action to be taken.

The program in the previous example demonstrated a technique for deciding among several possible alternatives, and using three possible codes: I, S, or C. Suppose a fourth code were entered, a fourth possibility not accounted for in the program: the possibility of an error.

One way to handle this error condition is writing a routine to print an error message, giving the user a chance to enter the data again. This routine is placed immediately after the sequence of IFs. It will only be entered when all the conditions being tested are false. If any one of the conditions is true, the GOTO in that IF statement will send the computer past the error routine, directly to the appropriate routine for that condition.

Example

We have modified the program from the previous example to include an error routine. Below is a partial listing of the program showing the modification.

```
10   REM ******** INCHES TO CENTIMETERS CONVERSION ********
20       INPUT "WHAT IS THE MEASUREMENT IN INCHES"; INCHES
30       PRINT "INCHES? SQUARE INCHES? CUBIC INCHES?"
40       INPUT "ENTER I, S, OR C"; CODE$
50   REM
100  REM ************ DETERMINE WHICH CODE **************
110      IF CODE$ = "I" THEN GOTO 200
120      IF CODE$ = "S" THEN GOTO 300
130      IF CODE$ = "C" THEN GOTO 400
140  REM
150  REM ************** ERROR ROUTINE ******************
160      PRINT CODE$; " IS INVALID. PLEASE RE-ENTER."
170      GOTO 40
180  REM
200  REM *********** INCHES TO CENTIMET
210      LET CENT = INCHES *
220      PRINT INC
230      GO
```

A portion of the block diagram for this program is also shown illustrating the flow of control involved in the error routine:

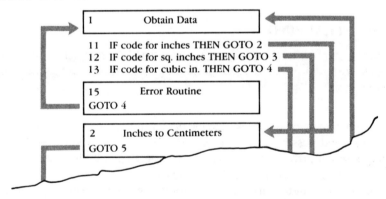

Think for a moment—what would have happened if an invalid code were entered before we included the error routine? Suppose the person at the keyboard meant to press C, but accidentally pressed X instead. The first IF test would have failed (CODE$ = "I" is false). The next IF test would have failed (CODE$ = "S" is false), and finally, the third IF test would also have failed (CODE$ = "C" is false).

After finding all these conditions false, the computer would continue in sequence to the next instruction. With no error routine in the program, it would enter the routine for converting inches to centimeters. An incorrect result would be produced, since the conversion intended was cubic inches to cubic centimeters.

If the keyboard operator did not catch this mistake, an incorrect measurement could be included in the drawings. The purpose of an error trap is to prevent such mistakes from occurring.

Let's run the modified program to test the function of the error routine.

```
RUN
WHAT IS THE MEASUREMENT IN INCHES?  87
INCHES?  SQUARE INCHES?  CUBIC INCHES?
ENTER I, S, OR C?  X
X IS INVALID. PLEASE RE-ENTER.
ENTER I, S, OR C?  7
7 IS INVALID. PLEASE RE-ENTER.
ENTER I, S, OR C?  C
 87 CUBIC INCHES = 1425.67 CC's

DO YOU HAVE MORE (Y OR N)?  N
END OF CONVERSION PROGRAM
```

The example shown here is only one kind of mistake for which an error trap should be considered. Wherever in a program an error can occur, we should include a routine to "trap" the error and halt the program until the error is corrected.

It is interesting to consider the error messages you sometimes receive from the BASIC Interpreter and DOS programs. Is it possible the program enters an error trap after failing to find the meaning of an instruction?

USING OR

The keyword OR can be used to combine two conditions in one IF statement if a single course of action depends on either one or both conditions being true.

OR can be used to combine conditions in an IF statement according to the following general format:

IF condition OR condition THEN statement

OR is called a "logical operator." The conditions on either side of OR must each be a condition in its own right—that is, each condition must contain two values separated by a relational operator.

When conditions are combined in an IF statement using the logical operator OR, the computer evaluates each individual condition. If *any* one of the conditions is *true*, the statement following THEN is executed. If *all* of the conditions are *false*, the statement following THEN is not executed.

Example

A company has a policy that purchase orders for more than $1000 must be approved by the department manager. Purchase orders for quantities over 100 items must also be approved by the department manager. This company uses a BASIC program for preparing and recording purchase orders. The following IF statement is included in the program; it prints a message on the order if the department manager's approval is needed.

```
IF QUANTITY > 100 OR TTLPRICE > 1000
    THEN PRINT "NEED MGR'S APPROVAL"
```

When both conditions are false, no message is printed. When one condition or both are true, the message will be printed.

USING AND

> The keyword AND can be used to combine two conditions in an IF statement when a course of action depends on both conditions being true.

AND is another logical operator used to combine conditions in an IF statement. The general format is:

IF condition AND condition THEN statement

When conditions are combined in an IF statement using the logical operator AND, the computer evaluates each individual condition. If *all* of the conditions are *true*, the command following THEN is executed. If *any* one of the conditions is *false*, the command following THEN is not executed.

Example

An insurance company sells automobile repair insurance for used cars. To qualify for the insurance, the car must be less than 5 years old and have less than 50,000 miles on it. The following IF statement could be used to determine if both conditions are true.

```
IF  AGE  <  5  AND  MILES  <  50000
        THEN  PRINT  "APPROVED  FOR  REPAIR  INSURANCE"
```

In this case, both conditions must be true for insurance to be approved. If one condition or both are false, the message is not printed.

FINDING VALUES IN A RANGE

The logical operator AND can be used in an IF statement to determine if a value is within a certain range. IF the value is greater than the lower limit AND the value is less than the upper limit, THEN the value is within that range.

Example

In the loan problem introduced at the beginning of this chapter, a maximum loan amount is calculated as a percentage of the customer's income plus a percentage of net worth. The percentages used in the calculation vary depending on the range of the income and the net worth.

The Loan Department has divided income into four possible ranges, as follows:

> Less than $15,000
> $15,000 to less than $35,000
> $35,000 to less than $100,000
> $100,000 and over

This is pictured graphically:

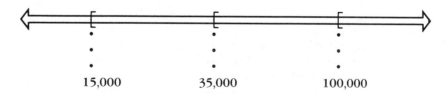

Before a maximum loan amount can be computed, we must determine which of these four possible ranges applies to the customer. To do this, a sequence of IF statements can be used, each testing the income for a value within one of the ranges.

The following simple program demonstrates the technique used in the loan program to determine the customer's income range.

```
10 INPUT "WHAT IS THE ANNUAL INCOME"; INCOME
20 IF INCOME < 15000
        THEN LET RANGE$ = "LOW"
30 IF INCOME >= 15000 AND INCOME < 35000
        THEN LET RANGE$ = "AVERAGE"
40 IF INCOME >= 35000 AND INCOME < 100000
        THEN LET RANGE$ = "HIGH"
50 IF INCOME >= 100000
        THEN LET RANGE$ = "VERY HIGH"
60 PRINT "THIS CUSTOMER'S INCOME IS "; RANGE$
```

Two sample RUNs of this program are shown:

RUN
```
WHAT IS THE ANNUAL INCOME? 17000
THIS CUSTOMER'S INCOME IS AVERAGE
```

RUN
```
WHAT IS THE ANNUAL INCOME? 250000
THIS CUSTOMER'S INCOME IS VERY HIGH
```

When using this type of decision structure, careful consideration must be given to the equal signs used in the conditions. The values 15000, 35000, and 100000 are the limits of the ranges. Each limit must be included in one range and only one.

If the equal signs were omitted from all the conditions, then an income of *exactly* 15000 would fail all four IF tests.

Incorrect:

```
20 IF INCOME < 15000
        THEN LET RANGE$ = "LOW"
30 IF INCOME > 15000 AND INCOME < 35000
        THEN LET RANGE$ = "AVERAGE"
40 IF INCOME > 35000 AND INCOME < 100000
        THEN LET RANGE$ = "HIGH"
50 IF INCOME > 100000
        THEN LET RANGE$ = "VERY HIGH"
```

If equal signs were included in all the conditions, then an income of 15000 would pass both the first test on line 20 and the second test on line 30.

Incorrect:

```
20 IF INCOME <= 15000
      THEN LET RANGE$ = "LOW"
30 IF INCOME >= 15000 AND INCOME <= 35000
      THEN LET RANGE$ = "AVERAGE"
40 IF INCOME >= 35000 AND INCOME <= 100000
      THEN LET RANGE$ = "HIGH"
50 IF INCOME >= 100000
      THEN LET RANGE$ = "VERY HIGH"
```

We must make sure that 15000 is included in one range, and only one. Each limit is correctly included in only one range by using the equal sign with the limit only once, as shown at the beginning of this example.

TEST YOUR UNDERSTANDING

5. The fare for a flight from Los Angeles to Phoenix is $43 for first class, $38 for economy class, and $35 for coach. Write a program which prompts for F, E, or C, tests the code that is entered, and prints the price of the fare. An error routine should be included to allow the code to be re-entered if incorrect. The output should appear in the following format:

```
LOS ANGELES TO PHOENIX
FIRST, ECONOMY OR COACH?
ENTER F, E OR C? S
PLEASE RE-ENTER
ENTER F, E OR C? C
COACH CLASS TICKET IS $35
```

Note: This sample output illustrates an incorrect response and execution of the error routine.

6. An automobile insurance company offers two rates for collision insurance. Applicants with no moving violations in the last three years and at least 21 years of age receive the preferred rate; all others receive the regular rate. Write a program which prompts for the applicant's age and number of moving violations, and prints either PREFERRED RATE APPLIES or REGULAR RATE APPLIES as appropriate.

7. A lumber company sells 2 × 4s in bulk at 38 cents per board-foot for quantities less than 2000 board-feet; 35 cents for quantities of 2000 to less than 5000 board-feet; and 31 cents for quantites of 5000 board-feet or more. Write a program to input the number of board-feet purchased and compute the total price.

Section 4. Complex Decisions

INTRODUCTION

The ability of the computer to perform a complex selection process depends only on the programmer's ability to write precise instructions. When decision problems become complex, we need additional techniques to analyze a decision process and implement a solution in BASIC.

In this section you will learn techniques to analyze a complex decision problem and write a BASIC program responding to a variety of conditions.

This section has four parts:

- Analyzing a Complex Decision
- Creating Indicators
- The ON. . .GOTO Statement
- The ON. . .GOSUB Statement

ANALYZING A COMPLEX DECISION

We can organize a solution for a complex decision problem by drawing a diagram illustrating the questions to be considered and the possible answers for each.

When there are several factors to consider and many possibilities for each, selecting a course of action can be complicated. In real life, the situation is worse because the problem often presents itself in a disorganized fashion. To solve the problem with a computer, we must organize the factors and the possiblities for each, then translate the resulting decision rules into BASIC instructions.

To organize a solution, we begin by identifying all questions considered in making a decision, then we choose one to be answered first. By drawing a diagram with that question at the top, we can list the possible answers below. This is our question at the first level.

Some outcomes for the first question may lead to a second question. We place these at the second level, and list the possible answers for each. This process continues until we have accounted for all questions and answers which concern us.

The result is a tree diagram of the decision process. Starting at the top, we can follow the questions and their answers until we arrive at a final course of action at the bottom of the diagram.

Example

A manufacturing company owns a large number of metal stamping machines in its main factory. When production schedules permit, one of these machines is taken out of service for maintenance. If the machine has been used less than 1000 hours, it is oiled and put back into service.

If the machine has recorded between 1000 and 49,999 hours, it is given either light or routine maintenance, depending on whether it is involved in a critical process. If not critical, the machine receives routine maintenance. Otherwise, it receives light maintenance unless it has never had routine maintenance, in which case routine maintenance must be done.

When a machine records between 50,000 and 99,999 hours of use, it is overhauled unless it has been overhauled before. In that case, it receives only routine maintenance.

Finally, if the machine has 100,000 hours or more, it must be totally rebuilt.

Let's assume that the chief engineer has asked us to write a program to determine whether a machine is to receive oiling, light maintenance, routine maintenance, overhauling, or rebuilding. This represents a complex decision process; we have several factors to consider and several possible courses of action. To develop a solution that can be implemented using the computer, let's begin by listing the factors.

Reading through the maintenance rules above, we discover four questions which bear upon a final decision.

> How many hours on the machine?
> Is it critical?
> Has it had previous routine maintenance?
> Has it had a previous overhaul?

Which of these questions would we like to consider first? We could pick any one, but we should consider first the one that most simplifies the problem. The questions concerning critical status, previous routine maintenance, and previous overhaul do not apply to every situation. Since the number of hours on the machine must be considered in every case, we start with that factor.

Our first question concerns the number of hours on the machine. The four answers with which we are concerned are shown as outcomes in this diagram:

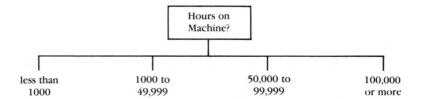

For hours less than 1000, we will only oil the machine. For hours between 1000 and 49,999, we must find out whether the machine is critical before determining what to do. Between 50,000 and 99,999 hours, we must know whether the machine has been overhauled before. Over 100,000 hours, the machine will be rebuilt.

Two of the four outcomes of this first question lead to a final result. Each of the other two outcomes leads to another question. This information as added to the second level of the diagram.

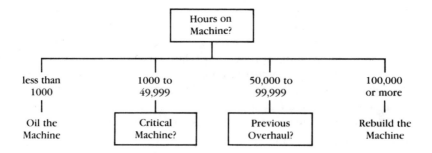

The question concerning critical status has two possible outcomes. If the answer is no, then the final result is to give the machine routine maintenance. If the answer is yes, we must determine if the machine has had routine maintenance before.

The question concerning a previous overhaul also has two outcomes. If previously overhauled, the machine receives routine maintenance. If no previous overhaul, it will be overhauled now.

This new information is added to the third level of our diagram.

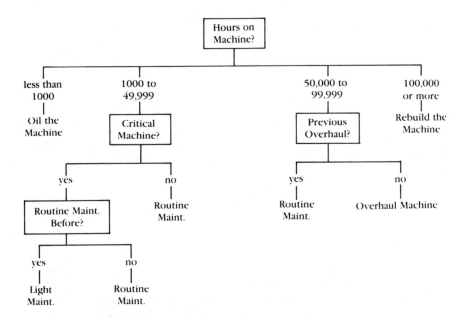

The question at the third level, previous routine maintenance, poses two possible outcomes. Each outcome leads to a final result as shown above.

We have illustrated the decision process for this problem using three levels of questions. Now that we have a clear picture of the questions to be considered, and the sequence in which to ask them, we can write a program to solve the problem.

First, we need a routine to obtain the necessary data: hours on the machine; critical status; whether the machine has had previous routine maintenance, and whether it has had a previous overhaul. Following that, we must write a routine to determine the range of hours. With four ranges to be tested, we can write a sequence of IFs, each containing a GOTO sending the computer to an appropriate routine for that range.

```
10   REM *************** OBTAIN DATA ****************
20      INPUT "HOW MANY HOURS ON THE MACHINE"; HOURS
30      INPUT "IS IT A CRITICAL MACHINE (Y OR N)"; CRITICAL$
```

```
40      INPUT "ROUTINE MAINTENANCE BEFORE (Y OR N)";
        ROUTINE$
50      INPUT "OVERHAULED BEFORE (Y OR N)"; OHAUL$
60      PRINT
70   REM
100  REM ************* HOW MANY HOURS? **************
110     IF HOURS < 1000 THEN GOTO 200
120     IF HOURS >= 1000 AND HOURS < 50000 THEN GOTO 300
130     IF HOURS >= 50000 AND HOURS < 100000 THEN GOTO 400
140     IF HOURS >= 100000 THEN GOTO 500
150  REM
```

For now, we can number the four routines by 100s, leaving us enough line numbers for all instructions. The first routine is simple; the first outcome leads to a final result, so we print a message and end the program.

```
200  REM *********** LESS THAN 1000 HOURS ***********
210     PRINT "OIL THE MACHINE"
220     END
230  REM
```

The routine for the second possible outcome requires a test of the critical status. This is an either/or situation, using the either/or structure illustrated earlier (see page 150). To determine the critical status, we use an IF statement to test the condition CRITICAL$ = "Y". When the condition is false, the machine is not critical; the routine for this condition is placed immediately following the IF. Since the machine receives routine maintenance if it is not critical, this routine prints a message and ends.

When the condition is true, we execute a GOTO sending the computer to a routine for that condition. For now, we will start that routine on line 340.

```
300  REM ********** 1000 TO 49,999 HOURS ************
310     IF CRITICAL = "Y" THEN GOTO 340
320     PRINT "GIVE THE MACHINE ROUTINE MAINTENANCE"
330     END
```

Referring back to our diagram, we see that if the condition (CRITICAL$ = "Y") is true, we must determine whether the machine has had routine maintenance before. Therefore, at line 340, we test the condition ROUTINE$ = "Y". If this condition is false, we give the machine routine maintenance; so, following the IF, we write instructions to print that message and end. If the condition is true, we give the machine only light maintenance; so we send the computer to a routine at line 370 which prints the appropriate message and ends the program.

```
340        IF ROUTINE$ = "Y" THEN GOTO 370
350        PRINT "GIVE THE MACHINE ROUTINE MAINTENANCE"
360        END
370        PRINT "GIVE THE MACHINE LIGHT MAINTENANCE"
380        END
```

To write the routine for the third category of hours, we again refer to our diagram. In this case, we must determine if the machine has been previously overhauled; so we test the condition OHAUL$ = "Y". If this condition is false, the machine is overhauled; so, following the IF statement, we write statements to print the corresponding message and end the program. If the condition (OHAUL$ = "Y") is true, we only give the machine routine maintenance; so we send the computer to a routine at line 440 to print that message and end the program.

```
400 REM ********** 50,000 TO 99,999 HOURS ***********
410     IF OHAUL$ = "Y" THEN GOTO 440
420     PRINT "OVERHAUL THE MACHINE"
430     END
440     PRINT "GIVE THE MACHINE ROUTINE MAINTENANCE"
450     END
460 REM
```

As we see on our diagram, the fourth category of hours leads to a final result, so the routine at line 500 simply prints the appropriate message and ends the program. The complete listing for this program and several sample runs are shown here:

```
10   REM *************** OBTAIN DATA ****************
20      INPUT "HOW MANY HOURS ON THE MACHINE"; HOURS
30      INPUT "IS IT A CRITICAL MACHINE (Y OR N)"; CRITICAL$
40      INPUT "ROUTINE MAINTENANCE BEFORE (Y OR N)"; ROUTINE$
50      INPUT "OVERHAULED BEFORE (Y OR N)"; OHAUL$
60   REM
100  REM ************* HOW MANY HOURS? **************
110     IF HOURS < 1000 THEN GOTO 200
120     IF HOURS >= 1000 AND HOURS < 50000 THEN GOTO 300
```

```
130     IF HOURS >= 50000 AND HOURS < 100000 THEN GOTO 400
140     IF HOURS >= 100000 THEN GOTO 500
150 REM
200 REM ********** LESS THAN 1000 HOURS ************
210     PRINT "OIL THE MACHINE"
220     END
230 REM
300 REM ********** 1000 TO 49,999 HOURS ************
310     IF CRITICAL = "Y" THEN GOTO 340
320     PRINT "GIVE THE MACHINE ROUTINE MAINTENANCE"
330     END
340       IF ROUTINE$ = "Y" THEN GOTO 370
350       PRINT "GIVE THE MACHINE ROUTINE MAINTENANCE"
360       END
370       PRINT "GIVE THE MACHINE LIGHT MAINTENANCE"
380       END
390 REM
400 REM ********** 50,000 TO 99,999 HOURS ***********
410     IF OHAUL$ = "Y" THEN GOTO 440
420     PRINT "OVERHAUL THE MACHINE"
430     END
440     PRINT "GIVE THE MACHINE ROUTINE MAINTENANCE"
450     END
460 REM
500 REM ********** 100,000 OR MORE HOURS **********
510     PRINT "REBUILD THE MACHINE"
520     END
```

RUN
HOW MANY HOURS ON THE MACHINE? **25287**
IS IT A CRITICAL MACHINE (Y OR N)? **N**
ROUTINE MAINTENANCE BEFORE (Y OR N)? **N**
OVERHAULED BEFORE (Y OR N)? **N**

GIVE THE MACHINE ROUTINE MAINTENANCE

RUN
HOW MANY HOURS ON THE MACHINE? **15121**
IS IT A CRITICAL MACHINE (Y OR N)? **Y**
ROUTINE MAINTENANCE BEFORE (Y OR N)? **Y**
OVERHAULED BEFORE (Y OR N)? **N**

GIVE THE MACHINE LIGHT MAINTENANCE

RUN
HOW MANY HOURS ON THE MACHINE? **65149**
IS IT A CRITICAL MACHINE (Y OR N)? **N**
ROUTINE MAINTENANCE BEFORE (Y OR N)? **Y**
OVERHAULED BEFORE (Y OR N)? **N**

OVERHAUL THE MACHINE

Notice that the answer to the first question on our diagram is determined using a sequence of IF's, each testing for a value of hours within one range. Two of the four outcomes lead to routines in which another question must be answered. The third routine contains a simple either/or decision structure. The second routine also contains an either/or decision structure, of which one outcome leads to an either/or structure at the third level.

We solved this problem by combining several different decision structures into one program, but by first diagramming the decision process, we could determine which structures were appropriate and their proper sequence.

Of course, there are many ways to solve a problem, and the program shown in this example is only one method. In fact, this program could be improved. How would you improve it?

CREATING INDICATORS

An indicator is a variable we create to control the operation of a program. At any point in the program, we can write a statement to store a value in the indicator. At some other point, we include a statement which tests the indicator and directs the operation of the program based on the value stored there.

Think of an indicator as a way to pass information from one part of a program to another. For instance, if we used a subroutine to carry out a sequence of tests, we would need some means of storing the outcome of those tests and sending the result back to the main program. We can create a variable to use as an indicator, and write the subroutine to assign a particular value to the indicator based on the outcome of the tests. When the computer returns from the subroutine, we can use the value in the indicator to determine what processing is to be performed next.

Example

A contracting company has two bulldozers used in excavation work. The smaller bulldozer is used whenever possible, but if the excavation is more than 2 yards deep or 1600 square yards in area, then the larger bulldozer must be used. Also, when the excavation involves more than 3000 cubic yards, the larger bulldozer is preferred.

The charge for excavating with the smaller bulldozer is $1.75 per cubic yard. For the larger bulldozer, the charge is $1.90 per cubic yard. The following program uses the length, width, and depth of an excavation to decide which bulldozer should be used and its cost.

```
10   REM ************* OBTAIN DIMENSIONS ***************
20      PRINT "ENTER THE DIMENSIONS OF THE EXCAVATION IN YARDS:"
30      INPUT "LENGTH"; LNGTH
40      INPUT "WIDTH"; WIDTH
50      INPUT "DEPTH"; DEPTH
60   REM ********* COMPUTE SIZE OF EXCAVATION **********
70      LET AREA = LNGTH * WIDTH
80      LET YARDS = AREA * DEPTH
90      LET SIZE$ = "SMALL" : REM SET INDICATOR FOR SMALL
100     GOSUB 200 : REM SEE IF LARGE ONE IS NEEDED INSTEAD
110  REM ************* COMPUTE CHARGES ***************
120     IF SIZE$ = "LARGE" THEN GOTO 150
130     PRINT "USE SMALL BULLDOZER. CHARGE IS $"; YARDS * 1.75
140     END
150     PRINT "USE LARGE BULLDOZER. CHARGE IS $"; YARDS * 1.90
160     END
170  REM
180  REM ************* SUBROUTINE SECTION *************
190  REM
200     IF DEPTH > 2 THEN LET SIZE$ = "LARGE"
210     IF AREA > 1600 THEN LET SIZE$ = "LARGE"
220     IF YARDS > 3000 THEN LET SIZE$ = "LARGE"
230     RETURN
```

(The variable LNGTH is used instead of LENGTH because LEN is a keyword in BASIC.)

We have created the indicator SIZE$ to indicate which bulldozer is to be used. Since the small bulldozer is used whenever possible, we give the indicator an initial value of SMALL (line 90), then send the computer to the subroutine to see if the large one is needed instead.

In the subroutine, we test the three conditions for using the large bulldozer, and change the value in the indicator to LARGE if any of the conditions is true. If none of the conditions is true, the indicator is not changed. At the end of this subroutine, the computer returns to line 110 in the main program section with the indicator either unchanged (SIZE$ = "SMALL") or changed (SIZE$ = "LARGE").

On line 120, we test the indicator to see if it has been changed. If the condition (SIZE$ = "LARGE") is true, we send the computer to line 150 where the charge for the large bulldozer is printed and the program ends.

If the indicator was not changed to LARGE, the condition in the IF statement (SIZE$ = "LARGE") is false. The computer ignores the remainder of the IF statement and continues with the next instruction in sequence. At line 130, the charge for the use of the small bulldozer is printed and the program ends.

The output of this program is shown in two sample runs:

```
RUN
ENTER THE DIMENSIONS OF THE EXCAVATION IN YARDS:
LENGTH?  45
WIDTH?  20
DEPTH?  1.5
USE SMALL BULLDOZER.  CHARGE IS $ 2362.5


RUN
ENTER THE DIMENSIONS OF THE EXCAVATION IN YARDS:
LENGTH?  42
WIDTH?  40
DEPTH?  1
USE LARGE BULLDOZER.  CHARGE IS $ 3192
```

THE ON . . . GOTO STATEMENT

The ON . . . GOTO statement functions as if it were a sequence of IF statements, wherein each IF contains a GOTO.

The general format of the ON. . . GOTO statement is:

ON numeric-variable-name GOTO line#, line#, line#, . . .

On most computers, we can list as many line numbers as we wish following the GOTO, up to a limit of approximately 256 total characters in the line. It is possible to get 40 or more line numbers within this limit.

When the ON . . . GOTO is executed, the computer checks the current value of the numeric variable that follows ON. If its value is 1, the computer goes to the first line number in the list; if its value is 2, the computer goes to the second line number in the list; if its value is 3, the computer goes to the third line number in the list, and so on. If the value of the numeric variable is not an integer, it is converted to an integer before a line number is selected from the list.

If the value of the numeric variable is zero, or if the value is greater than the number of lines listed, the computer does not branch. Instead, it continues in sequence to the instruction following the ON . . . GOTO.

If the value of the numeric variable is less than zero, or equal to or greater than 256, an error occurs. Depending on the computer, this error may be ILLEGAL FUNCTION CALL, or ILLEGAL QUANTITY ERROR.

Example

The following sequence of IF statements:

```
IF  CHOICE  =  1  THEN  GOTO  200
IF  CHOICE  =  2  THEN  GOTO  250
IF  CHOICE  =  3  THEN  GOTO  300
IF  CHOICE  =  4  THEN  GOTO  380
IF  CHOICE  =  5  THEN  GOTO  450
IF  CHOICE  =  6  THEN  GOTO  520
```

could be replaced by this single ON . . . GOTO statement:

```
ON  CHOICE  GOTO  200,250,300,380,450,520
```

If the value of the numeric variable CHOICE were 4, the fourth line number in the list would be selected and the computer would branch to line 380. If the value of CHOICE were 8, the computer would discover that there are not eight line numbers in the list, so it would continue with the next instruction in sequence. If the value of CHOICE were 0, the computer would ignore the remainder of the ON . . . GOTO and continue with the next instruction in sequence.

The ON . . . GOTO statement converts the value of the variable into an integer, if necessary, before selecting a line number from the list. If the value of CHOICE were 2.7, the integer value 2 would be used to select the second line number from the list, and the computer would branch to line 250.

We can illustrate the conditional transfer of control from an ON . . . GOTO by using a set of flow lines leading to the referenced routines. This is shown in the following "generic" block diagram.

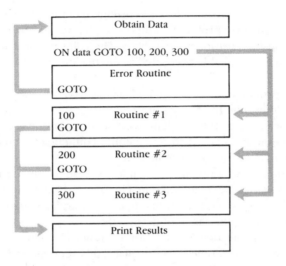

THE ON . . . GOSUB STATEMENT

The ON . . . GOSUB is similar to the ON . . . GOTO, except that after branching to one of the line numbers in the list, the computer will return to the statement following the ON . . . GOSUB when a RETURN statement is encountered.

The general format of the ON . . . GOSUB is:

ON numeric-variable-name GOSUB line#, line#, line#, . . .

The function of the ON . . . GOSUB is identical to the ON . . . GOTO, except that before going to the appropriate line number, a return address is saved. When a RETURN statement is encountered, the computer will return to the instruction following the ON . . . GOSUB statement.

As in the ON . . . GOTO, if the value of the numeric variable is zero, or greater than the number of lines listed, the computer continues with the next instruction in sequence. The value of the numeric variable must be not less than zero, but less than 256, to prevent the ILLEGAL FUNCTION CALL (or ILLEGAL QUANTITY ERROR) from occurring.

Example

We've now learned enough decision-making techniques to attempt a partial solution to the loan problem. In this example, we will solve the problem of determining the customer's loan class. The rules for this determination were illustrated in the table presented at the beginning of this chapter (see page 142).

To write a program determining the loan class, we should first analyze the problem to determine the factors under consideration and the possibilities for each. In analyzing this problem, we find that there are two factors to consider: income and net worth. Since either could be chosen for the question at the first level, let's choose income.

This question has four possible outcomes corresponding to the four established ranges of income. One outcome (Income < 15,000) leads directly to a final result (Class = 4). Each remaining outcome leads to a second-level question concerning the range of net worth.

To evaluate the question at the first level requires a sequence of IF tests to find the range of income. We can place this sequence of IF tests in a subroutine to simplify the main program section, but to do this, we must create an indicator to store the test outcome. Let's create the variable name LEVEL to use as an indicator and see how this portion of the program would look.

```
    •
    •
110     GOSUB 200 : REM DETERMINE INCOME LEVEL
    •
    •
200 REM *** SUBROUTINE TO DETERMINE INCOME LEVEL ***
210     IF INCOME < 15000 THEN LET LEVEL = 1
220     IF INCOME >= 15000 AND INCOME < 35000
            THEN LET LEVEL = 2
230     IF INCOME >= 35000 AND INCOME < 100000
            THEN LET LEVEL = 3
240     IF INCOME >= 100000 THEN LET LEVEL = 4
250     RETURN
260 REM
```

In this subroutine, one condition will be true, so a value of 1, 2, 3, or 4 will be assigned to the indicator LEVEL. When the computer RETURNs, we can use the value of LEVEL to direct it to the appropriate processing for one of the four income ranges. Let's write the instructions for the four possibilities as subroutines, then use an ON . . . GOSUB statement to send the computer to the indicated subroutine.

```
     .
     .
110     GOSUB 200 : REM DETERMINE INCOME LEVEL
120     ON LEVEL GOSUB 300, 400, 500, 600
130                 REM DETERMINE LOAN CLASS
     .
     .
```

In the subroutine section, we place four subroutines corresponding to the four possible income levels. If income was in the first range (income < 15000), the indicator LEVEL would have been assigned the value 1. The ON . . . GOSUB statement will send the computer to the first subroutine in the list, which we place at line 300.

Since the purpose of each subroutine is to determine the loan class, let's create a second indicator, CLASS. Looking at the table, we see that if income is less than $15,000, the loan class is 4. In this subroutine, no decision is necessary. We need only to assign the value 4 to the indicator CLASS and direct the computer to RETURN.

```
     .
     .
120     ON LEVEL GOSUB 300, 400, 500, 600
130                 REM DETERMINE LOAN CLASS
     .
     .
300 REM *** DETERMINE CLASS WHEN INCOME LEVEL = 1 ***
310     LET CLASS = 4
320     RETURN
330 REM
```

If income was in the second range, LEVEL would contain the value 2, and the ON . . . GOSUB would select the second line number from the list. In this subroutine, we must decide which range contains the net worth. For less than $20,000 net worth, the loan class is 4; between $20,000 and $149,999, the loan class is 3; at \$150,000 or more, the loan class is 2. We write a sequence of IFs to find the appropriate range of net worth and assign the proper value to CLASS.

```
    •
    •
120     ON LEVEL GOSUB 300, 400, 500, 600
130                 REM DETERMINE LOAN CLASS
    •
    •
400 REM *** DETERMINE CLASS WHEN INCOME LEVEL = 2 ***
410     IF NET < 20000 THEN LET CLASS = 4
420     IF NET >= 20000 AND NET < 150000
            THEN LET CLASS = 3
430     IF NET >= 150000 THEN LET CLASS = 2
440     RETURN
450 REM
```

If income level is in the third range, the LEVEL indicator will contain the value 3, causing the ON ... GOSUB to send the computer to the third line number in the list. As we see in the table, there are four possible loan classes for this income range, depending on the range of net worth. To determine which range of net worth applies, let's use four IFs in sequence. When the range is found, we assign the proper value to the indicator.

```
    •
    •
120     ON LEVEL GOSUB 300, 400, 500, 600
130                 REM DETERMINE LOAN CLASS
    •
    •
500 REM *** DETERMINE CLASS WHEN INCOME LEVEL = 3 ***
510     IF NET < 20000 THEN LET CLASS = 4
520     IF NET >= 20000 AND NET < 50000
            THEN LET CLASS = 3
530     IF NET >= 50000 AND NET < 150000
            THEN LET CLASS = 2
540     IF NET >= 150000 THEN LET CLASS = 1
550     RETURN
560 REM
```

If income is in the fourth range, LEVEL will contain the value 4 and the computer will be sent by the ON . . . GOSUB to the fourth subroutine in the list. In the fourth income range, the table shows us three loan classes are possible. The fourth subroutine must contain three IFs to determine which range contains the net worth. When the correct range is found, CLASS is assigned the appropriate value.

```
  •
  •
120    ON LEVEL GOSUB 300, 400, 500, 600
130                  REM DETERMINE LOAN CLASS
  •
  •
600 REM *** DETERMINE CLASS WHEN INCOME LEVEL = 4 ***
610    IF NET < 20000 THEN LET CLASS = 4
620    IF NET >= 20000 AND NET < 50000
             THEN LET CLASS = 2
630    IF NET >= 50000 THEN LET CLASS = 1
640    RETURN
```

Let's review how much we've accomplished in solving this problem. We have used a GOSUB to send the computer to a subroutine to determine the income level. This subroutine assigns a value of 1, 2, 3, or 4 to the indicator LEVEL, then RETURNs. Based on the value of LEVEL, an ON . . . GOSUB statement will then send the computer into one of four subroutines to determine the loan class.

When the computer returns from the appropriate subroutine, the variable CLASS will contain a value of 1, 2, 3, or 4, corresponding to the customer's loan class. All that remains is to print the result of this selection process. The complete listing for this program is shown, with two sample runs.

```
10   REM ************* OBTAIN DATA ****************
20     INPUT "WHAT IS THE ANNUAL INCOME"; INCOME
30     INPUT "WHAT IS THE NET WORTH"; NET
40     PRINT
50   REM
100 REM *** DETERMINE LOAN CLASS, DISPLAY RESULT ***
110    GOSUB 200 : REM DETERMINE INCOME LEVEL
120    ON LEVEL GOSUB 300, 400, 500, 600
130                  REM DETERMINE LOAN CLASS
```

```
140     PRINT "CUSTOMER QUALIFIES FOR CLASS"; CLASS; " LOAN"
150     END
160 REM
180 REM ********** SUBROUTINE SECTION **************
190 REM
200 REM *** SUBROUTINE TO DETERMINE INCOME LEVEL ***
210     IF INCOME < 15000 THEN LET LEVEL = 1
220     IF INCOME >= 15000 AND INCOME < 35000
            THEN LET LEVEL = 2
230     IF INCOME >= 35000 AND INCOME < 100000
            THEN LET LEVEL = 3
240     IF INCOME >= 100000 THEN LET LEVEL = 4
250     RETURN
260 REM
300 REM *** DETERMINE CLASS WHEN INCOME LEVEL = 1 ***
310     LET CLASS = 4
320     RETURN
330 REM
400 REM *** DETERMINE CLASS WHEN INCOME LEVEL = 2 ***
410     IF NET < 20000 THEN LET CLASS = 4
420     IF NET >= 20000 AND NET < 150000
            THEN LET CLASS = 3
430     IF NET >= 150000 THEN LET CLASS = 2
440     RETURN
450 REM
500 REM *** DETERMINE CLASS WHEN INCOME LEVEL = 3 ***
510     IF NET < 20000 THEN LET CLASS = 4
520     IF NET >= 20000 AND NET < 50000
            THEN LET CLASS = 3
530     IF NET >= 50000 AND NET < 150000
            THEN LET CLASS = 2
540     IF NET >= 150000 THEN LET CLASS = 1
550     RETURN
560 REM
600 REM *** DETERMINE CLASS WHEN INCOME LEVEL = 4 ***
610     IF NET < 20000 THEN LET CLASS = 4
620     IF NET >= 20000 AND NET < 50000
            THEN LET CLASS = 2
630     IF NET >= 50000 THEN LET CLASS = 1
640     RETURN
```

```
RUN
WHAT  IS  THE  ANNUAL  INCOME?  24000
WHAT  IS  THE  NET  WORTH?  50000

CUSTOMER  QUALIFIES  FOR  CLASS  3  LOAN


RUN
WHAT  IS  THE  ANNUAL  INCOME?  37000
WHAT  IS  THE  NET  WORTH?  65000

CUSTOMER  QUALIFIES  FOR  CLASS  2  LOAN
```

TEST YOUR UNDERSTANDING

8.   A real estate sales office pays its salespeople 1.5 percent commission on sales of single family homes. The commission is higher, however, on sales that exceed $100,000. A salesperson with the office for at least 12 months receives a 2 percent commission on a sale over $100,000. If the salesperson has been with the office less than 12 months, the commission rate is 1.7 percent for a sale over $100,000.

Identify the factors involved in determining the commission rate and draw a diagram representing the questions and possible outcomes for each.

9.   Draw a block diagram of the last sample program in this section (determining the loan class). Write the GOSUB and ON. . . GOSUB statements on the diagram, and indicate the transfer of control to and from the subroutines.

SECTION 5. THE LOAN PROGRAM

INTRODUCTION

The computer is only a machine that must be given step-by-step instructions. A program enabling the computer to make decisions cannot replace the decision-making ability of humans; to give the computer instructions for problem solving, a human had to solve the problem first.

To write a program solving a complex decision problem, we use a combination of simple decision structures. In this section, you will see how several decision structures have been combined to solve the loan problem.

This section has two parts:

- Structuring a Program
- The Loan Program

STRUCTURING A PROGRAM

When a program is well structured, we can easily identify the functions it performs, and easily locate the instructions to perform each function.

Any program can be written in a variety of ways. The objectives in designing a program are to: obtain the correct solution, make the program easy to read and understand, and make the program easy to modify, if necessary.

In a program which implements decisions, it may be possible to write the first-level decision structure as a subroutine. We can create an indicator to store the result of the decision, and use it to control further processing.

With an effective selection of indicators and indicator values, we can use an ON . . . GOSUB statement to direct the computer to one of several second-level decision subroutines, based on the outcome of the first-level decision. A second-level decision subroutine can also store decision results in an indicator—which can then be used in additional processing.

This approach simplifies the main program section, and makes it easier to understand. If the conditions for any particular decision must be altered, the subroutine handling that decision is easily located in the subroutine section.

The program in the last example—a partial solution to the loan problem—contained one subroutine to determine the income range, and four more to determine the loan class for a particular range of income. To complete the solution of the problem, we have to now compute the maximum loan amount based on the class.

Using the percentages given at the beginning of this chapter (see page 142) and creating the necessary variables, we can write the calculations:

```
Class 1:   LET  MAXAMOUNT  =  (INCOME  *  .20)  +  (NET  *  .25)
Class 2:   LET  MAXAMOUNT  =  (INCOME  *  .20)  +  (NET  *  .20)
Class 3:   LET  MAXAMOUNT  =  (INCOME  *  .15)  +  (NET  *  .20)
Class 4:   LET  MAXAMOUNT  =  (INCOME  *  .10)  +  (NET  *  .15)
```

The simplest method for telling the computer which calculation to perform is to place each LET . . . = statement in a separate subroutine, then use an ON . . . GOSUB statement to send the computer to the correct one. Since the variable CLASS has a value from 1 to 4, it can direct the ON . . . GOSUB to the correct subroutine. After the computer returns, all that remains is to print the result and end the program.

Even with nine subroutines in our final solution, the main program section contains only 10 lines of instructions. The subroutines and the ON . . . GOSUBs have been used to simplify the main program section considerably. Two indicators, LEVEL and CLASS, had to be created to store the results of decision subroutines. Of these, the LEVEL indicator controls selection of one of four subroutines to determine the loan class. The CLASS indicator then controls selection of one of four subroutines to calculate the maximum loan amount.

In any one run of the program, only three subroutines are used: the subroutine to determine income level, *one* subroutine to determine the loan class, and *one* subroutine to calculate the loan amount. Even though they are not all used on any one run, these subroutines are necessary to give the computer proper instructions to follow for every possible case. It is the program, however, that tests the data to determine which case applies.

THE LOAN PROGRAM

Review the program listing that follows, giving special attention to the use of indicators, how indicators are given values, and how they are used in the ON . . . GOSUB statements to control selection of appropriate subroutines.

```
10   REM  *********************************************************
20   REM                            REMARKS
30   REM  *********************************************************
40   REM   THIS PROGRAM COMPUTES THE MAXIMUM AMOUNT THAT MAY BE
50   REM   LOANED BASED ON THE ANNUAL INCOME AND NET WORTH.
60   REM   DEPENDING ON THE COMBINATION OF INCOME AND NET WORTH,
70   REM   THE LOAN IS ASSIGNED TO ONE OF FOUR CLASSES. FOR EACH
80   REM   CLASS, SPECIFIC PERCENTAGES OF INCOME AND OF NET WORTH
90   REM   ARE USED IN COMPUTING THE MAXIMUM LOAN AMOUNT.
100  REM  *********************************************************
110  REM                 LIST OF VARIABLES
120  REM INPUT
130  REM VARIABLES:  INCOME = CUSTOMER'S ANNUAL INCOME
140  REM                NET = CUSTOMER'S NET WORTH
```

```
150 REM PROGRAM
160 REM INDICATORS: LEVEL = 1, 2, 3, OR 4 DEPENDING ON
170 REM                      CUSTOMER'S INCOME
180 REM             CLASS = 1, 2, 3 OR 4 DEPENDING ON THE
190 REM                      COMBINATION OF INCOME AND NET WORTH
200 REM OUTPUT
210 REM VARIABLES:  MAXAMOUNT = MAXIMUM LOAN AMOUNT
220 REM ********************************************************
230 REM                    MAIN PROGRAM SECTION
240 REM ********************************************************
250 REM
260     PRINT "DETERMINING MAXIMUM LOAN AMOUNT"
270     PRINT
280     INPUT "WHAT IS THE ANNUAL INCOME"; INCOME
290     INPUT "WHAT IS THE NET WORTH"; NET
300     PRINT
310 REM    ******* DETERMINE INCOME LEVEL ***********
320     GOSUB 500
330 REM    ******** DETERMINE LOAN CLASS ***********
340     ON LEVEL GOSUB 600, 700, 800, 900
350 REM    ****** COMPUTE MAXIMUM LOAN AMOUNT *******
360     ON CLASS GOSUB 1100, 1200, 1300, 1400
370     PRINT "MAXIMUM LOAN AMOUNT IS $"; MAXAMOUNT
380     END
390 REM
400 REM ********************************************************
410 REM                    SUBROUTINE SECTION
420 REM ********************************************************
430 REM
440 REM ********* SUBROUTINE TO DETERMINE INCOME LEVEL *********
450 REM
500     IF INCOME < 15000 THEN LET LEVEL = 1
510     IF INCOME >= 15000 AND INCOME < 35000 THEN LET LEVEL = 2
520     IF INCOME >= 35000 AND INCOME < 100000 THEN LET LEVEL = 3
530     IF INCOME >= 100000 THEN LET LEVEL = 4
540     RETURN
550 REM
560 REM ***************************************************
570 REM                 LOAN CLASS SUBROUTINES
580 REM
600 REM ****** DETERMINE LOAN CLASS WHEN INCOME LEVEL = 1 ******
```

```
610 REM
620     LET CLASS = 4
630     RETURN
640 REM
700 REM ****** DETERMINE LOAN CLASS WHEN INCOME LEVEL = 2 ******
710 REM
720     IF NET < 20000 THEN LET CLASS = 4
730     IF NET >= 20000 AND NET < 150000 THEN LET CLASS = 3
740     IF NET >= 150000 THEN LET CLASS = 2
750     RETURN
760 REM
800 REM ****** DETERMINE LOAN CLASS WHEN INCOME LEVEL = 3 ******
810 REM
820     IF NET < 20000 THEN LET CLASS = 4
830     IF NET >= 20000 AND NET < 50000 THEN LET CLASS = 3
840     IF NET >= 50000 AND NET < 150000 THEN LET CLASS = 2
850     IF NET >= 150000 THEN LET CLASS = 1
860     RETURN
870 REM
900 REM ****** DETERMINE LOAN CLASS WHEN INCOME LEVEL = 4 ******
910 REM
920     IF NET < 20000 THEN LET CLASS = 4
930     IF NET >= 20000 AND NET < 50000 THEN LET CLASS = 2
940     IF NET >= 50000 THEN LET CLASS = 1
950     RETURN
960 REM
1000 REM **********************************************************
1010 REM              MAXIMUM LOAN AMOUNT SUBROUTINES
1020 REM
1100 REM ***************** LOAN CLASS 1 *********************
1110 REM
1120    LET MAXAMOUNT = (INCOME * .2) + (NET * .25)
1130    RETURN
1140 REM
1200 REM ***************** LOAN CLASS 2 *********************
1210 REM
1220    LET MAXAMOUNT = (INCOME * .2) + (NET * .2)
1230    RETURN
1240 REM
1300 REM ***************** LOAN CLASS 3 *********************
1310 REM
```

```
1320      LET MAXAMOUNT = (INCOME * .15) + (NET * .2)
1330      RETURN
1340 REM
1400 REM **************** LOAN CLASS 4 *********************
1410 REM
1420      LET MAXAMOUNT = (INCOME * .1) + (NET * .15)
1430      RETURN
```

Two sample runs of the loan program follow:

RUN
DETERMINING MAXIMUM LOAN AMOUNT

WHAT IS THE ANNUAL INCOME? **34900**
WHAT IS THE NET WORTH? **28700**

MAXIMUM LOAN AMOUNT IS $ 10975

RUN
DETERMINING MAXIMUM LOAN AMOUNT

WHAT IS THE ANNUAL INCOME? **14900**
WHAT IS THE NET WORTH? **20000**

MAXIMUM LOAN AMOUNT IS $ 4490

PROGRAMMING EXERCISES

Programming Problem 5A:

The Loan Manager has revised the rules for determining the loan class in the $35,000 to $99,999 income range (income level = 3). In this range, a class 3 loan applies to customers with a net worth between $20,000 and $99,999. It will now take a minimum of $100,000 net worth to qualify for the class 2 loan. Make the appropriate change to the program to implement the new rule.

Programming Problem 5B:

To generate more business, the Loan Manager has split the $15,000 to $34,999 income range into two ranges: $15,000 to $21,999 and $22,000 to

$34,999. The rules for determining loan class in the $22–34,999 range are the same as for the previous $15–34,999 range. In the new $15-21,999 category, however, a net worth of less than $50,000 qualifies for a class 4 loan, while a net of $50,000 or more qualifies for a class 3 loan. Revise the program to reflect this change.

ANSWERS TO "TEST YOUR UNDERSTANDING" EXERCISES

1.   A routine is a set of instructions performing a specific function.

2.   First routine (get data), lines 10–30; second routine (calculate growth of deposit), lines 40–70; third routine (print result), lines 80–90.

3.

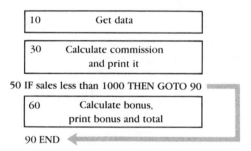

```
10              Get data

30        Calculate commission
              and print it

50 IF sales less than 1000 THEN GOTO 90

60          Calculate bonus,
         print bonus and total

90 END
```

4.   Suggested solution (GOTO approach):

```
10   INPUT "HOW MANY DAYS RENTED"; DAYS
20   INPUT "HOW MANY MILES DRIVEN"; MILES
30   IF DAYS > 7 THEN GOTO 70
40   LET DCHARGE = 15 * DAYS
50   LET MCHARGE = .10 * MILES
60   GOTO 90
70   LET DCHARGE = 14 * 7 + 12 * (DAYS - 7)
80   LET MCHARGE = .08 * MILES
90   PRINT "MILEAGE CHARGE IS $"; MCHARGE
100 PRINT "RENTAL CHARGE IS $"; DCHARGE
110 PRINT "FOR A TOTAL OF $"; DCHARGE + MCHARGE
```

Suggested solution (GOSUB approach):

```
10   INPUT "HOW MANY DAYS RENTED"; DAYS
20   INPUT "HOW MANY MILES DRIVEN"; MILES
```

```
30   IF DAYS > 7 THEN GOSUB 100
40   IF DAYS <= 7 THEN GOSUB 140
50   PRINT "MILEAGE CHARGE IS $"; MCHARGE
60   PRINT "RENTAL CHARGE IS $"; DCHARGE
70   PRINT "FOR A TOTAL OF $"; DCHARGE + MCHARGE
80   END
90   REM ******* OVER SEVEN DAYS ********
100  LET DCHARGE = 14 * 7 + 12 * (DAYS - 7)
110  LET MCHARGE = .08 * MILES
120  RETURN
130  REM ****** SEVEN DAYS OR LESS ******
140  LET DCHARGE = 15 * DAYS
150  LET MCHARGE = .10 * MILES
160  RETURN
```

5. Suggested solution:

```
10   PRINT "LOS ANGELES TO PHOENIX"
20   PRINT "FIRST, ECONOMY OR COACH?"
30   INPUT "ENTER F, E, OR C"; CODE$
40   IF CODE$ = "F" THEN GOTO 90
50   IF CODE$ = "E" THEN GOTO 120
60   IF CODE$ = "C" THEN GOTO 150
70   PRINT "PLEASE RE-ENTER"
80   GOTO 30
90   LET FARE = 43
100  LET CLASS$ = "FIRST"
110  GOTO 170
120  LET FARE = 38
130  LET CLASS$ = "ECONOMY"
140  GOTO 170
150  LET FARE = 35
160  LET CLASS$ = "COACH"
170  PRINT CLASS$; " CLASS TICKET IS $"; FARE
```

6. Suggested solution:

```
10 INPUT "AGE OF APPLICANT"; AGE
20 INPUT "HOW MANY MOVING VIOLATIONS IN LAST 3 YEARS"; VIOL
30 IF AGE >= 21 AND VIOL <= 0 THEN PRINT "PREFERRED RATE APPLIES"
40 IF AGE < 21 OR VIOL > 0 THEN PRINT "REGULAR RATE APPLIES"
```

7. Suggested solution:

```
10 INPUT "HOW MANY BOARD-FEET"; BOARDFEET
20 IF BOARDFEET < 2000 THEN LET PRICE = .38
30 IF BOARDFEET >= 2000 AND BOARDFEET < 5000 THEN LET PRICE = .35
40 IF BOARDFEET >= 5000 THEN LET PRICE = .31
50 LET TTL = PRICE * BOARDFEET
60 PRINT "TOTAL FOR "; BOARDFEET; " BOARD-FEET IS $"; TTL
```

8.

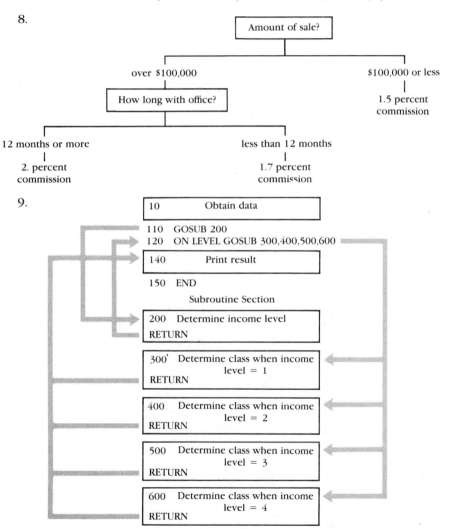

9.

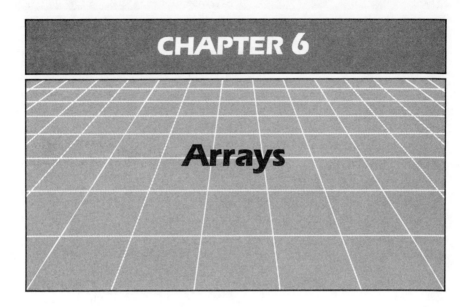

CHAPTER 6

Arrays

CHAPTER OBJECTIVE

To illustrate the methods of grouping related data items into an array structure, and the advantages of using arrays.

PROBLEM

The manager of the Delivery Department plans to streamline his area. He would like to use the computer to calculate delivery charges, prepare shipping documents, and compute total revenues for each truck leaving the warehouse. The problem he wants you to solve first, however, is how to use the computer to calculate delivery charges.

The cost of delivering merchandise is based on the area where the merchandise is sent. Ten different delivery areas have been established, each having a cost per pound for delivery figured against a minimum delivery charge. Given the area and the shipping weight, the delivery charge is computed by multiplying shipping weight by the delivery cost per pound for that area. If the computed charge is less than the minimum charge for that area, the minimum charge is applied.

Area	Delivery Charge (per lb.)	Minimum Charge
1	$ .75	$ 2.25
2	.84	2.70
3	.94	3.00
4	1.03	3.40
5	1.11	3.95
6	1.19	4.50
7	1.26	5.20
8	1.33	5.80
9	1.39	6.50
10	1.45	7.15

CHAPTER OVERVIEW

Solving the delivery charge problem efficiently by computer requires the use of arrays. Arrays are commonly used to simplify programs with a large number of similar data items. In this chapter, you'll learn what arrays are, how to create them, and how to use them. You will also learn two new BASIC statements, READ and DATA.

This chapter has four sections:

- **One-Dimensional Arrays**
- **Creating an Array**
- **Using Arrays**
- **The Delivery Charge Program**

Section 1. One-Dimensional Arrays

INTRODUCTION

Arrays can have one dimension, two dimensions, or more. Arrays with two or more dimensions are extremely useful in special situations, but the one-dimensional array is the most commonly used. Therefore, we will discuss only the one-dimensional array.

In this section, we discuss what comprises an array, how to refer to items stored in an array, and how to define an array.

This section has two parts:

- The Array
- Defining an Array with the DIM Statement

THE ARRAY

To humans, an array is a list of related items; to the computer, it's a series of storage spaces.

Let's look at an array from two points of view: what it represents to humans, and how it's stored in a computer.

We think of an array as a list of related items, but the terminology used for describing an array differs from that used for a list. We can illustrate this difference in terminolgy using a grocery list as an example, showing it first with its parts labeled in everyday terms:

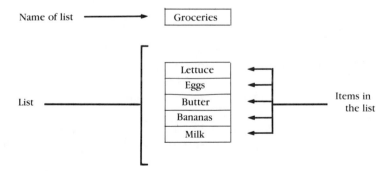

To see this grocery list as an array, we change the labels.

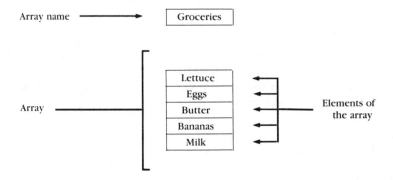

Using the list terminology, we'd say, "Milk is the fifth item on the list of groceries," but using array terms, we say "Milk is the fifth *element* of the *array* groceries."

In addition to specific terminology, arrays have one other important characteristic: the shorthand notation we use to refer to the elements of an array. To indicate a particular element of an array, we write the name of the array and the number of the element, such as "Groceries (2)," indicating the second element of the array—in this case, "Eggs."

Now let's discuss what an array means to the computer. Within the computer, an array is a series of storage spaces assigned a single array name. Each storage space is reserved for one element of an array. To identify any one of these storage spaces, we use the name of the array and an element number which we enclose in parentheses.

array-name (numeric-value)

The numeric value enclosed in parentheses is called a subscript; this identifies a particular element of the array (a particular storage space in the series). An array name followed by a subscript is sometimes called a "subscripted variable," since an array name must conform to the same rules as variable names.

If the array name ends with a dollar sign, it represents a series of string storage spaces; otherwise, it represents a series of numeric storage spaces.

Only when the name is followed by a subscript does the computer recognize it as referring to an array.

Example 1

Let's assume we've created an array using the array name PRICE. This is a numeric array; let's assume it has been created to hold 8 numeric values for the prices of eight products. In memory, a series of spaces is reserved for eight numeric values, which we picture as:

```
PR(1) ┌─────────┐
      │         │
PR(2) ├─────────┤
      │         │
PR(3) ├─────────┤
      │         │
PR(4) ├─────────┤
      │         │
PR(5) ├─────────┤
      │         │
PR(6) ├─────────┤
      │         │
PR(7) ├─────────┤
      │         │
PR(8) └─────────┘
```

(The computer still recognizes only the first two characters of the name.)

To store a value in one of these storage spaces, we must refer to it by the array name and the number of the space. For instance, executing the following statements,

```
LET PRICE(2) = 4.45
LET PRICE(7) = 12.05
```

would result in the indicated values being stored in the array:

```
PR(1) ┌─────────┐
      │         │
PR(2) ├─────────┤
      │  4.45   │
PR(3) ├─────────┤
      │         │
PR(4) ├─────────┤
      │         │
PR(5) ├─────────┤
      │         │
PR(6) ├─────────┤
      │         │
PR(7) ├─────────┤
      │  12.05  │
PR(8) └─────────┘
```

Let's assume we've assigned values to each element of the array:

PR(1)	3.99
PR(2)	4.45
PR(3)	.89
PR(4)	1.20
PR(5)	3.51
PR(6)	.78
PR(7)	12.05
PR(8)	.29

The following statements demonstrate several ways in which the elements of an array can be used.

Statements	Result When Executed
PRINT PRICE(5)	3.51
LET TTL = 5 * PRICE(7) PRINT TTL	60.25
IF PRICE(1) > PRICE(3) THEN PRINT PRICE(1)	3.99
LET ITEM = 8 PRINT PRICE(ITEM)	.29

As you can see from this example, a subscripted variable can be used in the same ways as an ordinary variable.

One advantage in using an array is that only one name is required. Without an array, we would have to create eight separate variable names for each of the eight values. By using an array, we need only one name for the entire list of values, and we can use a numeric subscript to specify which item from the list is to be used.

Notice in the last BASIC statement above that a variable name was used as a subscript. When a numeric variable name is used as a subscript, the current value of that variable will determine which element from the array is used.

Example 2

Let's assume we've created a string array named CITY$ to store the names of five cities. In memory, a series of five string storage spaces is reserved.

```
CI$(1)  ┌──────────┐
        │          │
CI$(2)  ├──────────┤
        │          │
CI$(3)  ├──────────┤
        │          │
CI$(4)  ├──────────┤
        │          │
CI$(5)  └──────────┘
```

We can assign a string value to any one of these storage spaces by using the name of the array and the number of the space we wish to use:

LET CITY$(5) = "MIAMI"

Execution of this statement results in the string of characters "MIAMI" being stored as the fifth element of the array CITY$.

```
CI$(1)  ┌──────────┐
        │          │
CI$(2)  ├──────────┤
        │          │
CI$(3)  ├──────────┤
        │          │
CI$(4)  ├──────────┤
        │          │
CI$(5)  └──────────┘
         MIAMI
```

Let's assume we've assigned a string value to each element of the array.

```
CI$(1)  ┌──────────┐
        │ SEATTLE  │
CI$(2)  ├──────────┤
        │ DALLAS   │
CI$(3)  ├──────────┤
        │ BOSTON   │
CI$(4)  ├──────────┤
        │ ST. PAUL │
CI$(5)  ├──────────┤
        │ MIAMI    │
        └──────────┘
```

The following statements demonstrate several ways in which the values in this array can be used.

Statements	Result When Executed
PRINT CITY$(4)	ST. PAUL
PRINT "FROM "; CITY$(2); " TO "; CITY$(5)	FROM DALLAS TO MIAMI
IF CITY$(3) = "BOSTON" THEN PRINT "FLIGHT DELAYED"	FLIGHT DELAYED
LET CHOICE = 1 PRINT CITY$(CHOICE)	SEATTLE

Example 3

It's possible to have an array and an ordinary variable with the same name. The computer recognizes a name as an array name only when it's followed by a subscript. Without a subscript, a name is just a variable name referring to a storage space in memory that's different from and unrelated to any array.

Running the following program may help to illustrate this point.

```
10 LET TEMP(1) = 77
20 LET TEMP(2) = 85
30 PRINT TEMP
40 LET TEMP = 54
50 PRINT TEMP, TEMP(1), TEMP(2)
RUN
0
54            77            85
```

After values are assigned to the array elements TEMP(1) and TEMP(2), we try to display these elements using the variable name TEMP. The PRINT statement on line 30 shows us nothing was assigned to the variable TEMP. Line 40 then assigns the value 54 to TEMP, and the next PRINT statement displays the values of the variable TEMP, and the array elements TEMP(1) and TEMP(2).

This demonstrates that assigning values to an array has no effect on the value of a variable which happens to have the same name. It also demonstrates that assigning a value to a variable has no effect on values contained in an array of the same name. The variable and the array are separate entities.

DEFINING AN ARRAY USING THE DIM STATEMENT

The DIM statement defines an array and the maximum number of elements it can contain.

An array can be defined implicitly or explicitly. Let's consider first how an array can be implicitly defined.

Recall that when a variable name is encountered in a program, the computer first checks to see if it has already reserved a storage space with that name. If it has, it uses that space. If it hasn't, it reserves a space and assigns the variable name to it.

The computer treats subscripted variables similarly. When it encounters a subscripted variable, it first checks to see if it has already reserved a series of storage spaces with that array name. If it has, it uses that space in the array corresponding to the subscript.

If it doesn't have an array by that name, the computer creates one and reserves enough storage space for us to use subscripts as high as 10. This is the implicit definition of an array, whereby the existence of the array is implied by the use of a subscripted variable. When an array is defined implicitly, 10 is the largest subscript we can use with the array.

NOTE: Since most computers consider zero a valid subscript, the first storage space in an array is numbered 0, the second is numbered 1, the third is numbered 2, and so on. Therefore, a subscript of 10 refers to the eleventh element of an array. To avoid confusion, we will ignore the existence of the 0th element. Thus, we will imagine a maximum subscript of 10 means there are 10 storage spaces reserved, although in reality there are 11.

If an array has been defined implicitly, it can contain no more than 10 elements. When we need an array containing more than 10 elements, we must define the array explicitly by using the DIM statement. DIM stands for *dimension*, and refers to the size of an array. The general format of this statement is:

DIM array-name (numeric-value)

The value in parentheses defines the largest subscript permitted for that array—or, viewed another way, it indicates the maximum number of elements that can be stored in the array. When this statement is executed, the computer creates an array and reserves enough storage space for the number of elements indicated in the parentheses.

One of the errors that may occur when arrays are used is BAD SUBSCRIPT ERROR (or perhaps SUBSCRIPT OUT OF RANGE, depending on your computer). This occurs when the computer encounters a statement containing a subscript value either negative or larger than the largest subscript permissible for that array.

Another error that may occur is the REDIMENSIONED ARRAY (or DUPLICATE DEFINITION) error. An array may be defined only once in any single run of a program. If the computer attempts to execute a DIM statement a second time for the same array name, or if it attempts to execute a DIM statement for an array already implicitly defined, this error occurs. To avoid it, use the DIM statement at the very beginning of a program, and keep DIM statements out of any kind of loop.

Example 1

When an array is not defined in a DIM statement, its first reference in a program causes the array to be implicitly defined with a maximum subscript of 10. The two arrays used in our previous examples, PRICE and CITY$, do not require DIM statements because the subscripts used are not larger than 10. It's a good practice, however, to always explicitly define an array regardless of the largest subscript.

These two arrays could have been defined using the following DIM statements:

```
DIM PRICE(8)
DIM CITY$(5)
```

Alternately, both arrays could have been dimensioned in one DIM statement, as follows:

```
DIM PRICE(8), CITY$(5)
```

Example 2

A business concern is going to use an array to store the names of 15 companies it does business with. It's possible the number of companies on this list might grow to 20 within the next year. The program using this array contains a DIM statement to define the array.

```
DIM COMPANY$(20)
```

Even though 15 is the largest subscript used for now, we have dimensioned the array to allow for future expansion of the list.

TEST YOUR UNDERSTANDING

1. When looking at a program listing, how can you tell the difference between a name referring to a variable and a name referring to an array element?

2. Write a LET. . .= statement to assign the value 3859 to the seventh element of the array SALES.

3. What's the largest subscript that may be used with an array name not defined in a DIM statement? What occurs when you use a subscript that's larger?

4. Assume you wish to use the following statements in a program:

```
80    LET NUM = 25
90    INPUT AREACODE (NUM)
100   INPUT PHNUMBER (NUM)
```

Write a DIM statement permitting these statements to be used without causing a BAD SUBSCRIPT ERROR.

Section 2. Creating an Array

INTRODUCTION

When the DIM statement is used to define an array, the computer only reserves space for the array; nothing is placed in that space. There are several ways to put values into an array, one of which is to use LET. . .= statements. However, an array of 30 elements would require 30 LET. . .= statements.

A more efficient method of loading values into an array uses READ and DATA statements, and a technique involving the FOR. . .NEXT loop.

This section has two parts:

- The READ and DATA Statements
- Loading Values into an Array

THE READ AND DATA STATEMENTS

The READ statement obtains a value from a DATA statement in the program and stores it in memory under a variable name.

The general format of the READ statement is:

READ variable-name, variable-name, variable-name,...

The keyword READ may be followed by one or more variable names up to a limit of approximately 256 characters in the line. A program containing a READ statement *must* contain a DATA statement. The general format of the DATA statement is:

DATA value, value, value,...

When more than one value is included in a DATA statement, the values must be separated by a comma. We must be careful with commas because of their function as separators. A comma can be included within a string of characters enclosed in quotes without being interpreted as a separator. Never include a comma in a numeric value, however, because the value will be treated as *two* values separated by the comma.

In the DATA statement, we can include as many values as we wish, up to a limit of approximately 256 characters in the line. If additional data is required, we can write a second DATA statement in the program, or as many as necessary to list all data.

A DATA statement is a *non-executable* statement. When it's encountered in a program, the computer does not execute the statement; it merely continues to the next instruction in sequence.

DATA statements may appear anywhere in the program, but are commonly placed either at the end of a program or immediately following a READ statement. Where the DATA statements are placed does not affect the computer's use of their values.

From the computer's point of view, all DATA statements in a program form a single data list, starting with the first value in the first DATA statement and continuing in sequence to the last value in the last DATA statement.

When a READ statement is executed for the first time in a program, the computer finds the first value in the data list and stores it under the first variable name appearing in the READ statement. A pointer is then set to indicate the next value in the data list.

If there are additional variable names in the READ statement, the second value in the data list is stored under the second variable name appearing in the READ statement, the third value under the third variable name, and so forth. As each value in the data list is used, the pointer advances to indicate the next available item in the list.

When a READ statement is executed more than once, the computer continues reading from the data list beginning with the next available data item, and advancing the pointer after each item is read.

Every time the computer is instructed to read a value into a variable, there must be a value in the data list that has not yet been read. If the computer is instructed to READ after the end of the data list has been reached, the error message OUT OF DATA is displayed.

The READ and DATA statements have applications beyond those demonstrated in this chapter. For instance, compare the function of the READ and DATA statements to the function of the INPUT # statement and the data file. Whereas we use the INPUT # statement to transfer values from a data file into memory—gradually working our way to the end of the file—we use the READ statement to transfer values from DATA statements within the program itself into memory—also gradually working our way to the end of the data list. In this way, the data a program is to use can be stored in DATA statements within the program instead of within a data file.

Example 1

The following simple program illustrates the function of the READ and DATA statements.

```
10 READ PRICE, QUANTITY
20 LET TTL = PRICE * QUANTITY
30 PRINT QUANTITY; " ITEMS AT $"; PRICE; " IS $"; TTL
40 DATA 3.55, 11
```

When this program is run, the output appears:

```
RUN
 11 ITEMS AT $ 3.55 IS $ 39.05
```

When the READ statement is executed, the computer searches the program for a DATA statement, finding it on line 40. The first value in the DATA
statement is stored under the first variable name in the READ statement,
PRICE. Then the second value in the DATA statement is assigned to the
second variable name in the READ statement, QUANTITY.

The READ and DATA statements have performed the same function as:

```
LET PRICE = 3.55
LET QUANTITY = 11
```

As you see from this program's output, 3.55 has been stored as the value
of PRICE and 11 has been stored as the value of QUANTITY, as a result of
the READ and DATA statements.

Example 2

In this example, we use an array to store the prices of four models of
portable stereos, then print a price list from the array. The following program
uses the READ and DATA statements to store the prices of each model in the
array, and a FOR. . . NEXT loop to retrieve the prices and print them.

```
10 DIM PRICE(4)
20 READ PRICE(1), PRICE(2), PRICE(3), PRICE(4)
30 DATA 19.99, 37.99, 54.99, 69.99
40 PRINT "MODEL NUMBER", "PRICE"
50 PRINT
60 FOR MDL = 1 TO 4
70  PRINT "MODEL"; MDL, "$"; PRICE(MDL)
80 NEXT MDL
```

When this program is run, the following price list is produced:

RUN
```
MODEL NUMBER      PRICE

MODEL 1           $ 19.99
MODEL 2           $ 37.99
MODEL 3           $ 54.99
MODEL 4           $ 69.99
```

The first instruction is a DIM statement defining PRICE as a 4-element
array. Even though we're not using a subscript greater than 10, the DIM

statement is used for documentation. When the READ statement is executed, the values in the DATA statement are assigned to corresponding elements in the array. Lines 40 and 50 then print a heading and a blank line.

To print each line of the price list, we have written a single PRINT statement and placed it in a FOR. . . NEXT loop. We've used the same variable name as both a counter variable and a subscript, so the program prints a different element from the array each time the loop is executed. Since the counter variable (which is also the subscript) starts at a lower limit of 1 and is incremented to 4, the first through fourth elements of the array are printed.

Notice that the READ and DATA statements have replaced the four following LET. . .= statements that could have assigned values to the subscripted variables.

```
20 LET PRICE(1)  =  19.99
25 LET PRICE(2)  =  37.99
30 LET PRICE(3)  =  54.99
35 LET PRICE(4)  =  69.99
```

Notice also that by using subscripted variables, we're able to use a FOR. . .NEXT loop to step through the array and print each of its elements. The counter variable in the loop is used as a subscript, causing a different element from the array to be printed on each pass through the loop. Without this FOR. . .NEXT loop, four PRINT statements would have been required to print each of the model numbers and prices.

LOADING VALUES INTO AN ARRAY

We can place a READ statement inside a FOR. . .NEXT loop to read a large number of values into an array.

The previous example demonstrated how the values in an array could be displayed using a FOR. . .NEXT loop. The counter variable in the loop is used as a subscript to step through each element of the array.

The FOR. . .NEXT loop can also be used to read values into an array. When a READ statement is placed in this loop and the array name is used with the counter variable as a subscript, every value from an appropriate DATA statement can be loaded into the array.

When the number of items in an array is large, this method very efficiently assigns values to an array.

Example

The following example program uses a FOR. . .NEXT loop to load 10 values into an array representing the cost per pound for delivering merchandise to each of 10 different delivery areas. The name of the array, RTE, stands for "rate." (AT is a BASIC keyword on some computers.) A FOR. . .NEXT loop is also used to print a table of delivery rates.

```
10   DIM RTE(10)
20   FOR ELEMENT = 1 TO 10
30        READ RTE(ELEMENT)
40   NEXT ELEMENT
50   DATA .75, .84, .94, 1.03, 1.11, 1.19, 1.26, 1.33, 1.39,
        1.45
60   PRINT "DELIVERY TO", "COST PER LB"
70   PRINT
80   FOR AREA = 1 TO 10
90        PRINT "AREA"; AREA, "$"; RTE(AREA)
100  NEXT AREA
```

The result when this program is run is:

```
RUN
DELIVERY TO             COST PER LB

AREA  1                 $ .75
AREA  2                 $ .84
AREA  3                 $ .94
AREA  4                 $ 1.03
AREA  5                 $ 1.11
AREA  6                 $ 1.19
AREA  7                 $ 1.26
AREA  8                 $ 1.33
AREA  9                 $ 1.39
AREA  10                $ 1.45
```

The FOR. . .NEXT loop causes the READ statement to be executed 10 times (for ELEMENT = 1 TO 10), resulting in the transfer of the 10 values in the DATA statement to the 10 elements of the array. Without the FOR. . .NEXT loop to read each value into the array, the READ statement would have needed 10 variable names.

```
30 READ RTE  (1) ,  RTE (2) ,  RTE (3) ,  RTE (4) ,  RTE (5) ,
   RTE (6) ,  RTE (7) ,  RTE (8) ,  RTE (9) ,  RTE (10)
```

This is one of the most significant advantages of arrays. Because of the numeric subscripts, loops can be used to step through the elements of an array for various purposes; such as loading, displaying, or searching an array.

Notice also that we loaded the array using the variable name ELEMENT as a subscript, but then printed the elements using AREA as a subscript. What's important is not the variable name used, but its *value.*

TEST YOUR KNOWLEDGE

5. Write a program using READ and DATA statements to assign the value 88.56 to the variable PRICE, 14 to the variable QTY, 12 to DISCOUNT, and 5 to TAX. The program is to then use those variables to print the following:

```
PRICE PER ITEM = $ 88.56
QUANTITY ORDERED = 14
DISCOUNT ON ORDER = 12%
SALES TAX = 5%
```

6. A refrigerator manufacturer has five distribution centers. The stock on hand at each center is shown below.

```
LOCATION            QUANTITY

CENTER  1            589
CENTER  2            315
CENTER  3            606
CENTER  4            248
CENTER  5            280
```

Write a program using READ and DATA statements to assign each of the five values above as elements of the array STCK, then using a FOR. . . NEXT loop to print a list in the format shown above.

7. The circulation totals for a monthly magazine are shown below, listed month by month. Write a program using a FOR. . . NEXT loop and READ and

DATA statements to load the array CIRCUL with the monthly circulation totals, and using another FOR. . . NEXT loop to print a list in the format below.

MONTH	CIRCULATION
1	7810
2	5655
3	4972
4	6841
5	6539
6	7285
7	8364
8	8900
9	8442
10	9117
11	9886
12	9567

Section 3. Using Arrays

INTRODUCTION

Arrays are useful for storing similar data items because of the variety of methods we can use to retrieve an element from an array. This section demonstrates the use of a variable subscript to access an array element, the use of two or more arrays to create a table, and a technique for searching an array.

This section has three parts:

- Using Variable Subscripts
- Creating a Table
- Looking Up Data in a Table

USING VARIABLE SUBSCRIPTS

Using a variable name for a subscript, we can write a program to retrieve any desired element from an array.

When an array has been created to store a list of values, any element from the array can be retrieved by using its subscript. If the subscript used in a program is a numeric variable name, the desired element from the array can be retrieved by inputting a value for the variable subscript, or by calculating a value from input data.

Example

A company has eight authorized service centers for the repair of its products. Each service center handles service calls for one of eight regions. When the company receives a service call, it is forwarded to the appropriate service center. The following program displays the name and phone number of the service manager for whichever region is needed.

```
10   REM ********** DEFINE AND LOAD ARRAY ************
20      DIM SERVICE$(8)
30      FOR NUM = 1 TO 8
40            READ SERVICE$(NUM)
50      NEXT NUM
60   REM ************* ACCEPT INQUIRY ***************
70      INPUT "SERVICE IN WHICH REGION"; REGN
80      IF REGN >= 1 AND REGN <= 8 THEN GOTO 130
90   REM ************* ERROR ROUTINE ****************
100     PRINT "INVALID REGION. PLEASE RE-ENTER. "
110     GOTO 70
120  REM ******* DISPLAY SERVICE INFORMATION *********
130     PRINT "CALL "; SERVICE$(REGN)
140     END
150  REM **************** DATA ********************
160     DATA "MICHAEL O'BRIEN 555-1719"
170     DATA "DOROTHY CRAY 555-2896"
180     DATA "JIM SIMS 555-7528"
190     DATA "ALLEN ROCATI 555-1592"
200     DATA "LOUISE PASS 555-8773"
210     DATA "JOAN ESBENSHADE 555-2169"
220     DATA "BOB FRANKLIN 555-4454"
230     DATA "MIKE DOSS 555-9892"
```

Here's a sample run of this program:

```
RUN
SERVICE IN WHICH REGION? 9
INVALID REGION. PLEASE RE-ENTER.
SERVICE IN WHICH REGION? 7
CALL BOB FRANKLIN 555-4454
```

When this program is run, the FOR. . .NEXT loop on lines 30−50 executes the READ statement eight times, causing all eight elements of the array to be loaded from the DATA. For clarity, eight DATA statements have been used, each containing one string value corresponding to one element of the array.

On line 70, the INPUT statement causes a prompt to be printed, and the computer stops to await data from the keyboard. After a number is entered, it's stored under the variable name REGN.

Line 80 checks the value of REGN to ensure it's a valid subscript value. This is necessary because REGN will be used as a subscript for the array SERVICE$. An improper value for the subscript could cause a BAD SUB-SCRIPT ERROR to occur.

If the value of REGN is not in the proper range, one of the conditions in the IF statement will be false. The computer will then continue with the next instruction in sequence and enter the error routine. If the value of REGN is in the proper range, the IF statement will send the computer directly to line 130 to print the desired information.

Line 130 causes the string "CALL " together with one of the elements of the array to be printed. The printed element corresponds to the number of the region entered at the keyboard.

CREATING A TABLE

A table of values can be stored in memory using one array for each column of the table.

A table consists of two or more columns of related data. Each table column can be represented as a one-dimensional array. By using a variable subscript, we can retrieve corresponding elements from each of the arrays, just as if we were reading across a row in the table.

Example

The following table of information represents the sales histories for five sales areas, and the current manager of each area.

Area	Manager	Last Year's Sales	Last Month's Sales
1	Tim Abrahams	479,000	12,870
2	Anne Garcia	512,000	14,190
3	Bill Wiggins	345,000	15,250
4	Bob Jones	289,000	10,600
5	Jane Roberts	435,000	11,350

This information can be stored in memory in three arrays. The following program stores this data in the arrays, then responds to an inquiry regarding the sales history for any one of the five areas.

```
10  REM ******** DEFINE AND LOAD THE ARRAYS ********
20      DIM MGR$(5), YRLAST(5), MOLAST(5)
30      FOR DTA = 1 TO 5
40          READ MGR$(DTA), YRLAST(DTA), MOLAST(DTA)
50      NEXT DTA
60  REM ************ ACCEPT INQUIRY **************
70      INPUT "SALES HISTORY FOR WHICH AREA"; AREA
80      IF AREA >= 1 AND AREA <= 5 THEN GOTO 200
90  REM ************ ERROR ROUTINE ***************
100     PRINT "INVALID AREA. PLEASE RE-ENTER."
110     GOTO 70
120 REM *********** DISPLAY INFORMATION ************
200     PRINT
210     PRINT "SALES MANAGER FOR AREA"; AREA; " IS ";
            MGR$(AREA)
220     PRINT "LAST YEAR'S SALES WERE $"; YRLAST(AREA)
230     PRINT "LAST MONTH'S SALES WERE $"; MOLAST(AREA)
240     END
300 REM **************** DATA ********************
310     DATA "TIM ABRAHMS", 479000, 12870
320     DATA "ANNE GARCIA", 512000, 14190
330     DATA "BILL WIGGINS", 345000, 15250
340     DATA "BOB JONES", 289000, 10600
350     DATA "JANE ROBERTS", 435000, 11350
```

Here's a sample run of this program:

```
RUN
SALES HISTORY FOR WHICH AREA?  0
INVALID AREA.  PLEASE RE-ENTER.
SALES HISTORY FOR WHICH AREA?  2

SALES MANAGER FOR AREA 2 IS ANNE GARCIA
LAST YEAR'S SALES WERE $ 512000
LAST MONTH'S SALES WERE $ 14190
```

This program is very similar in operation to the service center program in the last example. The difference is that three arrays have been used in this program to store three columns of information from a table. The subscript value was entered at the keyboard and used to retrieve the corresponding element from each of the three arrays.

LOOKING UP DATA IN A TABLE

The technique for finding data in a table when the subscript isn't known is called a *table search*. This technique involves comparing the item we are searching for to each item in an array until a match is found. The subscript is then known and all corresponding elements from the table can be retrieved.

In BASIC, a table search can be accomplished using a FOR. . .NEXT loop. An IF statement is used in the loop to compare the value searched for to one array element. If the condition in the IF statement is false, the computer continues with the next statement in sequence. This is the NEXT statement, which increments the counter variable and branches back to the IF statement again. The condition is then tested using the next element of the array.

When the condition in the IF statement is true, a match has been found. A GOTO is used in the IF statement to direct the computer to exit the FOR. . .NEXT loop. By exiting the loop, the counter variable is no longer incremented. The counter variable is "frozen" at the value of the subscript for the matching element, and can then be used as a subscript to retrieve the corresponding elements from each of the other arrays.

If the item we're searching for isn't in the array, the condition in the IF statement will never turn out to be true. When no match is found, the GOTO in the IF statement is never executed. The loop will terminate normally, and execution will pass to the instruction following the NEXT statement.

To handle the possibility there's no matching element in the array, we should place an error routine after the FOR. . .NEXT loop. The error routine will only be entered when the loop terminates normally after no match is found. This error routine should print a message that no match was found, then it could either end the program or send the computer back to get new data.

When a match *is* found, the GOTO in the IF statement will send the computer past the error routine and directly to the routine displaying the desired information.

Example

The following program responds to inquiries concerning airline flights. When a city name is entered, the computer searches an array of city names for a match. When a match is found, the corresponding flight information is displayed. If no match is found, an error routine is entered that prints a message and ends the program. This program uses three arrays to store the city name, the fare for the flight, and the departure time.

```
10   REM ********** DEFINE AND LOAD ARRAYS ************
20      DIM CITY$(6), FARE(6), TIME$(6)
30      FOR ROW = 1 TO 6
40            READ CITY$(ROW), FARE(ROW), TIME$(ROW)
50      NEXT ROW
100 REM ************* ACCEPT INQUIRY ***************
110     INPUT "WHAT IS YOUR DESTINATION"; DESTIN$
120 REM ******** SEARCH ARRAY OF CITY NAMES **********
130     FOR FLIGHT = 1 TO 6
140           IF DESTIN$ = CITY$(FLIGHT) THEN GOTO 200
150     NEXT FLIGHT
160 REM ************* NO MATCH FOUND ***************
170     PRINT "SORRY, NO FLIGHTS TO "; DESTIN$
180     END
200 REM ****** DISPLAY FARE AND DEPARTURE TIME *******
210     PRINT
220     PRINT "FLIGHT NUMBER"; FLIGHT; " TO "; CITY$(FLIGHT)
230     PRINT "DEPARTS AT "; TIME$(FLIGHT)
240     PRINT "FARE IS $"; FARE(FLIGHT)
250     END
300 REM ***************** DATA ********************
310     DATA "BOSTON", 145.85, "3:15 PM"
```

```
320     DATA "NEW YORK", 132.75, "8:45 AM"
330     DATA "AUSTIN", 82.55, "10:30 AM"
340     DATA "KANSAS CITY", 45.65, "9:50 PM"
350     DATA "SAN DIEGO", 110.15, "1:30 PM"
360     DATA "PORTLAND", 128.35, "6:20 PM"
```

Two sample runs of this program are shown below.

RUN
WHAT IS YOUR DESTINATION? **VANCOUVER**
SORRY, NO FLIGHTS TO VANCOUVER

RUN
WHAT IS YOUR DESTINATION? **SAN DIEGO**

FLIGHT NUMBER 5 TO SAN DIEGO
DEPARTS AT 1:30 PM
FARE IS $ 110.15

In this program, a DIM statement defines three arrays for a flight information table. The first array contains the names of the cities to which flights are available, the second contains the prices for flights to the corresponding cities, and the third contains the departure times for each flight.

A FOR...NEXT loop then loads the three arrays. The READ instruction is executed six times (for ROW = 1 TO 6). Each time the READ statement is executed, one element in each of the three arrays is assigned a value from the DATA list.

After these arrays have been loaded, they can be pictured as:

CI$(1)	BOSTON	FA(1)	145.85	TI$(1)	3:15 PM
CI$(2)	NEW YORK	FA(2)	132.75	TI$(2)	8:45 AM
CI$(3)	AUSTIN	FA(3)	82.55	TI$(3)	10:30 AM
CI$(4)	KANSAS CITY	FA(4)	45.65	TI$(4)	9:50 PM
CI$(5)	SAN DIEGO	FA(5)	110.15	TI$(5)	1:30 PM
CI$(6)	PORTLAND	FA(6)	128.35	TI$(6)	6:20 PM

The INPUT statement on line 110 prompts for the name of the desired destination. When a city name is entered, it's stored under the string variable name DESTIN$.

The computer then enters a FOR. . .NEXT loop to search the array CITY$ for a matching city name. The FOR statement assigns the value 1 to the counter variable FLIGHT, then the IF statement on line 140 compares the value of DESTIN$ to the value of CITY$(1). In the first RUN above, since VANCOUVER is not equal to BOSTON, the condition is false. The computer continues to the NEXT statement where the value of FLIGHT is incremented to 2, and the computer is sent back to repeat the instruction in the loop.

The IF statement next evaluates the condition (DESTIN$ = CITY$(2)). This is also false, since VANCOUVER is not equal to NEW YORK, so the loop is repeated for the next value of FLIGHT.

After comparing the value of DESTIN$ to each element of the array from CITY$(1) to CITY$(6), no match has been found. The loop terminates since the value of FLIGHT has reached the upper limit of 6, and the computer continues to the next instruction in sequence. Here, an error routine is entered which prints a message that no match was found, then ends the program.

In the second RUN above, the city name SAN DIEGO is entered and stored as the value of DESTIN$. In the FOR. . .NEXT loop, the IF statement compares the value of DESTIN$ to each element of the array CITY$. On the fifth pass through the loop (when the value of FLIGHT is equal to 5), the condition (DESTIN$ = CITY$(5)) is evaluated as true; CITY$(5) and DESTIN$ are both equal to SAN DIEGO. The GOTO in the IF statement is executed, causing the computer to exit the loop and enter the routine at line 200. Thus, the error routine is skipped over, and the value of FLIGHT is no longer incremented.

Lines 220–240 display the flight information, using the variable FLIGHT as a subscript to retrieve the appropriate elements from each array. Since the loop was exited with the value of FLIGHT equal to 5, the fifth element from each array is selected and the flight information for San Diego is printed.

TEST YOUR UNDERSTANDING

8. For this exercise, refer to the first sample program in this section (see page 209, this chapter). Two new service centers have been added to handle service calls in the new regions 9 and 10. The service manager for region 9 is Martha Sala (555-2816) and for region 10, Cheryl Collins (555-7596). Alter the program to add this data to the array, so the program will respond to inquiries for regions 1 through 10.

9. For this exercise, refer to the second sample program in this section (see page 211, this chapter). A fourth item of data, highest monthly sales, is

to be included in the program. The highest monthly sales figure for each sales area is as follows:

Area 1 = 13512　　　Area 3 = 15250　　　Area 5 = 13484
Area 2 = 14280　　　Area 4 = 11715

Create a fourth array, then alter the program so this new data is loaded into it, and the output is in this format:

```
SALES MANAGER FOR AREA 2 IS ANNE GARCIA
LAST YEAR'S SALES WERE $ 512000
LAST MONTH'S SALES WERE $ 14190
HIGHEST MONTHLY SALES $ 14280
```

10. Write a program to load two arrays; one containing people's names, the other containing their telephone numbers. Make up a list of at least 12 names and phone numbers to be included in your program's DATA statements. The program is to prompt for a person's name, then search the array of names for a match. When a match is found, your program is to print the name and corresponding phone number. Be sure to include an appropriate error routine.

Section 4. The Delivery Charge Program

INTRODUCTION

The problem introduced at the beginning of this chapter involved writing a program to compute the charge for delivering merchandise to any one of 10 different delivery areas. This program will eventually become part of a much larger program to prepare delivery documents and calculate total revenues for each truck leaving the warehouse.

The solution to this problem involves the use of arrays, convenient structures for storing large amounts of related data. There are many techniques for storing and retrieving data in an array, several of which we demonstrate in a program to solve the delivery charge problem.

This section has two parts:

- When to Use an Array
- The Delivery Charge Program

WHEN TO USE AN ARRAY

An array can simplify a program containing a group of five or more data items treated as belonging to a single list.

An array is a convenient structure for storing data, and under the proper circumstances, can simplify the solution to a problem. How do we determine if an array is appropriate?

Since an array is used to store data, we have to examine the data to be used in a program. The first step is to list all the needed constants and variables. These data items are then arranged into logical groups, and each group is examined.

If any group of data items could be considered items in the same list, and if a single name could be given to the list describing every item it, then that list of items could be treated as an array.

A list containing three items or less would probably be better treated as separate variables. A list containing five items or more would probably be better treated as an array. The deciding factor in any case is: Will the use of an array simplify the solution to the problem?

To decide if an array would simplify the solution, you'll have to imagine how the problem could be solved without an array, then with an array. Of course, experience in using arrays is a great benefit in making this decision. The following examples demonstrate some circumstances in which arrays can be used.

Example 1

A program is needed to read the names and addresses of a company's preferred customers from a data file, and print each name and address on an envelope. In the data file, the address contains the standard two-letter state abbreviation, but the president of the company insists the full state name be spelled out when the address is printed on the envelope.

One solution involves writing 50 IF statements in the program to check for every possible state abbreviation. When the matching abbreviation is found, then a LET...= statement could be used to substitute the full state name for that abbreviation.

•

•

```
310 IF STT$ = "AK" THEN LET STT$ = "ALASKA"
320 IF STT$ = "AL" THEN LET STT$ = "ALABAMA"
330 IF STT$ = "AR" THEN LET STT$ = "ARKANSAS"
340 IF STT$ = "AZ" THEN LET STT$ = "ARIZONA"
```

•   •   •   •

•   •   •   •

Another solution involves creating two arrays. One array contains the 50 state abbreviations, the other the corresponding full state names. A FOR. . .NEXT loop could do a table search through the array of abbreviations. When an abbreviation in the array matches the abbreviation in the address, the loop is exited, and the state name with the same subscript is then printed on the envelope.

A portion of the coding from such a program is shown below to illustrate the statements used in place of 50 IF statements.

•

•

```
50   FOR ST = 1 TO 50
60        READ ABBREV$(ST), SPELLED$(ST)
70   NEXT ST
```

•

•

```
300 FOR ST = 1 TO 50
310      IF ADDREST$ = ABBREV$(ST) THEN GOTO 520
320 NEXT ST
```

•

•

```
520 PRINT SPELLED$(ST)
```

•

•

```
1000 DATA AK, ALASKA, AL, ALABAMA, AR, ARKANSAS, AZ, ARIZONA
```

•

•

Lines 50−70 load two arrays with the 50 state abbreviations and the 50 full state names. A table search is illustrated on lines 300-320. When the state abbreviation in the address (ADDREST$) matches a state abbreviation in the array ABBREV$, the loop is exited. At line 520, the corresponding full state

name from the array SPELLED$ is printed. The data for the state abbrevia-
tions and full state names is listed in DATA statements beginning at line 1000.

This example demonstrates one type of situtation in which the use of
arrays can simplify the solution of a problem.

Example 2

The loan problem from the previous chapter (see page 184) contained
four subroutines for calculating the maximum loan amount for four classes
of loans. Since the calculations were identical except for the percentages
used in each case, we could have written a single statement to perform the
calculation using the appropriate elements from the following arrays:

IPERCENT (1)	.20	NPERCENT (1)	.25
IPERCENT (2)	.20	NPERCENT (2)	.20
IPERCENT (3)	.15	NPERCENT (3)	.20
IPERCENT (4)	.10	NPERCENT (4)	.15

Since the indicator CLASS contained a value of 1, 2, 3, or 4, this indicator
could have been used as a subscript to retrieve the correct percentages for
the maximum loan amount calculation.

Using arrays, the four subroutines to calculate the maximum loan amount
could be removed and the following coding inserted:

```
   •
   •
   •
272 REM ********** DEFINE AND LOAD ARRAYS ************
273    DIM IPERCENT(4), NPERCENT(4)
274    FOR ROW = 1 TO 4
275        READ IPERCENT(ROW), NPERCENT(ROW)
276    NEXT ROW
277    DATA .20, .25, .20, .20, .15, .20, .10, .15
   •
   •
320 GOSUB 500
330 REM ********* DETERMINE LOAN CLASS ***********
340 ON LEVEL GOSUB 600, 700, 800, 900
350 REM ****** COMPUTE MAXIMUM LOAN AMOUNT *******
360 LET MAXAMOUNT =
INCOME * IPERCENT(CLASS + NET * NPERCENT(CLASS)
```

```
370     PRINT "MAXIMUM LOAN AMOUNT IS $"; MAXAMOUNT
380     END
```
   •
   •

Using arrays for the loan percentages allows us to replace eight lines of instructions (in the four subroutines) with five lines of instructions to create and load the arrays. Line 360 is then changed from an ON. . .GOSUB statement to a LET. . .= statement to actually perform the calculation using the appropriate array elements.

Earlier, we stated that a list of 3 values or less would probably be better treated as separate variables; on the other hand, a list of 5 values or more would probably be better treated as an array. In this example, we have four values in each list. As you see, using arrays simplifies this problem to a small degree; on the other hand, the program may not be as clearly understood. In this case, it's a toss-up as to which approach is better.

If there were 15 loan classes, however, the subroutine approach would have required 15 subroutines containing 30 lines of instructions. Even with 15 elements, the array approach would still only require 5 lines of instructions to load the arrays. Under these circumstances, the use of arrays would significantly simplify the solution of the problem.

Example 3

The delivery charge problem involves two lists of values: the delivery rates for 10 delivery areas, and the minimum charge for delivery to the 10 areas. The charge for delivery to any one of these areas is equal to the shipping weight of the merchandise being delivered times the delivery rate for that area. If this charge is less than the minimum for that area, the minimum is applied.

Without using arrays, the variable representing the area of delivery could possibly be used in an ON. . .GOSUB statement, directing the computer to one of 10 subroutines for calculating the appropriate delivery charge. For example:

```
ON AREA GOSUB 300, 350, 400, 450, 500, 550, 600, 650, 700, 750
```

Using two arrays, however, we eliminate the need for 10 subroutines. Instead, the calculations can be performed using the variable AREA as a subscript to retrieve the appropriate delivery rate and minimum charge from the arrays. This approach is demonstrated in the program listing that follows (see page 222).

In examining the main program section of the delivery charge program, we see that the program defines and loads two arrays: one for the delivery rates, and one for the minimum charges. Ten elements fill each array, each element corresponding to one of the 10 delivery areas.

A heading is printed and the program then prompts for the shipping weight of the merchandise and the delivery area. After this data is entered, an IF statement checks the value entered for the delivery area. Since AREA is used as a subscript, we must check for a valid value in this variable to prevent any possible subscript error.

If AREA is less than 1 or greater than 10, it's not a valid value. One of the conditions in the IF statement will be false, so the computer will proceed to the next instruction in sequence. Here, the error routine is entered that prints an error message and sends the computer back to get the value for the AREA again.

When a valid value for AREA is obtained, the GOTO in the IF statement sends the computer past the error routine, directly to the routine to calculate the delivery charge. The first step in this calculation is multiplying the shipping weight by the delivery rate for the specified area. The variable AREA is used as a subscript to obtain the proper delivery rate from the array RTE.

At this point a yes-or-no decision is required; should the minimum charge be applied, or not? If the computed delivery charge is equal to or greater than the minimum charge, all that remains is to print the result. If the computed delivery charge is less than the minimum charge, the minimum is applied.

To accomplish this, we write an IF statement to compare the computed charge to the minimum. The condition (CHARGE => MINCHARGE(AREA)) uses AREA as a subscript to retrieve the appropriate value from the array of minimum charges.

When the computed delivery charge is less than the minimum for the area, the condition in the IF statement is false. The computer goes to the next statement in sequence, thereby entering the routine to apply the minimum charge.

When the computed delivery charge is equal to or greater than the minimum charge, the condition in the IF statement is true. The GOTO in the IF statement directs the computer past the minimum charge routine, directly to the routine that prints the charge.

The final routine in the program rounds off the charge to two decimal places, then prints the result.

THE DELIVERY CHARGE PROGRAM

Review this program listing, giving special attention to the use of the READ
and DATA statements for loading arrays, and the use of the variable subscript
to retrieve data from the arrays.

```
10  REM  **********************************************************
20  REM                                REMARKS
30  REM  **********************************************************
40  REM THIS PROGRAM COMPUTES THE CHARGE FOR DELIVERING
50  REM MERCHANDISE TO ONE OF TEN DELIVERY AREAS. TWO ARRAYS ARE
60  REM USED TO STORE DELIVERY RATES AND MINIMUM CHARGES FOR THE
70  REM AREAS. THE INPUT IS THE DELIVERY AREA AND THE SHIPPING
80  REM WEIGHT. THE AREA IS USED AS A SUBSCRIPT TO RETRIEVE THE
90  REM APPROPRIATE VALUES FROM THE ARRAYS. THE RATE FOR THE
100 REM AREA IS MULTIPLIED BY THE SHIPPING WEIGHT TO COMPUTE THE
110 REM DELIVERY CHARGE. IF THE COMPUTED CHARGE IS LESS THAN THE
120 REM MINIMUM CHARGE FOR THAT AREA, THE MINIMUM CHARGE APPLIES
130 REM  **********************************************************
140 REM                        LIST OF VARIABLES
150 REM
160 REM INPUT
170 REM VARIABLES: AREA = AREA TO WHICH MERCHANDISE IS DELIVERED.
180 REM                   USED AS A SUBSCRIPT TO ACCESS RATE
190 REM                   AND MINIMUM CHARGE FROM ARRAYS.
200 REM            SHIPWT = WEIGHT OF MERCHANDISE TO BE
210 REM                     DELIVERED (IN LBS.)
220 REM
230 REM ARRAYS:    RTE = AN ARRAY OF TEN CONSTANTS. EACH IS THE
240 REM                  COST PER LB. FOR DELIVERY TO THE
250 REM                  CORRESPONDING AREA.
260 REM            MINCHARGE = AN ARRAY OF TEN CONSTANTS. EACH
270 REM                        IS THE MINIMUM DELIVERY CHARGE FOR
280 REM                        DELIVERY TO THE CORRESPONDING AREA.
290 REM
300 REM OUTPUT
310 REM VARIABLES: CHARGE = COMPUTED COST FOR DELIVERY (OR
320 REM                     MINIMUM CHARGE, IF APPLIED.)
330 REM            SHIPWT = SHIPPING WEIGHT
340 REM
```

```
350 REM *********************************************************
360 REM                      MAIN PROGRAM SECTION
370 REM *********************************************************
380 REM
390 REM ************* DEFINE AND LOAD THE ARRAYS **************
400 REM
410     DIM RTE(10), MINCHARGE(10)
420     FOR TBL = 1 TO 10
430       READ RTE(TBL), MINCHARGE(TBL)
440     NEXT TBL
450     DATA .75, 2.25, .84, 2.70, .94, 3.00, 1.03, 3.40, 1.11
460     DATA 3.95, 1.19, 4.50, 1.26, 5.20, 1.33, 5.80, 1.39
470     DATA 6.50, 1.45, 7.15
480 REM
500 REM ************* PRINT HEADING AND GET DATA ***************
510 REM
520     PRINT "COMPUTING DELIVERY CHARGES"
530     PRINT
540     INPUT "WHAT IS THE SHIPPING WEIGHT"; SHIPWT
550     INPUT "WHAT IS THE DELIVERY AREA (1 - 10)"; AREA
560     PRINT
570     IF AREA >= 1 AND AREA <= 10 THEN GOTO 700
580 REM
590 REM ****************** ERROR ROUTINE *********************
600 REM
610     PRINT "INVALID AREA. PLEASE RE-ENTER."
620     GOTO 550 : REM INPUT AREA AGAIN
630 REM
700 REM *********** COMPUTE CHARGE AND PRINT RESULTS ***********
710 REM
720     LET CHARGE = SHIPWT * RTE(AREA)
730     IF CHARGE => MINCHARGE(AREA) THEN GOTO 900
740 REM
800 REM            ********* APPLY MINIMUM CHARGE *********
810 REM
820     PRINT "MINIMUM CHARGE APPLIES"
830     LET CHARGE = MINCHARGE(AREA)
840 REM
900 REM            ************* PRINT RESULT *************
910 REM
920     LET CHARGE = INT(CHARGE * 100 + .5) / 100
```

```
930     PRINT "DELIVERY CHARGE FOR"; SHIPWT; " LBS. IS $"; CHARGE
940     END
```

Here are two sample runs for the delivery charge program:

RUN
COMPUTING DELIVERY CHARGES

WHAT IS THE SHIPPING WEIGHT? **4.5**
WHAT IS THE DELIVERY AREA (1 - 10)? **11**

INVALID AREA. PLEASE RE-ENTER.
WHAT IS THE DELIVERY AREA (1 - 10)? **10**

MINIMUM CHARGE APPLIES
DELIVERY CHARGE FOR 4.5 LBS. IS $ 7.15

RUN
COMPUTING DELIVERY CHARGES

WHAT IS THE SHIPPING WEIGHT? **52**
WHAT IS THE DELIVERY AREA (1 - 10)? **6**

DELIVERY CHARGE FOR 52 LBS. IS $ 61.88

PROGRAMMING EXERCISES

Programming Problem 6A:

The delivery rates for three of the 10 delivery areas have been changed. The new rate for Area 4 is $1.05, for Area 5 is $1.14, and for Area 6 is $1.22. Change the program to put the new rates into effect.

Programming Problem 6B:

The minimum charge has been abolished. Instead, all delivery charges will be based on a fixed fee of $5.00 plus the computed delivery charge. Alter the program so that the minimum charge is no longer applied, and a fee of $5.00 is added to the computed charge for each delivery. Use the constant BASE when making this change.

SOLUTIONS TO "TEST YOUR UNDERSTANDING" EXERCISES

1. A name not followed by a subscript is a variable name; a name followed by a subscript (a numeric literal, or a numeric variable name, enclosed in parentheses) is an array element.

2. LET SALES(7) = 3859

3. The value 10 is the largest subscript permitted with an array not defined in a DIM statement. If a larger value is used, the BAD SUBSCRIPT ERROR (or SUBSCRIPT OUT OF RANGE error) occurs.

4. Suggested solution: DIM AREACODE(25), PHNUMBER(25)

5. Suggested solution:

```
10 READ PRICE, QTY, DISCOUNT, TAX
20 DATA 88.56, 14, 12, 5
30 PRINT "PRICE PER ITEM = $"; PRICE
40 PRINT "QUANTITY ORDERED = $"; QTY
50 PRINT "DISCOUNT ON ORDER ="; DISCOUNT; "%"
60 PRINT "SALES TAX ="; TAX; "%"
```

6. Suggested solution:

```
10 DIM STCK(5)
20 READ STCK(1), STCK(2), STCK(3), STCK(4), STCK(5)
30 DATA 589, 315, 606, 248, 280
40 PRINT "LOCATION", "QUANTITY"
50 PRINT
60 FOR CNTR = 1 TO 5
70   PRINT "CENTER"; CNTR, STCK(CNTR)
80 NEXT CNTR
```

7. Suggested solution:

```
10   DIM CIRCUL(12)
20   FOR DTA = 1 TO 12
30     READ CIRCUL(DTA)
40   NEXT DTA
50   DATA 7810, 5655, 4972, 6841, 6539, 7285
60   DATA 8364, 8900, 8442, 9117, 9886, 9567
```

```
70   PRINT "MONTH",  "CIRCULATION"
80   PRINT
90   FOR MNTH = 1 TO 12
100    PRINT MNTH, CIRCUL(MNTH)
110 NEXT MNTH
```

8. Suggested solution:

```
     •
     •
20   DIM SERVICE$(10)
30   FOR NUM = 1 TO 10
     •
     •
80   IF REGN >= 1 AND REGN <=10 THEN GOTO 130
     •
     •
240 DATA "MARTHA SALA 555-2816"
250 DATA "CHERYL COLLINS 555-7596"
```

9. Suggested solution:

```
     •
     •
20   DIM MGR$(5), YRLAST(5), MOLAST(5), HIMNTH(5)
     •
     •
40     READ MGR$(DTA), YRLAST(DTA), MOLAST(DTA), HIMNTH(DTA)
     •
     •
235 PRINT "HIGHEST MONTHLY SALES $"; HIMNTH(AREA)
     •
     •
310 DATA "TIM ABRAHMS", 479000, 12870, 13512
320 DATA "ANNE GARCIA", 512000, 14190, 14280
330 DATA "BILL WIGGINS", 345000, 15250, 15250
340 DATA "BOB JONES", 289000, 10600, 11715
350 DATA "JANE ROBERTS", 435000, 11350, 13484
```

10. Suggested solution:

```
10   DIM NM$(12), PH$(12)
20   FOR DTA = 1 TO 12
```

```
30    READ NM$(DTA), PH$(DTA)
40   NEXT DTA
50   INPUT "WHO'S PHONE NUMBER"; SEARCH$
60   FOR ROW = 1 TO 12
70     IF NM$(ROW) = SEARCH$ THEN GOTO 110
80   NEXT ROW
90   PRINT "SORRY. DON'T HAVE IT."
100 END
110 PRINT NM$(ROW); "'S NUMBER IS "; PH$(ROW)
120 DATA "CINDY HARRIS", "555-5432"
130 DATA "TOM SMALL", "555-9876"
  •    •       •            •
  •    •       •            •
```

APPENDIX A

Using a Data File on the Apple Computer

INTRODUCTION

The file concepts introduced in Chapter 4 apply, in general, to all computers, although the syntax of the file commands differs from machine to machine. This appendix illustrates some of the kinds of differences in BASIC file commands you may encounter when using various types of computers. Specifically, we illustrate the BASIC file commands used on the APPLE II+ computer.

This appendix has three parts:

- Putting Data into a File
- Getting Data from a File
- The Payroll Program

PUTTING DATA INTO A FILE

On the APPLE, the concepts of opening a file, writing to the file, and closing the file are the same. However, the APPLE command writing to a file turns off all screen output; to resume screen output, we must cancel the write command.

To open a file, either for input or for output, we use the OPEN command:

```
PRINT CHR$ (4);"OPEN filename"
```

Filenames may be up to 30 characters in length, and need not themselves be enclosed in quotes. PRINT CHR$ (4) is a signal to the computer that a Disk Operating System (DOS) command follows. The message inside the quotes is not printed on the screen, but is instead transmitted to the DOS for execution.

If the file already exists on the diskette, the computer locates it; if it doesn't exist, the computer creates an empty file with that name. In either case, after the file is opened, the computer is prepared to read or write to the file.

To write data to a file, we use the WRITE command:

```
PRINT CHR$ (4);"WRITE filename"
```

Executing this command turns on a "logical switch" within the DOS program, transferring all output normally appearing on the screen to the file instead. We'll call this the "write switch."

After executing the WRITE command, we write data to the file by using the normal PRINT statement. Because all output is directed to the file (including an INPUT statement's prompt), we must turn off the "write switch" before we can execute an INPUT statement or attempt to print anything on the screen. To turn it off we use:

```
PRINT CHR$ (4)
```

By turning the "write switch" on and off, we can alternate between writing to the file and printing on the screen. After we finish writing to the file, we execute a CLOSE command:

```
PRINT CHR$ (4);"CLOSE filename"
```

In addition to closing the file, this command also turns off the "write switch".

Example

When the "write switch" is turned on, nothing can be printed on the screen, not even INPUT prompts. In the program creating the payroll file, we'll have to input three data items, turn on the switch, write the data, turn off the switch, then go back for more. Other than this modified approach and the different file command syntax, this program is similar to its counterpart in Section 4 of Chapter 4 (see page 127). We've added quite a few remarks, though, to make this program's operation more clear. (You'll note that the APPLE doesn't support indenting.)

```
10   REM ***** PRINT INSTRUCTIONS, OPEN FILE *****
15   REM
20   PRINT "ENTER PAYROLL DATA"
25   PRINT "WHEN DONE, USE EMPLOYEE NAME = 'END OF DATA' "
30   PRINT  CHR$ (4);"OPEN PAYDATA"
35   REM
40   REM ******** GET DATA, CHECK FOR END ********
45   REM
50   INPUT "EMPLOYEE NAME? ";EMPLOYEE$
55   IF EMPLOYEE$ = "END OF DATA" THEN  GOTO 130: REM EXIT LOOP
60   INPUT "HOURS WORKED THIS WEEK? ";HOURS
65   INPUT "HOURLY PAY RATE? ";PAY
70   REM
75   REM ******** WRITE DATA TO THE FILE *********
80   REM
85   PRINT  CHR$ (4);"WRITE PAYDATA": REM TURN SWITCH ON
90   PRINT EMPLOYEE$
95   PRINT HOURS
100   PRINT PAY
105   PRINT  CHR$ (4): REM TURN SWITCH OFF
110   GOTO 50: REM GET MORE DATA
115   REM
120   REM ******** WRITE TRAILER RECORD *********
125   REM
130   PRINT  CHR$ (4);"WRITE PAYDATA": REM TURN SWITCH ON
135   PRINT "END OF DATA"
140   PRINT 0
```

```
145    PRINT 0
150    REM
155    REM ************ AND END ******************
160    REM
165    PRINT  CHR$ (4);"CLOSE PAYDATA": REM TURNS SWITCH OFF
170    PRINT "END OF PROGRAM": REM THIS NOW PRINTS TO THE SCREEN
175    END
```

Note that between execution of the WRITE command and PRINT CHR$
(4), you cannot cause anything to be printed on the screen. All PRINT
statements direct data to be "printed" into the file referred to in the WRITE
command. The effect of this program is identical to the effect of the similar
program in Chapter 4. After execution, there will exist a file on diskette with
the name PAYDATA (the APPLE does not use quotes around filenames), and
it will contain the data entered at the keyboard.

GETTING DATA FROM A FILE

The syntax of the commands for inputting data from a file is similar to
the syntax for writing data to a file.

To input data from a file, we first open it using the OPEN command introduced earlier:

```
PRINT CHR$ (4);"OPEN filename"
```

This command won't give the FILE NOT FOUND error because the computer creates the file if it doesn't already exist. The file would be empty,
however, as you'd discover when trying to input data from it.

Once the file is opened, we execute a READ command:

```
PRINT CHR$ (4);"READ filename"
```

After execution of this command, *all* INPUT statements obtain data from
the referenced file instead of from the keyboard. When we've finished inputting data, we close the file returning the INPUT statement to its normal
function:

```
PRINT CHR$ (4);"CLOSE filename"
```

Example

In the previous example, the "write switch" caused us to modify our file writing approach from that used in Chapter 4—we had to alternate from file to screen output, turning the "write switch" on and off.

The READ command also turns on a "switch", but it doesn't affect us as much in the program reading data from a file—we have no input coming from the keyboard, so there's no need to turn the switch on and off. Therefore, this program is very similar to its companion in Section 4 of Chapter 4 (see page 130). The significant differences are lines 50-55 (opening the file for input) and line 110 (closing the file).

```
10    PRINT "CONTENTS OF PAYDATA FILE"
20    PRINT
30    PRINT "NAME","HOURS","RATE"
40    PRINT
50    PRINT  CHR$ (4);"OPEN PAYDATA"
55    PRINT  CHR$ (4);"READ PAYDATA"
60    REM ********** INPUT LOOP **************
70    INPUT EMPLOYEE$,HOURS,WAGE
80    PRINT EMPLOYEE$,HOURS,WAGE
90    IF EMPLOYEE$ < > "END OF DATA" THEN  GOTO 70
100   REM ******** TERMINATE PROCESSING *******
110   PRINT  CHR$ (4);"CLOSE PAYDATA"
120   PRINT
130   PRINT "END OF PAYDATA FILE"
140   END
```

If all data has been read when an INPUT is executed for the file, the error OUT OF DATA occurs. Between execution of READ and CLOSE commands, INPUT accepts data only from the file referenced in the READ. The output of this program is virtually identical to that illustrated for the similar program in Chapter 4.

THE PAYROLL PROGRAM

We see below the listing of the main program section as written for the APPLE. The remainder of the program is similar to that illustrated in Chapter 4 (see page 135). However, using an APPLE with a 40-character screen, you'll note there are only three print zones—causing the fourth data item to be printed in the first print zone of the next line. Printing an item with 8 characters or more in the second zone also causes the next item to print on the line below, so we've modified the headings accordingly.

If you like, you may change line 690 of the program to print only three of the four data items, and change line 400 to print the appropriate headings—or try other output variations.

.

.

```
290   REM ********************************************************
300   REM                    MAIN PROGRAM SECTION
310   REM ********************************************************
320   REM
330   REM **** INITIALIZE CONSTANTS, OPEN FILE, PRINT HEADINGS **
340   REM
350   LET WRKWEEK = 40
360   LET FICA = .067
370   PRINT   CHR$ (4);"OPEN PAYDATA"
375   PRINT   CHR$ (4);"READ PAYDATA"
380   PRINT "PAYROLL REPORT"
390   PRINT
400   PRINT "EMPLOYEE","TOTAL","DEDUCT","NET PAY"
410   PRINT
420   REM
430   REM ************** INPUT AND PRINT LOOP ****************
440   REM
450   INPUT EMPLOYEE$,HOURS,WAGE
460   IF EMPLOYEE$ = "END OF DATA" THEN   GOTO 520: REM TERMINATE
  INPUT AND END
470   GOSUB 630: REM CALCULATE PAY AND PRINT RESULTS
480   GOTO 450: REM GET DATA FOR NEXT EMPLOYEE
490   REM
500   REM ************ TERMINATE INPUT AND END ****************
510   REM
520   PRINT
530   PRINT "END OF REPORT"
540   PRINT   CHR$ (4);"CLOSE PAYDATA"
550   END
```

.

.

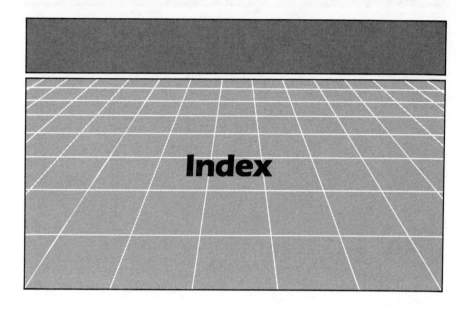

Index